Minitab Cookbook

Over 110 practical recipes to explore the vast array of
statistics in Minitab 17

Isaac Newton

BIRMINGHAM - MUMBAI

Minitab Cookbook

First published: February 2014

Production Reference: 1180214

Published by Packt Publishing Ltd.
Livery Place
35 Livery Street
Birmingham B3 2PB, UK.

ISBN 978-1-78217-092-1

www.packtpub.com

Cover Image by Asher Wishkerman (a.wishkerman@mpic.de)

Credits

Author

Isaac Newton

Reviewers

Srinivas R. Chakravarthy

Brad Cotton

Graham Errington

Mark Fidell

Gary Jing

Acquisition Editors

Edward Gordon

Gregory Wild

Content Development Editor

Susmita Panda Sabat

Technical Editors

Pooja Nair

Nikhil Potdukhe

Tarunveer Shetty

Copy Editors

Shambhavi Pai

Stuti Srivastava

Project Coordinator

Wendell Palmer

Proofreaders

Bridget Braund

Richard Warrell

Indexers

Hemangini Bari

Tejal Soni

Graphics

Ronak Dhruv

Disha Haria

Yuvraj Mannari

Production Coordinator

Aditi Gajjar

Cover Work

Aditi Gajjar

About the Author

It was probably inevitable that, after being gifted with the name Isaac, he discovered he was really good at mathematics and science.

Isaac Newton studied physics at Leicester University and is one of the few people to have an MPhys in Space Science and Engineering. MPhys degrees later changed to MSci after only two years. Yes, he has heard the joke or comment you are just thinking about. After a short stint of postgraduate studies at Birmingham University, he joined Minitab in 1999, where he has been helping the users of Minitab and taking training courses ever since.

Apart from introducing Minitab courses and the basic statistical tools, he has the pleasure of teaching reliability statistics, design of experiments, macro writing, and time series, among other subjects. Recently, he was extensively involved in mentoring others in their own projects and assisting them on getting the most out of their data.

I would like to thank Helen for putting up with me while I devoted my time to write this book. Our lovely daughter, Rosie, deserves a great big mention for arriving halfway through the work in progress. She's a great joy and distraction.

Also, a thank you to my parents for giving me one of the greatest names I could have, even when it was a little challenging at times.

Edward Gordon, Wendell Palmer, and everyone at Packt Publishing have been fantastic at keeping everything on track and helping get this book published.

Thanks to the reviewers for their time, effort, and suggestions.

About the Reviewers

Srinivas R. Chakravarthy is a professor and interim head of the Department of Industrial and Manufacturing Engineering, Kettering University, Flint, Michigan. He has a PhD in Operations Research, an MS in Statistics, and a BS in Mathematics. His research interests are in applied stochastic models, algorithmic probability, queuing, reliability, and inventory. He has published more than 95 papers in leading journals and presented several papers at national and international conferences. He has received NSF awards and organized the first and second International Conferences on Matrix-Analytic Methods in Stochastic Models. He received Kettering University Alumni Outstanding Teaching Award and Kettering University's Outstanding Researcher Award. He is a member of INFORMS, ASA, IIE, and Sigma Xi Research Society. He is currently an area editor for Simulation Modeling Practice and Theory, an associate editor of IAPQR Transactions, and a member of the advisory boards of many journals.

Brad Cotton is the owner and MD of Cotton Innovations Ltd. He worked as a mechanical engineer in the automotive industry in Coventry, UK, with Land Rover cars as an apprentice to the R&D and New Product Development Offices from 1978 to 1982. He led the R&D of component approval for all vehicles from 1982 to 1987. He moved to Jaguar Cars, initially to develop and lead their development programs in air bag systems and later to develop their core testing and capability protocols till 2004. As the component test center manager for both Jaguar and Land Rover, he managed the R&D vehicle crash and components safety labs with respect to protocol, office, and capability alignment.

He holds a Six Sigma Black Belt for Jaguar from 1998 to 2000. He has delivered projects that saved over one million Euros for Jaguar and Land Rover. He also holds a Six Sigma Master Black Belt with Smallpeice Enterprises Ltd, Leamington Spa, UK. Later, he worked with Smallpeice Enterprises, Accenture, and KM&T as a Master Black Belt.

Graham Errington is a Chartered Chemist, Member of the Royal Society of Chemistry, and a fellow of the Chartered Quality Institute, Chartered Quality Professional. He is also a member of the American Society for Quality. He holds an MBA degree and is a Six Sigma Master Black Belt.

He has over 30 years of experience in quality management and improvement, and has applied statistics in metals, semiconductor, polymer processing, automotive, and FMCG industries. Currently, he is the head of statistics and data management at British American Tobacco R & D center, Southampton, UK.

Mark Fidell has wide experience in training lean manufacturing and transactional, Lean Sigma, project management, and change management at the Master Black Belt level. A very experienced coach, he has supported participants in many sectors using Lean/Six Sigma frameworks for accelerated project delivery and full accreditations using Minitab Statistical Analysis and Quality Companion packages.

He has good experience in the industry, having worked at Textron David Brown Gears, FLS Aerospace, Ingersoll Dresser fluid handling, and Parsons Power Generation from green field sites to complete turnkey projects.

Gary Jing is an ASQ Fellow and MBA, and is a Lean Six Sigma deployment leader and Master Black Belt with extensive expertise in continuous improvement, quality, and reliability. As the founding MBB, he successfully anchored Lean Six Sigma deployment at two companies, Seagate TCO and Entegris. He created and managed the Lean Sigma group at Entegris. He is currently an MBB and DFSS deployment leader at TE Connectivity. He serves on the Editorial Review Board for Six Sigma Forum Magazine. He was an IQPC MBB of the Year finalist and trained dozens of Black Belts. He has authored/co-authored more than 20 journal articles and book chapters and holds two patents, and frequently speaks at conferences about Lean Six Sigma. You can take a look at his profile at http://www.linkedin.com/in/ggaryjing.

www.PacktPub.com

Support files, eBooks, discount offers and more

You might want to visit www.PacktPub.com for support files and downloads related to your book.

Did you know that Packt offers eBook versions of every book published, with PDF and ePub files available? You can upgrade to the eBook version at www.PacktPub.com and as a print book customer, you are entitled to a discount on the eBook copy. Get in touch with us at service@packtpub.com for more details.

At www.PacktPub.com, you can also read a collection of free technical articles, sign up for a range of free newsletters and receive exclusive discounts and offers on Packt books and eBooks.

http://PacktLib.PacktPub.com

Do you need instant solutions to your IT questions? PacktLib is Packt's online digital book library. Here, you can access, read and search across Packt's entire library of books.

Why Subscribe?

- ▶ Fully searchable across every book published by Packt
- ▶ Copy and paste, print and bookmark content
- ▶ On demand and accessible via web browser

Free Access for Packt account holders

If you have an account with Packt at www.PacktPub.com, you can use this to access PacktLib today and view nine entirely free books. Simply use your login credentials for immediate access.

Instant Updates on New Packt Books

Get notified! Find out when new books are published by following @PacktEnterprise on Twitter, or the Packt Enterprise Facebook page.

Table of Contents

Preface

Minitab® Statistical Software is a program with a long history. Its beginnings were at Penn State University in 1972, where three professors, namely, Barbara F. Ryan, Thomas A. Ryan, and Brian L. Joiner set about creating a statistics package to help their students learn and use statistics easily. This emphasis on trying to make statistics more accessible to everyone has continued through every iteration. Barbara Ryan still owns Minitab, the company that continues to create new versions of Minitab to make the use of statistics easier for everyone.

Over the years, Minitab has grown, each version adding new features and functionalities. Along with more advanced techniques that are added, there are also new easy-to-use features. In Minitab 13, the StatGuide™ was added to give quick references to the terminologies. In Version 16, the Assistant was added to help guide users to the right graph or statistical tool, continuing the trend of making statistics accessible.

After I obtained my Masters in Physics, I started working at Minitab. Most of my work has been concentrated on teaching how to use the software and how to understand the results, or when to use which statistical tool. The move from physics to statistics was made very easy by using Minitab. Its pedigree in being a teaching tool shows throughout, and it is still a powerful tool that is being used in many sectors of industry or business.

Part of the success of Minitab can be put down to the world's growing realization that understanding data and using data-driven decisions has become essential to success. This is epitomized with different business improvement programs such as Six Sigma and Lean Six Sigma. No matter which name is used to describe the improvement plan, the days of saying, "It looks like that made it better", or "If we do this it should work" are over. Increasingly, the questions are "Can we prove what should be changed?", or "Have we successfully improved the process". Minitab provides the tools that can be used to understand those variations and prove these differences if they exist.

In this book, I have attempted to try and find as much real data as possible to illustrate the use of each tool. This meant many nights of searching for different datasets and different data stores. Some data has just appeared at the right time, a serendipitous question on how to run some test or the other; others I have found from open source locations. Websites that keep a track of public data for use as examples, such as the Data and Story Library (DASL), have been invaluable sources. Quandl, for instance, is a website that holds a massive amount of data for financial, economic, and social information.

In a few places, it was not possible to provide real data. Of those datasets, most are based on real examples that are carefully recreated to hide the real study or to tidy up the example.

I wanted to show how varied the use of both Minitab as a tool and statistics can be. With this in mind, data has been picked from a wide variety of topics. This also provides another benefit for us. One problem new users of Minitab can face is how to insert the data correctly. What format should we use to enter our results? The worksheet does bear a similarity to an Excel spreadsheet, but anyone trying to use the worksheet like Excel will end up in a mess. The key is to enter data in columns. In each chapter, there are a few examples that show the formatting, right from getting this data into Minitab and into the right layout for use with that tool.

I hope you find this book useful. We want you to be able to pick a recipe and jump to that page and follow the example of interest to you.

What this book covers

Chapter 1, Worksheet, Data Management, and the Calculator, shows how to manage your datasets. We look at getting data into Minitab and at formatting tools, such as transposing or stacking data.

Chapter 2, Tables and Graphs, covers examples of creating graphs, and using some of the tabulation tools. The examples use bar charts, pareto charts, Tally, scatterplots, and more.

Chapter 3, Basic Statistical Tools, looks at the statistics in the basic statistics menu. We cover the use of the hypothesis test tools and look at chi-square tables.

Chapter 4, Using Analysis of Variance, covers the use of ANOVA from a simple one-way ANOVA, to general linear models, and to mixed effect models.

Chapter 5, Regression and Modeling the Relationship between X and Y, looks at how to use the regression tools. This covers the basic fitted-line plots before going into the more complex general regression tools using several predictors, model reduction tools, and binary logistic regression.

Chapter 6, Understanding Process Variation with Control Charts, shows how control charts are used to monitor the stability of a process. Here, we look at the use of the familiar Xbar-R, I-MR charts, and also go on to look at the more complex Laney control charts and rare event charts.

Chapter 7, Capability, Process Variation, and Specifications, looks at the tools used to assess a process to its specifications. We cover the use of normal and nonnormal data along with acceptance plans.

Chapter 8, Measurement Systems Analysis, covers the tools used to assess the quality of the measurement system. We look at the Gage R&R tools, including the expanded Gage R&R and attribute measurement studies.

Chapter 9, Multivariate Statistics, looks at the use of principal component analysis and factor analysis for reducing the number of variables or understanding associations in the data. Also, it covers cluster analysis tools, correspondence analysis, and discriminant analysis.

Chapter 10, Time Series Analysis, covers tools to fit to trends, seasonality, and then looks at what to use when no trends or seasonalities exist in the data.

Chapter 11, Macro Writing, looks at how to create simple macros and execs before it looks at the more complicated local macros.

Appendix, Navigating Minitab and Useful Shortcuts, lists navigating tools and useful shortcuts to be used in Minitab.

What you need for this book

Ideally, if you are using this book, you have Minitab available with you. This was written with users of Minitab 17 in mind. Datasets that are provided here can be opened in Minitab 16 and higher. The strategy for new versions of Minitab is to be least disruptive in user experience as possible. Anyone using earlier versions should find that a lot of the commands still run true; however, they may find certain tools here that are not available in previous versions of Minitab.

For instance, the Assistant appears in Minitab 16 and higher. Also, with Minitab 17, there have been big changes to the linear model tools.

Also, note that Laney control charts appeared in Version 16.2. For anyone using Minitab 16.1, you can update your version to the latest 16 version by using **Check for Updates** under **Help** or by talking to your IT department.

Who this book is for

The focus of this book is instructions on how to use Minitab. We do not explain how to interpret the statistics nor do we dig deep into the statistical formulas.

While it is not expected that the reader has in-depth knowledge of all the areas of statistics covered in this book, you should have a basic understanding of the tools that we want to use.

This book is for anyone who wants to know how Minitab likes to have data set up and how we can get Minitab to run those functions to get the most from the software. It is for anyone who feels a bit lost while looking at the worksheet or session folders and wonders what to do next.

If you find yourself asking, "How can I run a binary logistic regression to see the significant effects and present this output in a useful way?" or you run back to Excel to reformat a worksheet and then go back to Minitab, then we have the instructions for you here.

Minitab has become a very powerful and all-inclusive statistical package covering a lot of statistics. This is intended as a guide to help us find our way to the right menu and the right tool.

Conventions

In this book, you will find a number of styles of text that distinguish between different kinds of information. Here are some examples of these styles, and an explanation of their meaning.

Code words in text, database table names, folder names, filenames, file extensions, pathnames, dummy URLs, user input, and Twitter handles are shown as follows: "We can include other contexts through the use of the `include` directive."

When we are pointing to a URL then this is indicated as follows:

`http://lib.stat.cmu.edu/DASL/DataArchive.html`

A block of code is set as follows:

```
TSPLOT Data;
    Index;
    Connect:
    Symbol;
```

Any command-line input or output is written as follows:

`%Glayout`

New terms and **important words** are shown in bold. Words that you see on the screen, in menus, or dialog boxes for example, appear in the text like this: " Any worksheet is suitable, but be aware that the **Open Worksheet...** command".

Files to open use the code format as follows:

`Oxford Weather.txt`

Columns in the worksheet are referred to as follows:

`Year`

Warnings or important notes appear in a box like this.

Tips and tricks appear like this.

Reader feedback

Feedback from our readers is always welcome. Let us know what you think about this book—what you liked or may have disliked. Reader feedback is important for us to develop titles that you really get the most out of.

To send us general feedback, simply send an e-mail to feedback@packtpub.com, and mention the book title via the subject of your message.

If there is a topic that you have expertise in and you are interested in either writing or contributing to a book, see our author guide on www.packtpub.com/authors.

Customer support

Now that you are the proud owner of a Packt book, we have a number of things to help you to get the most from your purchase.

Downloading the example code

You can download the example code files for all Packt books you have purchased from your account at http://www.packtpub.com. If you purchased this book elsewhere, you can visit http://www.packtpub.com/support and register to have the files e-mailed directly to you.

Downloading the color images of this book

We also provide you a PDF file that has color images of the screenshots/diagrams used in this book. The color images will help you better understand the changes in the output. You can download this file from https://www.packtpub.com/sites/default/files/downloads/0921EN_ColoredImages.pdf

Errata

Although we have taken every care to ensure the accuracy of our content, mistakes do happen. If you find a mistake in one of our books—maybe a mistake in the text or the code—we would be grateful if you would report this to us. By doing so, you can save other readers from frustration and help us improve subsequent versions of this book. If you find any errata, please report them by visiting http://www.packtpub.com/submit-errata, selecting your book, clicking on the **errata submission form** link, and entering the details of your errata. Once your errata are verified, your submission will be accepted and the errata will be uploaded on our website, or added to any list of existing errata, under the Errata section of that title. Any existing errata can be viewed by selecting your title from http://www.packtpub.com/support.

Piracy

Piracy of copyright material on the Internet is an ongoing problem across all media. At Packt, we take the protection of our copyright and licenses very seriously. If you come across any illegal copies of our works, in any form, on the Internet, please provide us with the location address or website name immediately so that we can pursue a remedy.

Please contact us at copyright@packtpub.com with a link to the suspected pirated material.

We appreciate your help in protecting our authors, and our ability to bring you valuable content.

Copyright

Portions of information contained in this publication/book are printed with permission of Minitab Inc. All such material remains the exclusive property and copyright of Minitab Inc. All rights reserved.

The following are a trademark of Minitab Inc:

 ▸ StatGuide™

 ▸ ReportPad™

 ▸ Smart Dialog Boxes™

 ▸ Capability Sixpack™

MINITAB® and all other trademarks and logos for the company's products and services are the exclusive property of Minitab Inc. All other marks referenced remain the property of their respective owners. See minitab.com for more information.

Questions

You can contact us at questions@packtpub.com if you are having a problem with any aspect of the book, and we will do our best to address it.

1
Worksheet, Data Management, and the Calculator

In this chapter, we'll be covering the following recipes:

- ▶ Opening an Excel file in Minitab
- ▶ Opening data from Access using ODBC
- ▶ Stacking several columns together
- ▶ Stacking blocks of columns at the same time
- ▶ Transposing the columns of a worksheet
- ▶ Splitting a worksheet by categorical column
- ▶ Creating a subset of data in a new worksheet
- ▶ Extracting values from a date/time column
- ▶ Calculator – basic functions
- ▶ Calculator – using an if statement
- ▶ Coding a numeric column to text values
- ▶ Cleaning up a text column with the calculator

Introduction

This first chapter illustrates the use of a worksheet, data menu, and calculator tools. We start by bringing data in from other applications and then working on it using other data tools within the calculator menu. The emphasis is on getting data into Minitab and reformatting into a preferred structure for later studies.

↓	C1	C2	C3	C4	C5	C6	C7	C8
	Pulse1	Pulse2	Ran	Smokes	Sex	Height	Weight	Activity
1	64	88	1	2	1	66.00	140	2
2	58	70	1	2	1	72.00	145	2
3	62	76	1	1	1	73.50	160	3
4	66	78	1	1	1	73.00	190	1
5	64	80	1	2	1	69.00	155	2
6	74	84	1	2	1	73.00	165	1
7	84	84	1	2	1	72.00	150	3
8	68	72	1	2	1	74.00	190	2
9	62	75	1	2	1	72.00	195	2
10	76	118	1	2	1	71.00	138	2
11	90	94	1	1	1	74.00	160	1

As you can see in the preceding screenshot, Minitab prefers working in columns. This can be structurally a different approach to Excel, where the data is held in cells. We will start by bringing our data in from Excel and Access, and then move into reformatting the data. It should be noted that copying and pasting into Minitab can be a perfectly acceptable method of moving data from one application to another.

Opening an Excel file in Minitab

In this task, we will open a set of data in an Excel file. This can be either in `.xls` or `.xlsx` format. We will set options to help with reading the data in the Excel file as the correct type of data.

Getting ready

Preparation for this task is very simple. We only need a set of data saved in an Excel workbook. Any worksheet is suitable, but be aware that the **Open Worksheet...** command will open every worksheet in an Excel workbook at the same time. The formatting options that we will use here are applied across the entire workbook and cannot have separate format options for every worksheet. Minitab worksheets have a maximum limit of 4000 columns and a practical limit of 10 million rows.

We follow an example here using the `Pulse workbook.xlx` worksheet.

Downloading the example code

You can download the example code files for all Packt books you have purchased from your account at `http://www.packtpub.com`. If you purchased this book elsewhere, you can visit `http://www.packtpub.com/support` and register to have the files e-mailed directly to you.

How to do it...

The following instructions detail the steps for importing data from Excel by using the open worksheet command:

1. Within Minitab, go to the **File** menu and click on **Open Worksheet**.

2. Change the **Files of type** field to **Excel**, and navigate to the folder containing the Excel file.

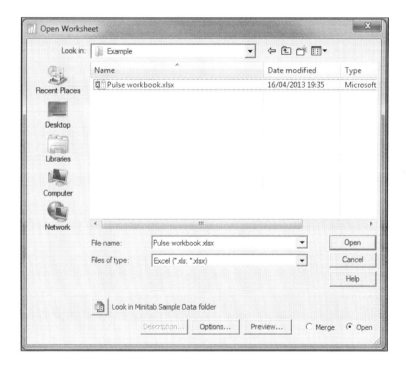

3. Select the Excel file by clicking on the workbook.

Double-clicking will open the workbook, but it is important to use **Preview** and **Options** as in the following steps.

4. Click on **Preview** to see the file structure, make a note of the row in which column names appear, and the data appears. In the following example, the column names are in the third row and the data starts from the fourth row.

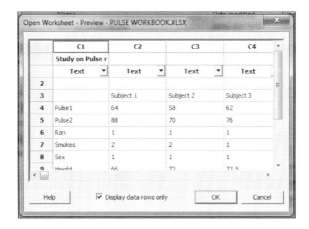

5. Click on **OK** and then select **Options**.

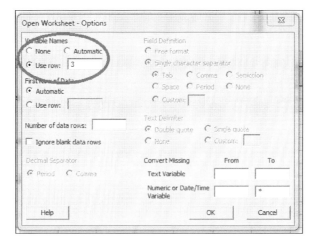

6. Select **Variable Names** to indicate the row of the column names. In this example we will use row **3**. The first row of data can be set to row **4**. The automatic setting will pick the next row with any data in it for the first row of data. Click on **OK**.

7. Click on **Preview**. We can check if this has helped with identifying the type of data. Further alterations to data type can be made. If further alterations need to be made, either change the data type from the drop-down list under each column name or return to **Options** to see what further changes need to be made.

8. Click on **Open**.

How it works...

The **Preview** screen will display the first 100 rows in the dataset. This can be a useful tool in seeing how the file is going to be opened and then deciding what needs to be changed in options.

Excel files can come in many different formats, and while options cannot correct everything, it is an important first step.

If a dataset contains summarized data rows such as means or standard deviations at the end of the worksheet, it is best to exclude them. This can be performed by limiting the number of rows that Minitab will open.

Another option that is useful is to ignore blank data rows. Any row that is completely empty will be left out as it is unnecessary to include them in a Minitab worksheet.

There's more...

Text files, CSV files, XML files, and more can be opened using the **Open Worksheet** option. While opening text files, column separators can be identified by using the field definition.

See also

▸ The *Opening data from Access using ODBC* recipe

Opening data from Access using ODBC

Here, we will show the instructions to pull data from a table within Access.

Getting ready

The instructions are left generic to enable us to use a suitable Access database. Try using these with your data.

How to do it...

The following instructions detail the steps for importing data from a database into Minitab:

1. Within Minitab, go to the **File** menu and click on **Query Database(ODBC)**.

2. Click on **Machine Data Source**, and select **MS Access Database** from the data source list. Then click on **OK**.

3. We can select the drive at the bottom of the next screen, and navigate to the folder containing the database.

4. Select the database and click on **OK**; fill in the username and password as required.

5. We will pick a table in the database from the drop-down control and then select the columns required from the selection on the left-hand side.

How it works...

ODBC stands for Open Database Connectivity and is aimed to allow transfer of data between databases independent of operating systems or database systems. Most databases supporting ODBC can be queried this way using Minitab.

Here, Minitab is constructing an ODBC command to ask Access for the data. The command that was sent from Minitab to Access can be seen by going into the `History` folder.

Stacking several columns together

Minitab will prefer data set up as columns, and often, it is better to stack data together, using one column for all the results, and a second or third column to group the information together. Here, we will stack several numeric columns together into one column.

Getting ready

We want to stack several columns together to give a column of results and an indicator column to identify the group they belong to.

We require a worksheet with several columns of the same data type. In this example, we use data from the `Party Membership of US Senators` file. This data can be found at

`http://mathforum.org/workshops/sum96/data.collections/datalibrary/`
`data.set6.html`.

This data is in the Excel file format. Download the file `senators.xls`. If you are copying and pasting data into Minitab, copy lines 3 to line 53. Alternatively, when following the instructions in the *Opening an Excel file in Minitab* recipe, set row 3 for the variable names.

The first column should be named `State`. Ensure that in Minitab the data appears as shown in the following screenshot:

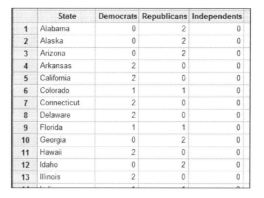

	State	Democrats	Republicans	Independents
1	Alabama	0	2	0
2	Alaska	0	2	0
3	Arizona	0	2	0
4	Arkansas	2	0	0
5	California	2	0	0
6	Colorado	1	1	0
7	Connecticut	2	0	0
8	Delaware	2	0	0
9	Florida	1	1	0
10	Georgia	0	2	0
11	Hawaii	2	0	0
12	Idaho	0	2	0
13	Illinois	2	0	0

How to do it...

The following instructions will stack the party columns together to create a single column for the number of US Senators:

1. Go to the **Data** menu and select **Stack**; then click on **Columns**.

2. Select the numeric columns, **Democrats**, **Republicans**, and **Independents** from the left-hand selection. They can be double-clicked on across into the section **Stack the following columns:**, alternatively select column **2** and drag down to column **4**. Then click on the **Select** button to move the columns as a group.

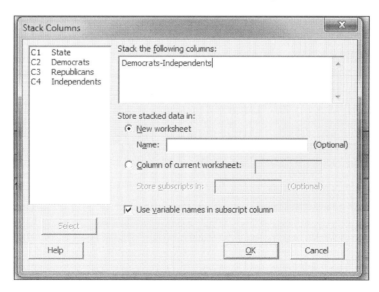

3. Name the worksheet `Stacked Data`, from the **New Worksheet** section and click on **OK**.

4. The worksheet will appear as in the following screenshot. As the columns will not be named from the stack command we need to rename them in the new worksheet. Column 1 **Subscripts** should be renamed to `Party`, and column 2 should be renamed to `Senators`.

↓	C1-T	C2
	Subscripts	
1	Democrats	0
2	Democrats	0
3	Democrats	0
4	Democrats	2
5	Democrats	2
6	Democrats	1
7	Democrats	2
8	Democrats	2
9	Democrats	1
10	Democrats	0
11	Democrats	2
12	Democrats	0

The preceding screenshot shows the stacked results that are created in a new worksheet. A useful tip here to avoid confusion while generating new worksheets, is to name the worksheet that will be generated in the stack column's dialog box.

How it works...

By default, the columns are created in a new worksheet, and an additional subscript column is created to differentiate the groups in the data. This can be deselected and will identify the stacked data by numeric values: 1 for the first column, 2 for the second, and so on. Alternatively, the data can be stacked into the same worksheet.

See also

-   The *Stacking blocks of columns at the same time* recipe
-   The *Transposing the columns of a worksheet* recipe

Stacking blocks of columns at the same time

With some datasets, we may want to keep several columns together while running a stack command rather than running several individual stack commands to stack blocks of columns.

In the previous recipe, the data for senators was stacked, but we didn't keep the information about the states in the new worksheet. Stacking blocks of columns can keep the information about the states with the stacking command.

Getting ready

We will use the senators data from the previous recipe. This can be found from the following location:

```
http://mathforum.org/workshops/sum96/data.collections/datalibrary/
data.set6.html
```

The *Getting ready* section of the *Stacking blocks of columns at the same time* recipe has details on how to import the data.

How to do it...

The following instructions will stack the party membership details and retain information about the state at the same time:

1. Navigate to **Data | Stack** and then click on **Blocks of Columns**.

2. In the first field, enter `Democrats` and select the `State` columns.

3. In the second field, enter `Republicans` and select the `State` columns

4. In the third field, enter `Independents` and select the `State` columns

5. In the **Store stacked data in** section, name the new worksheet `Stacked Data` and click on **OK**.

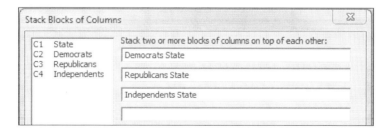

6. As with the stack command, the columns created in the new worksheet are not named. We will need to rename these columns, go to the section above the data in column one and name it `Party`, column two as `Senators`, and column three as `State`.

How it works...

The stack blocks of columns commands will stack columns vertically by order in each row. The number of senators for Democrats will be placed in the second column at the top, those for Republicans will placed below it, and finally, the Independent senators will appear. The `State` column is placed in each row to ensure that the stacked data has the correct state next to each count of senators in the second column.

The optional selection of **Use variable names in subscript column** uses the name of the first column in each row to identify where the data has come from in the new worksheet and places this in the first column. Hence, in the stacked worksheet, column 1 lists Democrats, then Republicans, and finally, Independents.

↓	C1-T	C2	C3-T
	Subscripts		
1	Democrats	0	Alabama
2	Democrats	0	Alaska
3	Democrats	0	Arizona
4	Democrats	2	Arkansas
5	Democrats	2	California
6	Democrats	1	Colorado
7	Democrats	2	Connecticut
8	Democrats	2	Delaware

The preceding screenshot shows the worksheet generated up to step 5 in the instructions. The column names are stored in the subscript column, `C1`. If we do not want the name of the parties to appear in column **1**, then unselecting this option will create the subscript column with numbers instead.

As the stack commands do not name the columns, we should use step 6 to ensure that we can identify each column when we use these later in dialogs.

See also

▶ The *Stacking several columns together* recipe
▶ The *Transposing the columns of a worksheet* recipe

Transposing the columns of a worksheet

Data is often structured with categories denoted in a row and multiple observations of these dimensions in subsequent columns. This can be a popular format used in Excel worksheets. Here, we will transpose this into the column format that is preferred by Minitab in the following manner:

↓	C1-T	C2	C3	C4	C5	C6	C7
		Subject 1	Subject 2	Subject 3	Subject 4	Subject 5	Subject 6
1	Pulse1	64	58	62.0	66	64	74
2	Pulse2	88	70	76.0	78	80	84
3	Ran	1	1	1.0	1	1	1
4	Smokes	2	2	1.0	1	2	2
5	Sex	1	1	1.0	1	1	1
6	Height	66	72	73.5	73	69	73
7	Weight	140	145	160.0	190	155	165
8	Activity	2	2	3.0	1	2	1

In the preceding screenshot, we can see that different individuals are listed starting from the second column. Their resting pulse is in first row, and after activity in second row, it is preferable for this data to be transposed.

Getting ready

The data used in this example is in the `Pulse workbook.xlx` file. To get this data into Minitab, follow the *Opening an Excel file in Minitab* recipe.

How to do it...

The following instructions will transpose the numeric columns of the `Pulse workbook` file:

1. Click on the **Data** menu and then click on **Transpose Columns**.

2. Select the subject columns in the left-hand column panel by selecting **C2** and dragging down through the columns till the end of the column list. Then click on **Select**.

> The left-hand pane in the following screenshot will show the available columns that can be selected. We could double-click on each column across, but here it is faster by dragging and selecting to highlight the columns we want. We could also use *Shift* or *Ctrl* to allow multiple column selection.

3. In the **Create variable names using column** section, enter C1 and click on **OK**.

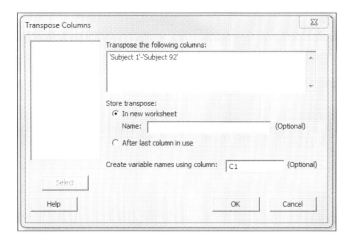

How it works...

Columns of different data types cannot be transposed with this command. We cannot transpose column 1 from the original data into the numeric data held by the subject columns. Row one of the original worksheet becomes column one of the transposed worksheet. Mixing data types will generate an error. Instead, variable names should be optionally identified by the row categories if they are given in a column of the original worksheet. Here, we use column one to identify the column names of the transposed data.

See also

▸ The *Opening an Excel file in Minitab* recipe

▸ The *Stacking several columns together* recipe

▸ The *Stacking blocks of columns at the same time* recipes

Splitting a worksheet by categorical column

In this recipe, we will create several new worksheets from a grouping column. Split worksheet is a great way of quickly separating data out into separate worksheets.

Getting ready

We will use the file `pulse.mtw` from the sample Minitab data folder. Here, we will split the worksheet into two new worksheets: one for those who ran and the other for those who didn't run.

To open the pulse file, go to **File** and then click on **Open Worksheet**. Click on the button **Look in Minitab Sample Data folder**. Then find the file `pulse.mtw`. If the file does not show up, make sure the file type is set to **Minitab (*.mtw; *.mpj)**.

How to do it...

The following instructions will split a worksheet by a categorical column:

1. Go to the **Data** menu and click on **Split Worksheet**.
2. In the **By variables** section, select the `Ran` column, and click on **OK**.

How it works...

Split worksheet is a very quick command to generate new worksheets for each grouping level of a column. If we had data on temperature measurements over time from different weather stations, the Split worksheet could generate a new worksheet for each weather station to enable us to analyze the data separately.

See also

> ▶ The *Creating a subset of data in a new worksheet* recipe

Creating a subset of data in a new worksheet

Here, we will want to obtain a smaller set of data from a large worksheet. This is useful when we do not want to analyze all the data, or maybe only a small portion is of interest to us. We will create a subset of this worksheet to look only at the most recent years, that is, from 2000 onwards.

Getting ready

The data shown in the following screenshot is from the Met office (`http://www.metoffice.gov.uk/climate/uk/stationdata/`) and shows weather details for the Oxford weather station on a monthly basis from 1853. We will subset the data to view the results from 2000 onwards. Select the Oxford station data and copy the data into Minitab.

 When copying the data into Minitab from the website, only select the information for the year and weather. Copying the column header information will create text columns. Minitab only allows one header for column names, and the dataset here has a header for names and a second header for units. It is advised that we only grab the information for now and rename the columns afterwards.

The `Oxford weather (cleaned).mtw` file is provided in the code bundle.

↓	C1-T	C2-T	C3	C4	C5	C6
	Year	Month	T Max (C)	T Min (C)	AirFrost (Days)	Rain (mm)
1	1853	1	8.4	2.7	4	62.8
2	1853	2	3.2	-1.8	19	29.3
3	1853	3	7.7	-0.6	20	25.9
4	1853	4	12.6	4.5	0	60.1
5	1853	5	16.8	6.1	0	59.5
6	1853	6	20.1	10.7	0	82.0
7	1853	7	21.2	12.2	0	86.2
8	1853	8	20.2	10.8	0	72.3
9	1853	9	17.3	8.4	0	51.3
10	1853	10	13.9	7.4	0	102.3
11	1853	11	8.7	2.3	10	49.6
12	1853	12	3.7	-1.3	19	10.7
13	1854	1	6.7	1.5	11	54.5
14	1854	2	8.0	0.6	12	22.6
15	1854	3	11.2	2.2	8	10.6

How to do it...

The following instructions will generate a new worksheet of weather data 2000 onwards:

1. Go to the **Data** menu and click on **Subset Worksheet**.

2. Rename the new worksheet as `Temperature for 2000 onwards` and click on the **Condition** button.

3. In the **Condition** section, double-click on the **Year** column to move this into the **Condition** section, and then add >= 2000, as shown in the following screenshot. Then click on **OK** twice.

How it works...

Subset worksheet can create a new worksheet based on an entered condition, row numbers, or selected data that we have brushed on a chart.

This gives a bit more control than split worksheet, and we only generate one worksheet.

There's more...

With this command, data can be excluded or included very quickly.

Row numbers can be specified in the **Row numbers** field, either singly, with a space between each value (for example, `2 4 8 9 10`), or a range of row numbers can be entered by using a colon (for example, `100:150`).

The **Condition** section works in the same way as the calculator. Multiple conditions can be added with the use of **And**, **Or**, and **Not**. Text values should be referred to within double quotes (for example, `"April"`) and date formatted data should be used as `DATE("05/11/2000")`.

See also

▶ The *Splitting a worksheet by categorical column* recipe

Extracting values from a date/time column

Often, it can be useful to find values such as day, month, or hour of the day from a date column. This can help later on while trying to find out about the variation in our results, finding effects based on day of the week or month of the year.

Getting ready

The data column displayed in the following screenshot shows dates in the mm/dd/yyyy format. To run this recipe, type the following data into a new column and label the column as `Date`. We will then create a new column displaying the months from the dates.

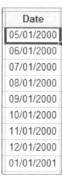

Date
05/01/2000
06/01/2000
07/01/2000
08/01/2000
09/01/2000
10/01/2000
11/01/2000
12/01/2000
01/01/2001

How to do it...

The following steps will create a column for the month from the dates in the worksheet:

1. Navigate to **Data | Extract from Date/Time | Extract to Text**.

2. In the dialog box, enter the date column in the **Extract from date/time column** section. Enter Month into the **Store text column in** section.

3. Tick the **Month** selection and click on **OK**.

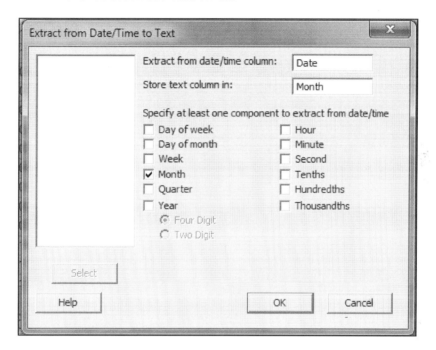

How it works...

If the worksheet does not contain a column called Month already, it will create a new column for us. The selected fields will then populate this column in the worksheet. The **Extract to Text** option will create months and days of the week by their names, where the **Extract from date/time to Numeric** option will create a column of numbers.

Calculator – basic functions

The e-calculator tool is analogous to formulas in Excel. In Minitab, we will run calculations on the columns one at a time. Using the weather data from the Oxford station, we will create a new column for the hours of sunlight in a month divided by the amount of rainfall (in millimeters) for that month.

C6	C7
Rain (mm)	Sun (Hours)
67.7	189.8
19.4	164.6
28.5	161.2
58.3	209.4
87.2	126.1
119.5	83.9
99.1	69.2
99.8	51.9
57.4	83.3
68.6	85.0

Getting ready

We will be using data from Oxford weather station; it can be obtained from `http://www.metoffice.gov.uk/climate/uk/stationdata/`. Select Oxford weather station data and copy the data into Minitab. Only copy the data and not the column headers. Then, rename the columns as `Year`, `Month`, `T Max`, `T Min`, `Airfrost(days)`, `Rain(mm)`, and `Sun(Hrs)`.

Inspect the data that we copy to ensure that the columns have the right data type. The column header `C1-T` will indicate text, `C1-D` will indicate data, and `C1` without the hyphen is a numeric column.

Also, note that a few of the values in the data will be recorded as missing; this is where text values are supplied next to the number. A cleaned worksheet is provided in the `Oxford weather (cleaned).mtw` file.

How to do it...

The following instructions will create a new column for the hours of sunlight to amount of rainfall in a month ratio:

1. Go to the **Calc** menu and click on **Calculator**.

2. In the dialog box, enter a name for the new column into the **Store result in Variable** section. We will name it as `'Sun(Hrs)/Rain(mm)'`.

3. Select the section labeled **Expression**, and then double-click on `Sun (Hours)` to move it across, enter `/`, and then move the `Rain(mm)` column over.

4. Tick the box labeled **Assign as formula** and click on **OK**.

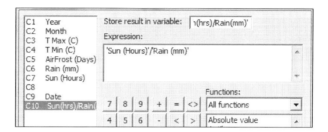

How it works...

The results of this function are generated in the selected column. The checkbox **Assign as a formula** will create a formula in the worksheet that will keep updating it. By default, this is not selected to avoid problems with circular or self-referencing formulas. When a formula is stored in a column, a green cross is placed at the top of the column to indicate the presence of a formula. The green cross indicates that this is up-to-date, while a red cross would indicate a problem in updating the formula.

C10 ✓
Rain/Sun
0.72021
0.59160
1.61597
1.87447

There's more...

The calculator in Minitab has a plethora of functions available. We can choose from the function list on the right in the calculator screen. These include several statistical, mathematical, and text functions. They can be filtered with the drop-down list at the top. The help function for the calculator includes a list of functions and how to use them.

See also

▸ The *Calculator – using an if statement* recipe

▸ The *Cleaning up a text column with the calculator* recipe

Calculator – using an if statement

If statements can be useful tools in extracting information from a column or in reformatting data. Here, we will recode the values in the pulse worksheet.

In the pulse dataset, the C4 smokes column indicates if an individual is a smoker. **1** indicates a regular smoker and **2** stands for those who do not smoke. We will use an if statement to replace the numeric values for smokers and nonsmokers.

Getting ready

The data used here is one of the example files that come with Minitab. Open the pulse. mtw worksheet from the sample Minitab data folder by going to the **File** menu and clicking on **Open Worksheet**. Select the icon **Look in Minitab Sample Data folder**.

Pulse1	Pulse2	Ran	Smokes	Sex	Height	Weight	Activity
64	88	1	2	1	66.00	140	2
58	70	1	2	1	72.00	145	2
62	76	1	1	1	73.50	160	3
66	78	1	1	1	73.00	190	1
64	80	1	2	1	69.00	155	2
74	84	1	2	1	73.00	165	1

How to do it...

The following instructions will convert the values of 1 and 2 in the Smokes column to Smokes and Non-Smoker

1. Go to the **Calc** menu and select **Calculator**.

2. In **Store result in variable**, enter the column Smokes.

3. In the **Expression** text box, enter IF('Smokes' = 1, "Smoker", "Non-Smoker").

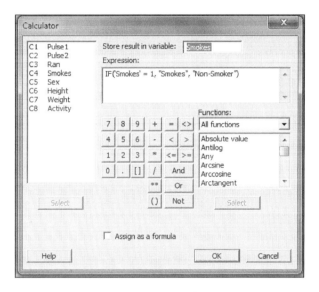

4. Click on **OK**.

How it works...

An if statement is entered in the following format: IF(Logical statement, TRUE, FALSE); the value entered after the first comma being the true for the statement. Numeric values for the response are entered purely as numbers without any double quotes. Text is always entered inside double quotes, for example, "True". Column names are used with single quotes, for example, 'Pulse1'.

Column names can be typed, double-clicked, or selected in the column from the available list on the left of the dialog box. While single quotes are used to denote columns, they are not always necessary. A column name, that is, a single name without special characters or spaces in the name does not need to be referred to with single quotes. The column Ran can be used as Ran or 'Ran'. Selecting a column from the list will automatically enter single quotes where necessary.

There's more...

The IF statements can be generalized to multiple IF conditions very simply. A general IF statement would have the following syntax:

```
IF(Statement1, True1, Statement2, True2... StatementN, TrueN, False)
```

When identifying missing values in the worksheet, the code must be used as the first statement. These values can be identified with the code Miss() or '*'.

For example, the following will identify a missing result in the Smokes column as Unknown, 1 as Smoker, and all others as Non-Smoker:

```
IF('Smokes' = '*', "Unknown", 'Smokes' = 1, "Smoker",
"Non-Smoker")
```

See also

- ▶ The *Calculator – basic functions* recipe
- ▶ The *Coding a numeric column to text values* recipe

Coding a numeric column to text values

In the pulse worksheet, the Activity column lists the usual level of activity of the students in the study, where 1 denotes slight activity, 2 is moderate activity, and 3 stands for a lot of activity.

We will change the numeric values of Activity from 1, 2, and 3 into Slight, Moderate, and High.

Getting ready

Use **File** and **Open Worksheet** to open the pulse.mtw dataset worksheet from the sample Minitab data folder.

How to do it...

The following instructions will convert the values of 1, 2, and 3 in the Activity column to Slight, Moderate, and High:

1. In the **Data** menu, navigate to **Code | Numeric to Text**.

2. Enter the Activity column into **Code data from columns**.

3. Enter the Activity column into the section **Store coded data in columns**.

4. In the **Original values** section, enter 1 in the first line, 2 in the second line, and 3 in the third line, as shown in the following screenshot:

5. In the **New** section, enter Slight in the first line, Moderate in the second line, and High in the third line.

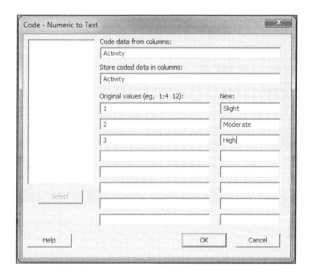

6. Click on **OK**.

How it works...

The code tools work like an IF statement. The code tools cannot be set as an updating formula in the worksheet like the IF statements can be set from the calculator.

In this example, we are replacing the numeric values in the Activity column and putting the new results back into the same column. This will change the data type of the Activity column from Numeric to Text.

There's more...

Ranges of numbers can be entered using colons. If we wish to change the values from 0 to 30 as low, 30 to 60 as medium, and 60 and above as high, then we would enter these as shown in the following screenshot:

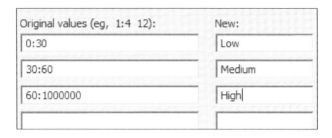

The code tool does not accept symbols such as >, <, or =, and therefore, we can use a large number, such as 100000, to create a greater than statement.

See also

> ▸ The *Calculator – using an if statement* recipe

Cleaning up a text column with the calculator

In the dataset shown in the following screenshot, volunteers are listed with their first and last names:

Volunteer
Joan Sherrif
Nicholas Kouiden
Robert thompson
katie mclane
Sarah roberts

Throughout the column, there are errors in the capitalization of names. We will apply the correct case to the names and separate the names into new columns for first and last name.

Getting ready

Enter the names in the screenshot into a new column in Minitab. Name the column `Volunteer`.

How to do it...

The following instructions will use the proper word commands in the calculator to create a column of correctly capitalized surnames:

1. In the **Calc** menu, click on **Calculator**.

2. In the section **Store result in variable**, create a new column called `Surname`.

3. Filter the function list by selecting the text functions from the drop-down list. Then look for the function `Proper`. Double-click on the function to move it into the calculator.

4. Next, find the function `Word` in the text function list. Double-click on this to highlight and replace the section `text` in the calculator. This should look like the following screenshot:

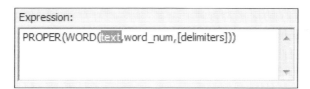

5. Double-click on the column `Volunteer` to bring it into the expression and replace the section labeled **text**.

6. Replace `word_num` with 2 and delete the delimiters and brackets. The expression should look like the following screenshot:

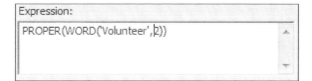

7. Click on **OK** to create a column of surnames capitalized correctly.

Volunteer	Surname
Joan Sherrif	Sherrif
Nicholas Kouiden	Kouiden
Robert thompson	Thompson
katie mclane	Mclane
Sarah roberts	Roberts

How it works...

The text function `Proper` returns a capital letter at the start of each word. The rest are set to lowercase. The `Word` function is used to locate a word in a text string. The `Word 2` function finds the second word in a cell, using spaces as delimiters by default.

Nesting the `Word` function inside the `Proper` command tells Minitab to find the second word for the text in the column `Volunteer` and then set the first letter in each word as a capital and all others as lowercase.

There's more...

There is a list of calculator functions within the **Help** menu for the calculator. The text functions include a number of useful tools. Note, `Item` is similar to the `Word` function but allows the separator to be specified. For example, `A_123_tx` could be used with an `Item` function such as `Item(c1,2,"_")` to define the separator of the items as an underscore.

It is also worth noting that **Find** and **Replace** work in the worksheet as they do in other applications. Press *Ctrl + F*, and *Ctrl + H* or they can be found in the **Editor** menu.

2
Tables and Graphs

In this chapter we will cover the following recipes:

- ▶ Finding the Tally of a categorical column
- ▶ Building a table of descriptive statistics
- ▶ Creating Pareto charts
- ▶ Creating bar charts of categorical data
- ▶ Creating a bar chart with a numeric response
- ▶ Creating a scatterplot of two variables
- ▶ Generating a paneled boxplot
- ▶ Finding the mean to a 95 percent confidence on interval plots
- ▶ Using probability plots to check the distribution of two sets of data
- ▶ Creating a layout of graphs
- ▶ Creating a time series plot
- ▶ Adding a secondary axis to a time series plot

Introduction

Minitab has a very powerful and flexible range of charts that can be created. In this chapter, we will make use of some simple tabulation tools, such as Tally or Descriptive Statistics tables and then explore some of the many graphs that are available to us.

There are many more charts available in Minitab than the ones shown here. Hopefully, seeing the range of charts and editing will give us ideas about what is possible.

We will also explore some of the editing options for graphs. This is a fairly simple routine. Most editing options are made available by double clicking on the item on the chart to edit, or from the right-click menu. Editing a scale on the chart is performed by double-clicking on the scale axis of interest. To add items not already a graph, we would go to the right-click menu. To place data labels on a bar chart, we would right click on the bar chart, go to the **Add** menu, and select **Data Labels**.

As is so often true in Minitab, there is more than one method to edit charts and on the right-click menu, there is an **Edit** item option.

We also have a graph-editing toolbar. This contains a quick select drop-down menu, and a quick select add menu. The following figure shows us the graph editing toolbar illustrating the select and add drop-down menus.

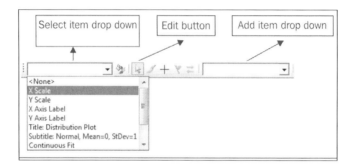

Most of the tools used in this section are found in the **Graph** menu. We will also use a few **Stat** menu items. Tally and **Descriptive statistics** tables are located under **Tables** within the **Stat** menu.

Finding the Tally of a categorical column

The Tally tool can be useful for quickly summarizing counts or percentages. Tally is found in **Tables** under the **Stat** menu. We will open one of the sample data files that come with Minitab and find the count and percentages of males and females listed in the dataset.

How to do it...

The following instructions will open the Department.MTW worksheet and then display the counts and percentages of male and female staff:

1. Go to the **File** menu and select **Open Worksheet...**.
2. Click on the button labeled **Look in Minitab Sample Data folder**.
3. Open the Department.MTW worksheet.

4. Navigate to **Stat | Tables** then **Tally individual Variables....**

5. Enter Gender into the **Variables:** section.

6. Check the box for **Percents** as shown in the following screenshot. We should have both **Counts** and **Percents** selected.

7. Click on **OK**.

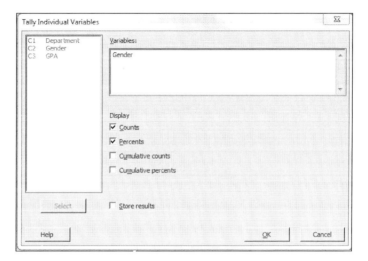

How it works...

Tally can be used very quickly to show counts and percentages of data in columns:

Tally for Discrete Variables: Gender

Gender	Count	Percent
F	26	52.00
M	24	48.00
N=	50	

The results in the preceding screenshot show us that 52 percent of the 50 total individuals listed are female. We could also select cumulative counts/ percentages and store the results back into the worksheet.

See also

▸ The *Building a table of descriptive statistics* recipe

Building a table of descriptive statistics

In the previous recipe, we tallied the number of male and female staff in the department's dataset. Here, we will use a table to count the number of male and female staff in each department. We will also find the mean of the GPA column.

The descriptive statistics tables within Minitab are found with the **Stat** menu under the sub menu **Tables**. This menu also includes cross tabulation and Chi-square statistics.

How to do it...

The following instructions will create a table consisting of the department and gender sections. The table will contain the mean GPA score and the count of observations.

1. Go to the **File** menu and select **Open Worksheet...**.
2. Click on the button labeled **Look in Minitab Sample Data folder**.
3. Open the `Department.MTW` worksheet.
4. Go to the **Stat** menu, select **Tables**, and then select **Descriptive Statistics...**.
5. Enter `Department` in the **For Rows:** section.
6. Enter `Gender` in the **For columns:** section, as shown in the following screenshot:

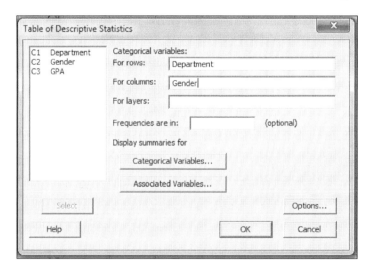

7. Click on **Associated Variables...** and then enter `GPA` in the **Associated variables:** section and select **Means**.
8. Click on **OK** in each dialog box.

How it works...

The levels of department are used to build rows of a table in the session's window and the `Gender` column creates the columns of this table. Summaries of categorical variables can be used to display percentages by the row, column, or by total. The default option here is to count the number of observations.

Numeric columns will be entered into the **Associated variables:** section and can be summarized with Means, Medians, Sums, and more.

```
Tabulated statistics: Department, Gender

Rows: Department    Columns: Gender

                 F       M     All

Economics     2.833   3.070   2.928
                 15      10      25

Stats         3.027   2.793   2.896
                 11      14      25

All           2.915   2.908   2.912
                 26      24      50

Cell Contents:   GPA  :   Mean
                          Count
```

The preceding results show the means of GPA and counts of individuals, classified by gender and department. Multiple summaries can be included in each cell of the table.

See also

▶ The *Finding the Tally of a categorical column* recipe

▶ The Using *Cross tabulation and Chi-Square* recipe in *Chapter 3, Basic Statistical Tools*

Creating Pareto charts

A Pareto chart is a bar chart that is displayed in descending order by default. It is typically used to display the largest defect types. Here, we will create a Pareto defect chart with a frequency column. The data used in this example will look at manufacturing defects for textiles.

Column 1 contains the nature of the defect and column 2 contains the number of defects recorded.

How to do it...

The following instructions will create a Pareto chart from a table of defect and frequency:

1. Go to the **File** menu and select **Open Worksheet...**.

2. Click on the button labeled **Look in Minitab Sample Data folder** and then open the `ClothingDefect.MTW` worksheet.

3. Go to the **Stat** menu and select **Quality Tools...** and then select **Pareto Chart...**.

4. In the **Defects or attribute data in:** section, enter `Defect`.

5. In the **Frequencies in:** section, enter `Count`.

6. Select the **Do not combine** option and click on **OK**.

How it works...

Pareto charts always order the bars in descending order, showing the highest frequency first with the cumulative frequency displayed by the red line, as shown in the following screenshot:

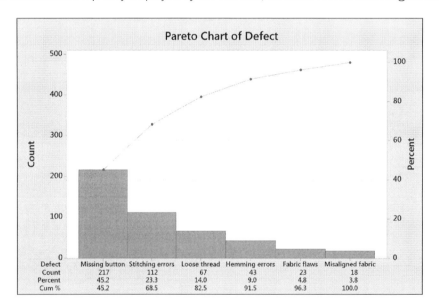

The data shown in this example was created as a table using types of defect and its frequency. Alternatively, the data could be left as a raw format and the Pareto chart command would count up the occurrence of each category.

The **BY variable in:** section can be used to split the chart out into separate graphs. This is useful if, for example, we wanted to show Pareto charts for different departments.

The **Combine remaining defects into one category after this percent:** and **Do not combine** options can be used to tidy up a graph. Combining the smallest categories into one column called `Other` is a great way to shrink a large number of small defect types into one category. When creating a Pareto chart, this is initially set to 95 percent. This means that a chart will show up only when the category crosses 95 percent; it will include only this category in the chart. Everything else will be put into a remainder bar called `Other`.

There's more...

A weighted Pareto chart can be created by looking at the cost or value. Here, we have results of total cost in column 4. By using this column instead of the frequency, the Pareto chart shows us the most categories with the most costly defect first.

If we have a worksheet without a total cost column, we will use the calculator to multiply them together.

See also

- ▶ The *Calculator – basic functions* recipe in *Chapter 1, Worksheet, Data Management, and the Calculator*
- ▶ The *Creating bar charts of categorical data* recipe
- ▶ The *Creating a bar chart with a numeric response* recipe

Creating bar charts of categorical data

The bar chart tools in Minitab offer some of the most flexible graphs for use. Many different styles of bar charts are available. The choices here allow us to use categorical data with the **Counts of unique values** selection. We could create bars of mean values, totals, medians of a set of numeric data from the **Function of a variable** option, or plot the values from a table.

Here, we will create a bar chart of the data in the `Pulse.MTW` worksheet. We will display the number of smokers and nonsmokers by gender for a group of students. As the columns are categorical, we will use the **Counts of unique values** bar charts.

How to do it...

The following instructions will create a stacked bar chart showing the number of smokers and nonsmokers among a group of male and female students.

1. Go to the **File** menu and select **Open Worksheet...**.
2. Click on the button labeled **Look in Minitab Sample Data folder**.
3. Open the `Pulse.MTW` worksheet.

4. Go the to **Graph** folder and select **Bar Chart...**.

5. From the displayed charts, select the **Stack** style of the bar chart.

6. Enter `Sex` first and `Smokes` second; the dialog should appear as follows.

7. Click on **OK**.

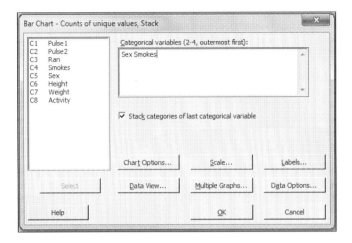

How it works...

The first column is used as the outermost or the lowest category on the x axis. Here this is the `Gender` column. The final column is used as the stacked column. In the following graph, we will see the value of smokes being stacked inside the results for gender. The values of **Sex** are **1** for male and **2** for female; the values of **Smokes** are **1** for regular smokers and **2** for nonregular smokers. Up to four categorical columns can be used in stacked or unstacked bar charts

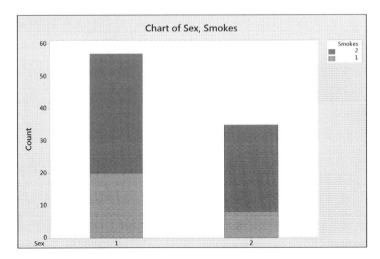

There's more...

The results can also be displayed as a percentage of all the data or as a percentage within each gender.

The option to show the results as a percentage can be found by right-clicking on the chart and then selecting **Graph Options...** from the right-click menu.

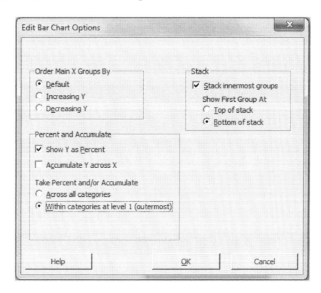

Across all categories will display each level as a percentage of the total result. For example, female smokers represent 8.7 percent of the students.

Within categories at level 1 (outermost) displays the levels of smokers as a percentage within that of gender. For example, 22.86 percent of females part of this study smoke.

You can use the example of coding data to convert numeric values to text present in *Chapter 1, Worksheet, Data Management, and the Calculator*, to display text instead of numbers on this chart.

See also

▶ The *Coding a numeric column to text values* recipe in *Chapter 1, Worksheet, Data Management, and the Calculator*

▶ The *Creating a bar chart with a numeric response* recipe

▶ The *Creating Pareto charts* recipe

Creating a bar chart with a numeric response

Bar charts can also be used with numeric responses. Using the graphs with the selected function of a variable, we can find the mean of a numeric column. Here, we will use the pulse data to see the difference in the mean pulse rate for the previous and next activity columns. We will also split the bars into those who ran on the spot and those who didn't.

How to do it...

The following instructions will create a bar chart of `Pulse1` and `Pulse2` clustered together within the `Ran` column:

1. Go to the **File** menu and select **Open Worksheet…**.
2. Click on the button labeled **Look in Minitab Sample Data folder**.
3. Open the `Pulse.MTW` worksheet.
4. Go to the **Graph** menu and select **Bar Chart…**.
5. Change the selection for **Bars represent:** to **A function of a variable**.
6. Select the **Cluster** bar chart under **Multiple Y's** and select **OK**.
7. Make sure the **Function:** section is set to **Mean** and then select the **Graph variables:** section. Enter `Pulse1` and `Pulse2` into the graph variables.
8. Select the **Categorical variables for grouping (1-3, outermost first):** section, enter `Ran`.
9. Choose the option under **Scale Level for Graph Variables** to **Graph Variables displayed innermost on scale**.
10. Click on **OK**.

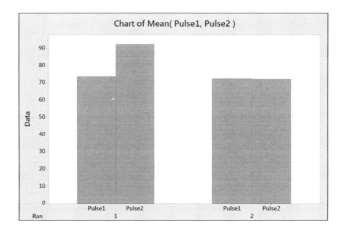

How it works...

The graph that is created will appear as shown in the previous screenshot. We chose the **Multiple Y's** option when selecting the graph so that we could use both the `Pulse1` and `Pulse2` columns on the same chart. The `Ran` column is used as the categorical scale. Numeric columns used with this type of bar chart can be displayed as means, totals (sum), count, medians, and more.

The position of the categories on the x axis can be selected from the options of the scale level for graph variables. Graph variables refer to the numeric columns, outermost refers to the lowest category on the x axis, and innermost refers to the highest category on the x axis. By putting graph variables innermost, we tell Minitab to place the columns of `Pulse1` and `Pulse2` within each category of `Ran`.

There's more...

The following instructions can be used to color the bars of `Pulse1` and `Pulse2` separately and tidy up the graph by removing extra labels on the x axis:

1. Double-click on the bars on the chart.
2. Select the tab labeled **Groups**.
3. Choose the **Assign attributes by graph variables** option (graph variables refers to columns and attribute refers to the bar color).
4. Click on **OK**.
5. Double-click on the y axis.
6. Select the tab labeled **Show**.
7. Uncheck the selection for **Graph variables** under **Show labels by Scale Level**.

See also

- ▶ The *Creating bar charts of categorical data* recipe
- ▶ The *Creating Pareto charts* recipe

Creating a scatterplot of two variables

We will use a `Scatterplot` command to visualize the relationship between a resting pulse and the pulse after a group of students' activity.

How to do it...

The following instructions create a scatterplot of `Pulse1`—the resting pulse, `Pulse2`—the pulse after activity, and the `Ran` column. The `Ran` column indicates whether a student ran in his/her place or not:

1. Go to the **File** menu and select **Open Worksheet...**.
2. Click on the button labeled **Look in Minitab Sample Data folder**.
3. Open the `Pulse.MTW` worksheet.
4. Go to the **Graph** menu and select **Scatterplot...**.
5. From the graph selection screen, select the **With Groups** scatterplot.
6. Enter `Pulse2` as the y variable and `Pulse1` as the x variable.
7. Next, enter `Ran` as **Categorical variable for grouping (0-3):**. Then click on **OK**.

How it works...

In the graph, we have created our y variables that are placed on the vertical y axis, and the x variables along the horizontal x axis. The y axis most commonly plots outputs to our responses in the data. Predictors, which are our inputs, are entered on the x axis.

By entering the `Ran` column as a grouping variable, we change the style of points on the graph. Here, **1** under `Ran` is shown as circles, and **2** as squares. Our results in the scatterplot may lead us to believe that it was the first group that exercised.

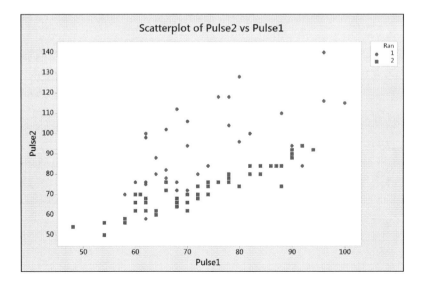

There's more...

Least squares regression lines can be added to the scatterplot by right-clicking on the chart and selecting **Add | Regression Fit...**. A regression line added this way will not report the coefficient tables or analysis of variance tables.

The fitted model can be viewed with a pop-up textbox when hovering the cursor over the line. For statistical information on the model, use fitted line plots in regression.

The **Crosshairs** feature can be found from the right-click menu and is very useful for finding coordinates on the graph. The brushing tool is also a powerful tool to use in scatterplots. This is available from the right-click menu and is used to highlight individual or groups of data points. By default, it will report row numbers and can also be used to display row information from the worksheet.

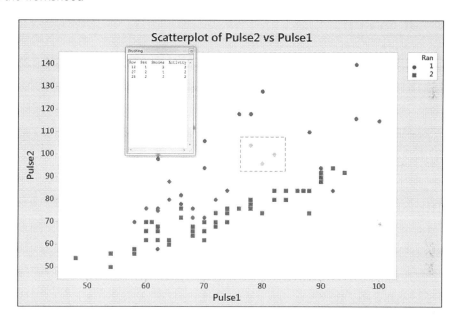

An example of brushing is shown in the previous screenshot. To brush the chart, right-click on the chart and select **Brush**. To add row information from the columns in the worksheet, right-click on the graph once more and select **Set ID Variables...** from the right-click menu. Then, double-click on the **Sex**, **Smokes**, and **Activity** columns in the **Variables:** section. Click on **OK** and highlight a few points on the chart to observe the values of the columns entered as variables in brushing.

▶ The *Visualizing simple regressions with fitted line plots* recipe in *Chapter 5, Regression and Modelling the Relationship between X and Y*

▶ The *Multiple regression with linear predictors* recipe in *Chapter 5, Regression and Modelling the Relationship between X and Y*

Generating a paneled boxplot

Boxplots can offer a very clear way to observe location and spread of data. When comparing different groups of results, they are often more intuitive than histograms.

We will use a boxplot to investigate the average values for a set of data and see the range of values. In this recipe, we will create a boxplot of the mean maximum and minimum temperatures by month.

This example will also use the paneling options within Minitab to generate two separate graphs on one page.

Getting ready

We will use the data for the Oxford weather station in this example. This data is from the Met Office and is found at the following location:

`http://www.metoffice.gov.uk/climate/uk/stationdata/`

Select the Oxford station. The data is also made available in the `Oxford data.txt` file, which preserves the format from the website. Also, the `Oxford weather (Cleaned).mtw` Minitab file is correctly imported into Minitab for us.

How to do it...

The following instructions will copy the data from the website before generating boxplots of the mean maximum and minimum temperatures by month.

1. Follow the previous link to the Met Office weather station site.
2. Choose the **Oxford 1853-** station.
3. In your web browser, save the file as a text file.
4. In Minitab, go to **File** and select **Open Worksheet...**.
5. Change **Files of type:** to **Text (*.txt)**.
6. Select the file that we have just saved, or the provided `Oxford Data.txt` file.

7. Click on the **Preview...** button to see how the data will be imported. Notice that the data starts on line 8, and the variable names on row 6. All the data appears in one column.

8. Click on **OK** and select the **Options...** button.

9. In the **Variable Names**, select **Use row:** and enter 6.

10. For the **First Row of Data**, select **Use row:** and enter 8.

11. Set **Field Definition** to **Free format**.

12. Click on **OK** in each dialog.

13. Go to the **Graph** menu and select **Boxplot...**.

14. From the graph selection, choose the **With Groups** chart under **One Y**.

15. Enter the mean maximum temperature, Tmax, and the mean minimum temperature, Tmin, in **Graph Variables:**.

16. Enter the month column, mm, in **Categorical Variables for grouping (1-4, outermost first):**.

17. Select the **Multiple Graphs...** button and choose the **In separate panels of the same graph** option in **Show Graph Variables**. Then tick the button for **Same Y** under **Same Scales for Graphs**.

How it works...

Steps 1 to 12 help us bring the text data into Minitab correctly. They can be skipped if we open the provided Minitab worksheet with the results in it. This is useful to show how we can use the **Open Worksheet...** command to bring text data in and ensure that the format is correct before opening. The use of **Variable Names** and **First Row of Data** helps us define where the data starts. We also used the **Free format** option to identify how to split out columns, but we could also use **Tab**, **Comma**, and other options to separate out columns.

Copy and paste will work as a method to import data. To copy and paste the weather data, we should select just the data without column headers. Copy this block into Minitab and then rename the columns. This is done because the text file has two column headers. These include the line for the column names and the line for units. We have only one column header in Minitab.

By default, the **One Y** selection for a graph creates a new graph page for each variable. The **Multiple Graphs...** options can be used to place separate graphs on the same page. In this scenario, it was also useful to set the y axis scales to remain fixed. The default option is independent scaling.

The maximum temperature graph is then displayed next to the minimum temperatures.

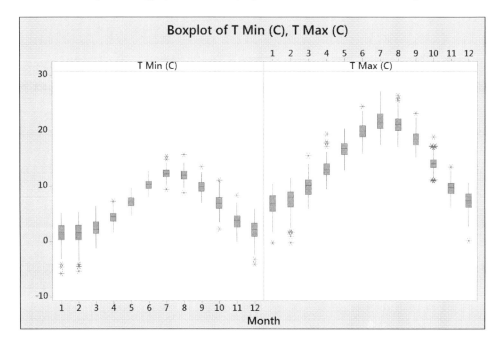

There's more...

We created a paneled graph page of maximum and minimum monthly mean temperatures. The previous graph shows the result of this side-by-side view. The same results can be displayed in a very different format by changing column orders or using a different boxplot style.

Try using the **With Groups** chart under **Multiple Y's**. This will place both variable columns within the same chart. Changing the option for graph variables that are displayed outermost on the scale to innermost will change the style of the chart from the side-by-side temperature columns to the maximum and minimum temperatures together within the month.
Edit the colors of the boxplot by double-clicking on one of the boxes. Within the **Edit box** tab, select the **Groups** section. Check the **Assign attributes by graph variables** option to color the boxes that are by the two separate columns.

See also

▸   The *Finding the mean to a 95 percent confidence on interval plots* recipe

Finding the mean to a 95 percent confidence on interval plots

Interval plots are used to display the mean of a group of data and an interval bar around the mean. The intervals can be either standard error bars or confidence intervals.

Here, we will use the `Camshaft2.MTW` worksheet from the Minitab example data folder. The data shows a recorded length of camshaft from the two suppliers. The interval plot is used to display the mean and confidence interval of the mean for each supplier.

How to do it...

The following instructions will create an interval plot showing 95 percent confidence intervals around the mean value.

1.   Go to the **File** menu and select **Open Worksheet...**.

2.   Click on the button labeled **Look in Minitab Sample Data folder**.

3.   Open the `Camshaft2.MTW` worksheet.

4.   In the **Graph** menu, go to **Interval Plot...**.

5.   Select the **With Groups** chart under **One Y**.

6.   Enter `Length` into the **Graph variables:** section.

7.   Enter `Supplier` into the **Categorical variables for grouping (1-4, outermost first):** section and then click on **OK**.

How it works...

By default, the interval plot displays the data means and the 95 percent confidence intervals around the mean. The results in this graph reveal that supplier **B** has a wider interval because of greater variation in the data for B:

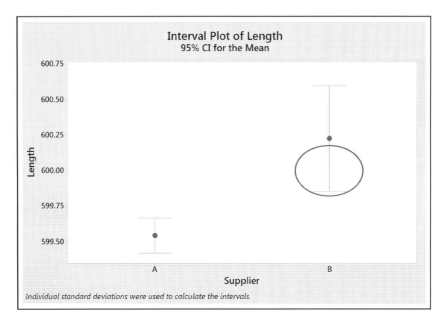

Double-clicking on **Confidence interval** as it is circled in the graph will allow us to change the options for this interval as shown in the following screenshot:

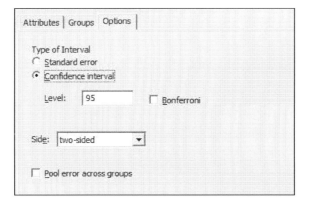

We can choose to display **Standard error** or **Confidence interval**. **Confidence interval** can be set as **Bonferroni** intervals and we can also adjust the confidence level.

The option to pool errors across groups would be used if we knew that sigma, the population standard deviation, is expected to have a similar value between the groups. The confidence intervals plotted here are such that they have an individual error rate of 1- the confidence interval. Bonferroni confidence intervals are used when we want to set the confidence intervals such that the simultaneous error rate across all groups would be a fixed value.

See also

▸   The *Generating a paneled boxplot* recipe

Using probability plots to check the distribution of two sets of data

We will use the probability plot tool to check if data from two suppliers could be normally distributed. The results are stacked in the second column, Length, where the first column, Supplier, informs us which supplier the result comes from. Probability plots from the graph menu allow more options than the normality test in the basic statistics tools. Using the probability plot, we can generate a chart for each supplier.

How to do it...

The following instructions will generate a probability plot for the results of two suppliers:

1.   Go to the **File** menu and select **Open Worksheet...**.

2.   Click on the button labeled **Look in Minitab Sample Data folder**.

3.   Open the Camshaft2.MTW worksheet.

4.   Go to the **Graph** menu and select **Probability Plot...**.

5.   Select the **Single** graph option.

6.   Enter Length as the graph variables.

7.   Select the **Multiple Graphs...** button and then select the **By Variables** tab in the new subdialog.

8.   Enter Supplier into the section labeled **By variables with groups in separate panels:**.

9.   Click on **OK** in each dialog box to create the graphs.

How it works...

The **Single** chart option that we selected by default creates a probability plot of the columns entered into the graph variables. The Length column, though, is divided into two suppliers. To allow us to check if both suppliers A and B could follow a normal distribution, we have to split the chart. The options for multiple graphs allow us to split the graph into separate panels on one page, as the previous instructions show, or to create a new page for each level of the supplier column.

There's more

The **Probability plots...** option has more flexibility than just checking if data could be distributed normally. Within the graph dialog using options under the **Distribution...** button, we can change the type of distribution to be used and enter historical data for that distribution.

Creating a layout of graphs

The layout tool is a clever way to bring several graphs together onto one graph page. This can be a powerful way of presenting data or making comparisons.

Getting ready

The only requirement to run this example is to have a Minitab session open with at least two graphs available. The greater the amount of charts, the better this example.

How to do it...

Let's get started with the steps to bring several graphs together on to one graph page:

1. Make a graph an active window by selecting it with a left-click.

2. Go to the **Editor** menu, which will show you the editing options for graphs and select the **Layout Tool...** option.

3. Select a graph from the left-hand list, and double-click on it or click on the right arrow to move the chart across into the layout.

4. If you have more charts to add, select them from the list and double-click on them to add.

5. Once all the required graphs are in the layout, click on **Finish** to create the new page.

How it works...

Selected graphs will be moved into the section with the blue border. The following screenshot shows us that the next graph that is added would be placed in the lower-left section:

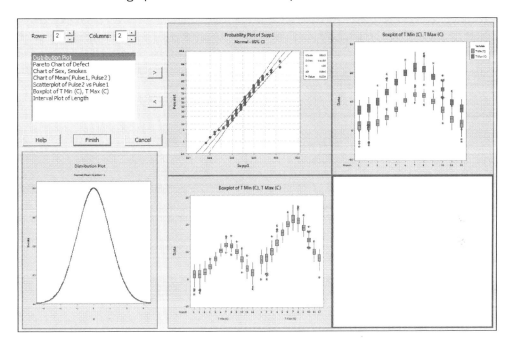

Charts already added to the layout can be orientated on the page by dragging them into the position.

The page is very flexible to change its set up. Notice in the screenshot the top-left corner provides a section for rows and columns. The default value for rows and columns is **2** creating a 2 x 2 panel of graphs. The values here can be changed from 1 to 9 allowing any combination of graphs up to a 9 x 9 layout.

Clicking on the **Finish** button fixes the charts in position and creates the page.

There's more...

The boxplot used in the screenshot for this section can be created by following the steps in the *There's more...* section of the *Generating a paneled boxplot* recipe.

To quickly move the layout in to PowerPoint, right click on the finished page and select the option **Send Graph to Microsoft PowerPoint**.

See also

▸ The *Generating a paneled boxplot* recipe

Creating a time series plot

Time series plots will generate a graph showing the values by their row number in the worksheet. As such, they will always generate a graph with an even distribution on the x axis.

In the following example, we will plot the mean maximum temperature that is recorded monthly at the Oxford weather station. As this data starts from 1853, we will subset this to all results from 2000 onwards.

Getting ready

We will use the data for the Oxford weather station in this example. This data is from the Met Office website and can be found at the following location:

`http://www.metoffice.gov.uk/climate/uk/stationdata/`

Select the Oxford station. The data is also made available in the `Oxford data.txt` file, which preserves the format from the website. Also, the `Oxford weather (Cleaned).MTW` Minitab file is correctly imported into Minitab for us.

When copying the data into Minitab, copy just the data starting at 1853. Then, paste it in the first row of the worksheet. After pasting the data, rename the columns.

For instructions on opening this data from a saved text file, see the *Generating a paneled boxplot* recipe.

How to do it...

The following instructions will create a time series plot of temperatures from the year 2000 to the end of the worksheet. We also stamp the year and month onto the x axis:

1. Go to the **Graph** menu and select **Time Series Plot...**.
2. Choose the **Simple** time series plot.
3. Enter the column for mean maximum temperature into the **Series:** section of the dialog box.
4. Click on the **Time/Scale...** button.

5. From the options, select **Stamp** and complete the dialog as shown in the following screenshot:

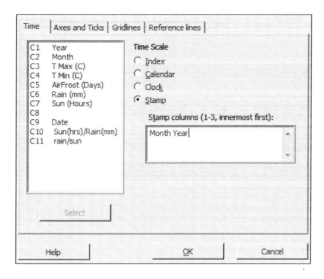

6. Click on **OK** and select the **Data Options...** button.

7. Make sure that the **Specify which rows to Include** option under **Include or Exclude** is selected.

8. Then, select the **Rows that match** option and click on the **Condition...** button.

9. In the **Condition:** section, enter the values as shown in the following screenshot:

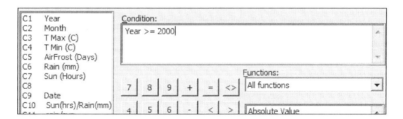

10. Click on **OK** thrice to create the chart.

How it works...

Time series plots display the results by row number. We should ensure that the data is in its correct time order before using a time series plot.

By selecting the scale and stamp button, it allows us to change the default time scale from the row number to year and month. The first column entered is at the top of the x axis and subsequent columns in the stamp section are placed below the previous columns. This shows only the relevant value in the year and month columns; it does not display the results in the date order if they are sorted differently.

Data options allows us to filter the data displayed on a graph. This option is available for all graphs created from the **Graph** menu. By setting the condition for the year to be greater than or equal to 2000, we display only the temperatures from 2000 onwards.

There's more...

When generating the time series plot for the data from the Met Office website or the saved text file, we notice that there are some missing points on the chart and in the worksheet. Check the data in the text that we copied; some of the results are indicated with *. These are provisional results. We would need to correct these manually in the worksheet or remove * from the original file.

The `Oxford weather (cleaned).MTW` worksheet provides this data with the missing data points corrected.

See also

> ▶ The *Adding a secondary axis to a time series plot* recipe

Adding a secondary axis to a time series plot

Time series plots and scatterplots can be used with a secondary axis. Here, we will use the Oxford weather station's data to plot the temperature and hours of sunlight on the same chart. `Temperature` will be displayed on the left y axis; `Sun(Hours)` will be displayed on the right axis.

Getting ready

As done in the previous recipe, we will use the Oxford weather station's data. See the details in the *Creating a time series plot* recipe. Most of the steps in this example will be similar to the time series plot instructions, except the use of the multiple time series plots instead of a single one.

How to do it...

Let's get started with the steps that would help us add a secondary axis to a time series plot:

1. Go to the **Graph** menu and select **Time Series Plot...**.

2. Select the **Multiple** chart.

3. Enter the column for mean maximum temperature and the column for hours of sunlight into the section labeled **Series:**.

4. Follow the steps in the previous example to add the year and month on the x axis, and for the condition to display only the results from 2000 onwards, that is, from step 4 to step 9.

5. The graph should appear as shown in the following screenshot:

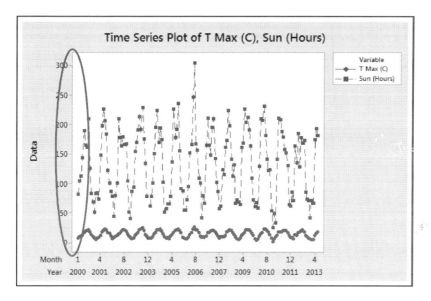

6. Double-click on the y axis to edit the scale as indicated on the screenshot.

7. From the **Edit** y axis options, choose the **Secondary** tab and use the dropdown to put the hours of sunlight column on the **Secondary** axis, as shown in the following screenshot:

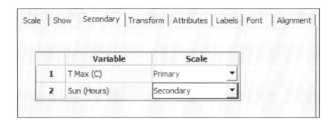

How it works...

Multiple charts that are overlaid are displayed on the same graph. When the scales are very different, as in this case where temperatures are in degree Celcius and sunlight hours in hours of sunlight in a month, then one response can appear disproportionate to the other. The secondary axis allows independent scaling of both axes while using the same x axis.

This can be a useful tool to display correlations in the data.

Basic Statistical Tools **3**

In this chapter, we will cover the following recipes:

- ▶ Producing a graphical summary of data
- ▶ Checking if data follows a normal distribution
- ▶ Comparing the population mean to a target with a 1-Sample t-test
- ▶ Using the Power and Sample Size tool for a 1-Sample t-test
- ▶ Using the Assistant menu for a 1-Sample t-test
- ▶ Looking for differences in the population means between two samples with a 2-Sample t-test
- ▶ Using the Power and Sample Size tool for a 2-Sample t-test
- ▶ Using the Assistant menu to run a 2-Sample t-test
- ▶ Finding critical t-statistics using the probability distribution plots
- ▶ Finding correlation between multiple variables
- ▶ Using the 1 Proportion test
- ▶ Graphically presenting the 1 Proportion test
- ▶ Using the Power and Sample Size tool for a 1 Proportion test
- ▶ Testing two population proportions with the 2 Proportions test
- ▶ Using the Power and Sample Size tool for a 2 Proportions test
- ▶ Using the Assistant menu to run a 2 Proportions test
- ▶ Finding the sample size to estimate a mean to a given margin of error
- ▶ Using Cross tabulation and Chi-Square
- ▶ Using equivalence tests to prove zero difference between the mean and a target
- ▶ Calculating the sample size for a 1-Sample equivalence test

Introduction

In this chapter, we will explore how to use inferential statistical tools in Minitab. The emphasis of this chapter is on discovering population parameters and comparisons of these parameters to targets or between two groups of data. The majority of the tools used in this chapter can be found by navigating to the **Stat | Basic Statistics** menu within Minitab. This is shown in the following screenshot:

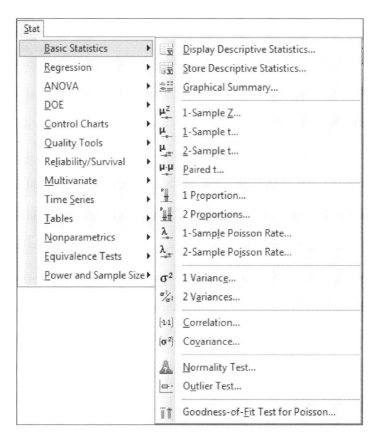

Producing a graphical summary of data

The **Graphical Summary...** tool is a quick way of producing an overview of a column of data. The following example shows us the output comprising a histogram, the Anderson-Darling test for normality, mean, standard deviation, and more.

Here, we will use the data from the Oxford weather station and produce a summary of the amount of rainfall in mm for each month, for all the results from 1853 onwards.

Getting ready

We will use the data from the Oxford weather station in this example. This data is from the Met Office website and can be found at `http://www.metoffice.gov.uk/climate/uk/ stationdata/`. Select the Oxford station.

The data is made available in the `Oxford Weather.txt` file; this preserves the format from the website. This data is also available in the Minitab `Oxford weather (cleaned).mtw` file, and using this worksheet correctly imports itself into Minitab for us.

How to do it...

The following steps will import the weather station's data and then produce a summary of rainfall seen in each month from 1853 to 2013:

1. Follow the previously mentioned link to the Met Office weather station website.

2. Choose the Oxford (**Oxford 1853-**) station.

3. In your web browser, save the file as a text file.

4. In Minitab, go to **File** and select **Open Worksheet...**.

5. Change **Files of type** to **Text (*.txt)**.

6. Select the file that we have just saved or select the provided `Oxford Weather.txt` file.

7. Click on the **Preview...** button to see how the data will be imported. Notice that the data starts on line **8** and the variable names on row **6**. All the data appears in one column.

8. Click on **OK** and select the **Options...** button.

9. In the **Variable Names** section, select **Use row:** and enter 6.

10. For the **First Row of Data** section, select **Use row:** and enter 8.

11. Set the **Field Definition** option to **Free format**.

12. Click on **OK** in the **Open Worksheet** dialog box and then click on **Open**.

13. Go to the **Stat** menu, then **Basic Statistics** and then click on **Graphical Summary...**.

14. In the dialog box, enter the column for rainfall amount as the **Variables:** field, and the column for month into the **By Variables** field.

15. Click on **OK**.

How it works...

The columns in **Variables** populate the summary statistics and the optional selection of **By variables (optional)** allows us to split a set of data into separate summaries. Using the month as **By variables (optional)** creates a summary for each month. The following screenshot shows us the results for July:

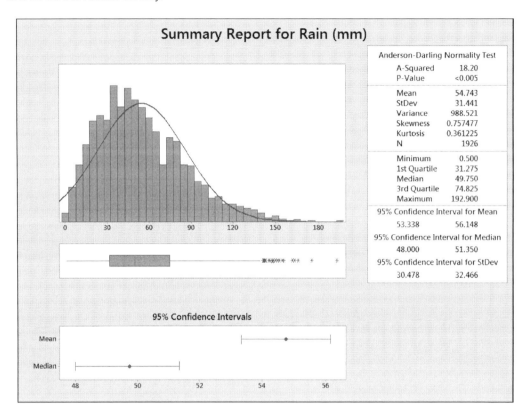

There's more...

If we want to view the results from only one month, say July, instead of generating a summary for all months, we can use the **Split Worksheet...** or **Subset Worksheet...** tools. These can be used to generate new datasets using the results contained within a single month.

See also

▶ The *Splitting a worksheet by categorical column* recipe in *Chapter 1, Worksheet, Data Management, and the Calculator*

▶ The *Creating a subset of data in a new worksheet* recipe in *Chapter 1, Worksheet, Data Management, and the Calculator*

Checking if data follows a normal distribution

The normality test in basic statistics is a tool that is similar to the probability plot used in *Chapter 2, Tables and Graphs*. It is limited to testing normality but it does offer us the choice between Anderson-Darling statistics, Kolmogorov-Smirnov, and Ryan-Joiner tests.

Here, we will use the data from the Oxford weather station and check the normality of the mean maximum temperature for July.

Getting ready

The data for this example can be found on the Met Office website at
`http://www.metoffice.gov.uk/climate/uk/stationdata/oxforddata.txt`.

The data is made available in the Oxford Weather.txtfile; this preserves the format from the website and also the Minitab Oxford weather (cleaned).mtwfile. This worksheet is correctly imported into Minitab for us. Follow steps 1 to 12 in the *Producing a graphical summary of data* recipe to import the results.

How to do it...

1. Go to the **Data** menu and select **Split Worksheet...**.
2. In the **By variables** section, enter the column for month (**C2 mm**).
3. Click on **OK**.
4. From the new worksheets, select the worksheet for July.
5. Go to the **Stat** menu and then **Basic Statistics** and click on **Normality Test...**.
6. In the dialog box, enter the column for mean maximum temperature in the **Variable** field.
7. Click on **OK**.

How it works...

The output will give us means, standard deviation, the test statistic, and the P-value. The Anderson-Darling test is more sensitive to deviations from normality in the tails of the distribution.

See also

▸ The *Splitting a worksheet by categorical column* recipe in *Chapter 1, Worksheet, Data Management, and the Calculator*

▸ The *Using probability plots to check the distribution of two sets of data* recipe in *Chapter 2, Tables and Graphs*

▸ The *Producing a graphical summary of data* recipe

Comparing the population mean to a target with a 1-Sample t-test

We will use the **1-Sample t-test** to investigate the population mean for measures of the economy. The data here is for the UK Gross Domestic Product (GDP). This is often used as a measure of the health of an economy. We will test to see if the percentage growth of GDP per quarter for the UK is equal to zero.

Getting ready

The data for this example was obtained from the Guardian newspaper's website and can be found at `http://www.guardian.co.uk/news/datablog/2009/nov/25/gdp-uk-1948-growth-economy`.

A direct link to the Google Docs spreadsheet is provided at `https://docs.google.com/spreadsheet/ccc?key=0AonYZs4MzlZbcGhOdG0zTG1EWkVPX1k1VWR6LTd1U3c#gid=10`.

Enter the results shown in the following screenshot into the worksheet.
The UK GDP file1.mtw file is also provided on the Packt Publishing
website at http://www.packtpub.com/support.

C1-T	C2-T	C3	C4
Year	Quarter	GDP % growth	GDP - seasonally adjusted
2009	Q2	-0.2	349261
2009	Q3	0.4	350643
2009	Q4	0.4	352091
2010	Q1	0.6	354177
2010	Q2	0.7	356701
2010	Q3	0.6	358885
2010	Q4	-0.4	357324
2011	Q1	0.5	359114
2011	Q2	0.1	359405
2011	Q3	0.6	361599
2011	Q4	-0.1	361130
2012	Q1	-0.1	360880
2012	Q2	-0.4	359538
2012	Q3	0.9	362914
2012	Q4	-0.3	361846
2013	Q1	0.3	362932

The percentages given in the previous screenshot are rounded figures. To obtain a more
precise estimate of the change in percentage, we will calculate this figure. Then, we will
run the t-test.

How to do it...

The following example will calculate the percentage change in GDP from the seasonally
adjusted data before using a t-test to compare the mean percentage growth to 0:

1. Go to the **Calc** menu, select **Calculator...**, and enter the expression as shown in the
    following screenshot:

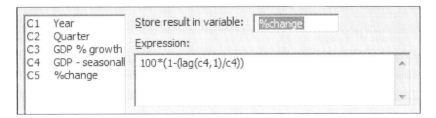

2. Click on **OK**.

3. Go to the **Stat** menu and then **Basic Statistics** and select **1-Sample t...**.

4. Enter the **%change** column into the section for the variables as shown in the following screenshot:

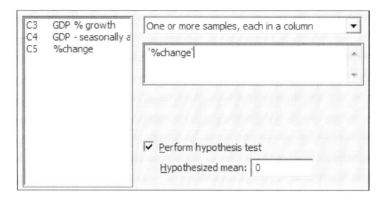

5. Check the option for **Perform hypothesis test** and enter a mean of 0.

6. Click on the **Graphs...** button, select **Individual value plot**, and click on **OK** twice.

How it works...

The calculator is used in the first step to find the percentage change using the `lag` function. The **lag(c4,1)** function moves the results of column 4 one row down, allowing a comparison of a column with itself one row later.

The null hypothesis of this test is set to a mean of 0 percent. The results come out with a mean of 0.255 percent and a 95 percent confidence interval between 0.017 percent and 0.493 percent. Finally, the P-value for this test is 0.038.

This indicates that the mean `%change` per quarter is not zero.

The drop-down box above the variables section allows us to choose between using data entered as columns in the worksheet or summarized values of means and standard deviations.

There's more...

We should check the assumptions of running a t-test. It is random, independent data, and that the population follows a normal distribution, although t-tests are relatively robust to greater than 20 samples that lack normality.

It is useful to run a time series plot to observe variation over time and a normality test.

See also

▸ The *Time series plot* recipe in *Chapter 2, Tables and Graphs*

▸ The *Checking if data follows a normal distribution* recipe

▸ The *Finding critical t-statistics using the probability distribution plot* recipe

Using the Power and Sample Size tool for a 1-Sample t-test

In the previous example, we ran a t-test to compare the population mean against a hypothesized value. The results of the t-test on the data entered showed us a mean of 0.255 with a standard deviation of 0.43. In this example, we will check the size of difference that a 1-Sample t-test using 15 samples and a standard deviation of 0.43 can detect with 80 percent or 90 percent power.

Getting ready

We will use the results of the mean, standard deviation, and the sample size from the *Comparing the population mean to a target with a 1-Sample t-test* recipe. We would like to know the type of difference that this test can observe.

How to do it...

The following steps will generate the size of effect that we could observe using 80 percent or 90 percent of the results in the previous recipe:

1. Go to the **Stat** menu and select **Power and Sample Size**; it is last option in the menu.

2. Then select **1-Sample t...**.

3. In **Sample sizes:**, enter 15; in **Power values:**, enter 0.8 and 0.9; and in **Standard deviation:**, enter 0.43 as shown in the following screenshot:

Specify values for any two of the following:

Sample sizes:	15
Differences:	
Power values:	0.8 0.9
Standard deviation:	0.43

How it works...

The result here indicates that if the population mean was really 0.3346 different from the target, we would be able to prove this difference 80 percent of the time we ran a 1-Sample t-test with 15 results. If the population was really 0.387 different from the hypothesized mean, this test would have a 90 percent chance of observing this difference.

By entering a difference that we would be interested in finding and a power value with which we would want to see that effect, we can obtain a suggested sample size.

Multiple values can be entered into the sample size, differences, or power values sections. They only need to be separated by a space. Power values should also be entered as a proportion rather than a percentage.

See also

▶ The *Comparing the population mean to a target with a 1-Sample t-test* recipe
▶ The *Using the Assistant menu for a 1-Sample t-test* recipe

Using the Assistant menu for a 1-Sample t-test

The Assistant menu offers us an alternative route to a t-test. In general, the Assistant tools offer us a lot more guidance in both the use and interpretation of results than the Stat menu. The Assistant tools are designed to be more accessible and because of this, there are less options to choose from, compared to the equivalent tool in the **Stat** menu.

Here, we will use the same economic results as the 1-Sample t-test.

Getting ready

The data for this example is from the UK GDP figures from 2009 to 2013. Enter the data shown in the following screenshot into the worksheet. Alternatively, open the data `UK GDP file1.mtw` file.

C1-T	C2-T	C3	C4
Year	Quarter	GDP % growth	GDP - seasonally adjusted
2009	Q2	-0.2	349261
2009	Q3	0.4	350643
2009	Q4	0.4	352091
2010	Q1	0.6	354177
2010	Q2	0.7	356701
2010	Q3	0.6	358885
2010	Q4	-0.4	357324
2011	Q1	0.5	359114
2011	Q2	0.1	359405
2011	Q3	0.6	361599
2011	Q4	-0.1	361130
2012	Q1	-0.1	360880
2012	Q2	-0.4	359538
2012	Q3	0.9	362914
2012	Q4	-0.3	361846
2013	Q1	0.3	362932

How to do it...

The following steps will use the Assistant tools to run the 1-Sample t-test:

1. In the **Assistant** menu, select **Hypothesis Tests...**.

2. From the screen that asks us what our objective is, select **1-Sample t** from the **Compare one sample with a target** field.

3. In the **Data column:** field, enter the percentage change results.

4. Enter 0 for the **Target** field.

5. Under **What do you want to determine?**, select **Is the mean of '%change' different from 0**.

6. Click on **OK**.

How it works...

The Assistant tool starts from a selection screen to guide us to a test. If we wanted more information on the presented choices, we would click on the top field under the first objective screen. Here, we would be presented with a decision tree to help us pick the right tool. Further guidance is found within each decision diamond.

> When entering the fields in the 1-Sample t-test, the text for one-sided or two-sided tests is updated to reflect the column name being used and target entered.

By entering a difference that is of practical importance to us, the power of the test is calculated with the results and the suggested alternative sample sizes.

The output that is generated comprises several graphical report cards. The first page contains any warnings about the study. The second page contains diagnostic checks, a time series plot, and the power study. The last page contains the results of the t-test with an individual value plot, means, and confidence intervals, plus comments on whether we can conclude that the mean is different from the target or not.

See also

> ▸ The *Comparing the population mean to a target with a 1-Sample t-test* recipe

> ▸ The *Using the Power and Sample Size tool for a 1-Sample t-test* recipe

> ▸ The *Finding critical t-statistics using the probability distribution plot* recipe

Looking for differences in the population means between two samples with a 2-Sample t-test

For this recipe, we will use a 2-Sample t-test to compare two groups of data. The null hypothesis for the 2-Sample t-test is that the population means are the same.

Here, we will look at comparing the pulse rate of a group of students that exercised against a group that didn't.

Getting ready

The data is in the Minitab `Pulse.mtw` worksheet. The file can be found in the Minitab `Sample Data` folder.

How to do it...

The following steps will compare the mean pulse rate of two groups of students:

1. To open the worksheet, go to the **Stat** menu and select **Open Worksheet...**.
2. Click on the **Look in Minitab Sample Data folder** button.
3. Open the `Pulse.mtw` worksheet.
4. Go to the **Stat** menu and select **Basic Statistics**, then click on **2-Sample t...**.
5. In **Samples**, enter the **Pulse2** column.
6. In **Sample IDs:**, enter **Ran**.
7. Select the **Graphs...** button and check the option for **Boxplots of data**.
8. Click on **OK** twice.

How it works...

The 2-Sample t-test here uses the sample column for all the pulse measurements; the subscripts are then used to identify if a result was from the group that ran (1) or the group that didn't run (2). Alternatively, the two groups could have been in separate columns or we could have just entered the summarized results of sample size, mean, and standard deviations.

In Minitab v17, we can choose between samples in one column, different columns, or summarized data from the drop-down box at the top of the dialog.

There is also an option to run the test assuming equal variances; we use Welch's t-test for unequal variances by default.

There's more...

The 2 variance test under **Basic Statistics** can be used to test the assumption of equal variance.

See also

▶ The *Using the Power and Sample Size tool for a 2-Sample t-test* recipe
▶ The *Using the Assistant menu to run the 2-Sample t-test* recipe

Using the Power and Sample Size tool for a 2-Sample t-test

Here, we will use the power and sample size tools to find the number of samples needed to observe a difference in the means between two populations.

We will not need to open a dataset for this recipe. Using a standard deviation that has been set to 1, we will discover the number of samples required to observe a 1, 2, or 3 standard deviation difference between two population means.

How to do it...

The following steps will help us find the sample size required to detect differences of 1, 2, or 3 standard deviations between the means of two samples:

1. Go to the **Stat** menu and then **Power and Sample Size** and then select **2 Sample t...**.

2. Fill out the dialog box as shown in the following screenshot:

Specify values for any two of the following:		
Sample sizes:		
Differences:	1 2 3	
Power values:	.8 .9	
Standard deviation:	1	

3. Click on **OK**.

How it works...

The differences are stated in terms of the value of the standard deviation from the results shown in the following screenshot:

Difference	Sample Size	Target Power	Actual Power
1	17	0.8	0.807037
1	23	0.9	0.912498
2	6	0.8	0.876418
2	7	0.9	0.929070
3	4	0.8	0.938936
3	4	0.9	0.938936

The sample size is for each group.

To observe a 1 standard deviation difference between the population means of two samples, we would need 17 samples to have an 80 percent chance of observing this difference or 23 samples to have a 90 percent chance of observing the difference. This sample size is for both groups of data.

The options for this test allow us to specify a one-sided test or change the significance level.

Using the Assistant menu to run the 2-Sample t-test

We can also use a 2-Sample t-test from the Assistant menu. Like the other Assistant tools, this provides a simpler interface and graphical report cards for the output. Here we will use the `Pulse` dataset as shown in the earlier example. We will compare the results of `Pulse2` with the groups in the **Ran** column.

How to do it...

The following steps will help us compare the mean pulse rates of two groups of students using the Assistant tools. Initially, we will unstack the data before running the t-test:

1. To open the worksheet, go to the **File** menu and select **Open Worksheet...**.
2. Click on the **Look in Minitab Sample Data folder** button.
3. Open the `Pulse.mtw` worksheet.
4. Go to the **Data** menu and select **Unstack Columns...**.
5. Enter the **Pulse2** column in the **Unstack the data in:** field.
6. Enter the **Ran** column in the **Using subscripts in:** section.
7. Click on **OK**.
8. Go to the **Assistant** menu and select **Hypothesis Tests...**.
9. Select **2-Sample t**.
10. In the dropdown for **How are your data arranged in the worksheet?**, select the option for **Each sample is in it own column**.
11. Enter the **Pulse2_1** column in the section **First sample column:**.
12. Enter the column **Pulse2_2** in the **Second sample column:** section.
13. Choose the option for **Is the first mean of 'Pulse2_1' different from the mean of 'Pulse2_2'?**.
14. Click on **OK**.

How it works...

The unstacked columns can be used to put the unstacked data into a new worksheet or after the last columns of the current worksheet. By default, it will name the new columns using the name of the unstacked column along with the grouping value used to unstack the data. Here, the grouping column for **Ran** has the levels 1 or 2. So, the columns are named **Pulse2_1** and **Pulse2_2**.

In Minitab v17, we could also have used the data without unstacking the columns using the **Both samples are in one column, IDs are in another column.** option.

Assistant can also be used to help pick the type of test to be used with the **Help me choose** selection.

See also

▸ The *Looking for differences in the population means between two samples using a 2-Sample t-test* recipe

▸ The *Using the Power and Sample Size tool for a 2-Sample t-test* recipe

Finding critical t-statistics using the probability distribution plot

The critical t-statistic can be found from either the **Calc** menu tools under **Probability Distributions**, or from the **Graph** menu and **Probability Distribution Plot...**. Here, we will find the critical t-statistic using the graphical tools used in probability distribution plots. In this recipe, we will find the critical t-statistic with 14 degrees of freedom for a two-sided test.

How to do it...

The following steps will show us how we can use the probability distribution plot tools to find the critical t-statistic:

1. Go to the **Graph** menu and select **Probability Distribution Plot...**.
2. Choose the **View Probability** chart.
3. From the **Distribution:** dropdown, select **t** and under **Degrees of freedom:**, enter 14.
4. Select the tab for **Shaded Area**. Ensure that the option for **Define Shaded Area By** is already **Probability**.
5. For a two-sided test, select **Both Tails**. Leave the **Probability** at 0.05.
6. Click on **OK**.

How it works...

Probability distribution plots allow us to easily create a graph of a distribution curve based on the parameters entered. Using the option to view probability, we will generate a distribution curve with a shaded area under the curve.

The previous steps created the t-distribution curve and shaded the area below 0.025 and above 0.975. Overall, 5 percent of the curve is shaded and the position of the 0.025 and 0.975 in T is displayed. This is our critical t-statistic for a t-test, as shown in the following screenshot:

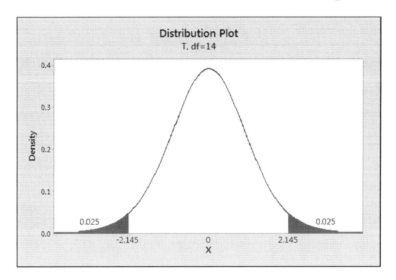

From the graph, the critical t for a two-sided test with df equal to 14 is 2.145.

There's more...

Under the **Calc** menu, the tools found under probability distributions can be used to calculate the probability's density functions, CDF, or inverse CDF. The same critical t-statistics can be calculated using the t-distribution and the inverse CDF.

Finding correlation between multiple variables

The correlation tool is used to investigate linear relationships between variables. In this recipe, we will use the example from the Oxford weather station and check the correlation between the mean maximum temperature, mean minimum temperature, air frost days, rainfall, and hours of sunlight.

Getting ready

The data from the Oxford weather station can be obtained from the Met office website at `http://www.metoffice.gov.uk/climate/uk/stationdata/`.

Open the `Oxford weather (cleaned).mtw` file. This is available on the Packt Publishing website. For more on importing this data directly, see the *Producing a graphical summary of data* recipe.

How to do it...

The following steps will generate the Pearson correlation coefficient and P-value for the results of the weather station data:

1. Go to **Stat**, click on **Basic Statistics**, and select **Correlation...**.
2. Enter the columns for maximum temperature, minimum temperature, rainfall, and hours of sunlight into the **Variables:** section.
3. Click on **OK**.

How it works...

The output generates a table that compares all of the variables to one another. The top number is the correlation score and the lower number the P-value. Correlation scores range from -1 to +1, and a score of 0 indicates no correlation. The null hypothesis for this test is that there is no correlation; the alternative is that there is correlation. Strong correlations should be seen between the temperature columns and hours of sunlight.

There's more...

With a lot of variables, the correlation table can often be wider than the page width of the session window. The results are then displayed across multiple output tables. The session window's output width can be changed in **Options...** under the **Tools** menu.

Correlations can also be visualized very quickly using a matrix plot. This chart will plot a scatterplot of each variable versus one another.

Spearman Rank correlation is also available in Minitab v17 by changing the **Method:** option to **Spearman rho.**

See also

- ▸ The *Producing a graphical summary of data* recipe

Using the 1 Proportion test

In this recipe, in the pulse dataset, we will look at the proportion of students who smoke regularly. We want to check if the proportion is different now from a historical figure of 25 percent of students who smoke regularly. Additionally, we will convert the numeric values in the **Smokes** column to text. This step is not necessary for the proportions test but can be useful to display the results.

Getting ready

Open the `Pulse.mtw` dataset from the Minitab `Sample Data` folder. The column **Smokes** has values of 1 and 2; 1 refers to those who smoke regularly and 2 refers to those who don't smoke regularly.

How to do it...

The following steps will recode the values in the smokes column to categories of **Smokes** and **Does not Smoke** before checking to see if the proportion of smokers is different from the historical proportion of 0.25:

1. Go to the **Data** menu, click on **Code**, and select **Numeric to Text...**.

2. Enter the data shown in the following screenshot into the dialog box:

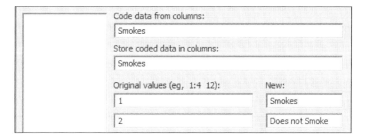

3. Click on **OK**.

4. Go to **Stat** and then **Basic Statistics** and select **1 Proportion...**.

5. Enter the **Smokes** column as the **Samples in columns:**.

6. Tick the option for **Perform hypothesis test**. Enter the **Hypothesized proportion** as `0.25`.

7. Click on **OK**.

How it works...

It is not essential to code the **Smokes** column from numeric values to text but this can be a useful step in the interpretation of the results. Steps 1 to 3 on coding data from numeric to text could be skipped if we want to go straight to the proportion test.

We have used the 1 Proportion test to count the frequency of observations in the **Smokes** column. It is also possible to use the 1 Proportion test with summarized results by entering the number of events and the number of trials.

The options for the 1 Proportion test can be used to change the confidence interval and choose between a one-sided or two-sided test.

The null hypothesis for this test is no different from the hypothesized proportion. The alternative hypothesis is that there is a difference. Here, we fail to reject the null hypothesis with a P-value of 0.278.

See also

▸ The *Graphically presenting the 1 Proportion test* recipe

▸ The *Using the Power and Sample Size tool for a 1 Proportion test* recipe

▸ The *Coding a numeric column to text values* recipe in *Chapter 1, Worksheet, Data Management, and the Calculator*

Graphically presenting the 1 Proportion test

We can represent the results of the 1 Proportion test in the previous example using a probability distribution plot. Using the binomial distribution, we can show where the results of the study are in relation to the historical figures of 25 percent.

Getting ready

Following on from the previous example, we will use the figures of 92 students in total, out of which 28 smoke regularly. It is not necessary to open the dataset but it may be beneficial to run the previous example to compare the results.

How to do it...

The following steps will use probability distribution plots to generate a binomial distribution for 92 trials and an event probability of 0.25:

1. Go to the **Graph** menu and select **Probability Distribution Plot...**.
2. Select the **View Probability** graph.

3. From the dropdown for **Distribution:**, select **Binomial**.

4. Under **Number of trials:**, enter 92 and for **Event probability:**, enter the hypothesized probability of 0.25.

5. Select the tab for **Shaded Area**, choose **X Value**, and select **Both Tails**.

6. For the **X value** field, enter 28.

7. Click on **OK**.

How it works...

The probability distribution plot creates a histogram of the probability density function. For our observed results of 28, we have shaded the area of the distribution above 28. This indicates that we have 0.1399 in the tails of the distribution above 28. As this is a two-sided test and we are checking for a difference, the values of 18 and lower are shaded as well. The area in the distribution below 18 is 0.1383.

Add the two tails together to obtain the P-value of the 1 Proportion test, 0.1383 plus 0.1399 equals 0.2782 - the result of previous example.

For a one-sided test, we can choose to shade just one tail of the distribution.

See also

▶ The *Comparing the population mean to a target with a 1-Sample t-test* recipe

▶ The *Using the Power and Sample Size tool for a 1 Proportion test* recipe

Using the Power and Sample Size tool for a 1 Proportion test

In the 1 Proportion test example, we have 92 students and 28 smokers in the group. The sample shows 30.4 percent of the group as smokers. The results from a 1 Proportion test will indicate that we cannot reject the null hypothesis.

For this recipe, we want to know how many students we need to sample in order to be able to observe a difference of 2.5 percent or 5 percent between the hypothesized and actual proportions that have a power of 80 percent. We will use a hypothesized proportion of 25 percent and differences of 2.5 and 5 percent.

How to do it...

The following steps will help us find the number of samples needed to identify a difference of 2.5 percent or 5 percent with at least an 80 percent chance of identifying this difference:

1. Go to the **Stat** menu, click on **Power and Sample Size**, and select **1 Proportion....**

2. Enter .25 in the **Hypothesized proportion:** field.

3. Enter .2 .225 .275 .3 in the **Comparison proportions:** field and .8 in the **Power values:** field.

4. Click on **OK**.

How it works...

To achieve a power of 80 percent to observe a population with a different proportion to 0.25, we would require a sample size of over 2300 for a 0.025 difference or around 600 samples for a 0.05 difference.

We should also note that we require less samples for the same power to observe a decrease than an increase in the proportion. The results show us that we need 2305 samples to see a proportion of 0.225 or 2399 for a proportion of .275.

By specifying two of the values of **Sample sizes:**, **Power values:**, and **Comparison proportions:**, Minitab will calculate the third value. Each of these three fields will accept multiple values.

Try thinking about the difference that could be observed with only 300 surveyed students. This test can also be made more sensitive by changing the alternative from different to a one-sided test.

See also

- ▶ The *Using the 1 Proportion test* recipe
- ▶ The *Graphically presenting the 1 Proportion test* recipe

Testing two population proportions with the 2 Proportions test

Using the data in the Pulse worksheet, we previously checked to see if the number of regular smokers in a group of students was different to a historical proportion of 0.25. We will use the 2 Proportions test to check if the proportion of regular smokers is different by gender.

Getting ready

Open the `Pulse.mtw` dataset from the Minitab `Sample Data` folder. The **Smokes** column has values of **1** or **2**; **1** refers to students who smoke regularly and 2 refers to students who don't smoke regularly. The **Sex** column uses **1** for male and **2** for female.

How to do it...

The following steps will help us compare the proportion of smokers and nonsmokers between male and female students:

1. Go to the **Stat** menu and then **Basic Statistics** and select **2 Proportions...**.

2. Enter the **Smokes** column as **Samples:** and the **Sex** column as **Sample IDs:**.

3. Click on **OK**.

How it works...

The results will show **Event** as level **2** in the response column. **2** refers to the nonsmokers, the **X** values in the table indicate the count of nonsmokers, and the **Sample p** values indicate the proportion of nonsmokers in the group. The following screenshot indicates where this event is indicated:

```
Event = 2


Sex   X   N   Sample p
1     37  57  0.649123
2     27  35  0.771429



Difference = p (1) - p (2)
Estimate for difference:  -0.122306
95% CI for difference:  (-0.308592, 0.0639809)
Test for difference = 0 (vs not = 0):  Z = -1.29  P-Value = 0.198
```

Event is alphabetically chosen as the last value by default. The preceding screenshot shows **2** as the event, that is, the nonsmokers. 65 percent of the male students were nonsmokers, compared to 77 percent of female students. If we coded the columns to text values as in the *Using the 1 Proportion test* recipe, *Smokes - Does Not Smoke*, then the Event would be Smokes.

The P-value is calculated from a standard normal approximation, which is the Z-score in the previous output. This can be inaccurate if there are less than 5 events or nonevents in either of the samples. Fisher's exact test is also calculated and can be used when the normal approximation is not valid.

The dialog can also accept data as summarized results or separate columns by changing the options available in the drop-down box.

The null hypothesis for the 2 Proportions test is *p1-p2* = 0. The alternative for the two-sided test is p1-p2 ≠ 0.

See also

▸ The *Using the 1 Proportion test* recipe

▸ The *Using the Power and Sample Size tool for a 2 Proportions test* recipe

▸ The *Using the Assistant menu to run a 2 Proportions test* recipe

Using the Power and Sample Size tool for a 2 Proportions test

In the previous recipe, we checked if we could prove a difference in the population of smokers between a group of students. Now, we will check how many students we need to sample to observe a difference of 5 percent or 10 percent between smokers of each gender.

Getting ready

We will use the figures from the previous recipe, *Testing two population proportions with the 2 Proportions test*, but there is no need to open a dataset.

How to do it...

The following steps will find the number of male and female students that need to be included in a sample to be able to observe a difference in the proportion of smokers in each group of 0.05 or 0.1 with at least 80 percent or 90 percent power:

1. Go to the **Stat** menu, select **Power and Sample Size**, and click on **2 Proportions...**.

2. Enter 0.25 in the **Baseline proportion (p2):** field; in **Comparison proportions (p1):**, enter 0.15 0.2 0.3 0.35.

3. In **Power values:**, enter .8 .9.

4. Click on **OK**.

How it works...

The sample size that is calculated is for each group, not overall. To have an 80 percent chance of seeing a population difference of 0.25 to 0.35 in the proportion of smokers, we would need 329 male and female students.

▸ The *Testing two population proportions with the 2 Proportions test* recipe

▸ The *Using the Assistant menu to run a 2 Proportions test* recipe

Using the Assistant menu to run a 2 Proportions test

The Assistant tool also provides us with a 2 Proportions test. We will enter summarized results and check if there is a difference between the observed number of defectives before and after a process change.

No dataset is needed for this recipe as we will be using summarized results. We will use the results for a **Before** group of 200 samples and 21 defective items. After a change was made, we took a sample of 150 items and observed only 6 defectives.

How to do it...

The following steps will use the Assistant tool to run a 2 Proportions test to check the difference between 6 defective items in 150 and 21 in 200:

1. Go to the **Assistant** menu and select **Hypothesis Tests...**.

2. Choose the **2-Sample % Defective** option from under the **Compare two samples with each other** group.

3. Complete the dialog box as shown in the following screenshot:

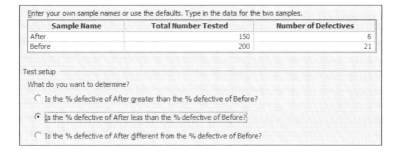

4. Click on **OK**.

How it works...

The Assistant test for 2 percent defectives only uses summarized data, but provides a series of report slides as the output. The Assistant can also make the choice of a one-sided or two-sided test very simple. The choice of what we want to determine will be updated to reflect the sample names that have been entered.

See also

▶ The *Testing two population proportions with the 2 Proportions test* recipe

▶ The *Using the Power and Sample Size tool for a 2 Proportions test* recipe

Finding the sample size to estimate a mean to a given margin of error

Here, we want to obtain the sample size required to estimate a population parameter to a given margin of error. We will not use specific values but will find the number of samples required to estimate a mean with a confidence interval ±0.5 and ±1 standard deviation wide.

How to do it...

The following steps will identify the number of samples required to find an estimate of the population mean to a confidence interval of +/- 0.5 and +/-1 standard deviations wide:

1. Go to the **Stat** menu, go to **Power and Sample Size**, and select **Sample Size for Estimation...**.

2. In the **Parameter** section, select **Mean (Normal)** from the dropdown.

3. Under **Planning Value**, enter **Standard deviation:** as 1.

4. In **Margins of error for confidence intervals:**, enter 0.5 and 1 (separated by a space).

5. Click on **OK**.

How it works...

We are trying to find the sample size required to estimate the population mean as +/- 0.5 or 1 standard deviations. Eighteen samples would give us a confidence interval that is 1 standard deviation wide; seven samples would give us a confidence interval of 2 standard deviations wide. This tool does not tell us the number of samples required to prove a difference, only the number of samples required for a given confidence interval.

We have entered the standard deviation in the dialog box as 1 and then entered the margin of error as a ratio of the standard deviation. We could have used actual standard deviations and margins of error. If we use the example of the GDP figures in the UK from 2009 to 2013, we will find a standard deviation of 0.43 from the *Comparing the population mean to a target with a 1-Sample t-test* recipe. By entering the standard deviation as 0.43, we could check how many samples are needed to estimate the mean percentage growth to a margin of error of 0.1 percent.

See also

▶   The *Comparing the population mean to a target with a 1-Sample t-test* recipe

Using Cross tabulation and Chi-Square

We can use a Chi-Square test to check if proportions are equal across several groups of data. The example here is of the proportion of enlisted men and women in the US armed forces. Does the proportion of men and women in the US armed forces differ by service?

The data is obtained from the Statisticbrain website and can be found at `http://www.statisticbrain.com/demographics-of-active-duty-u-s-military/`.

Getting ready

Enter the data into a blank worksheet as shown in the following screenshot:

Enlisted	Service	Gender
392392	Army	Male
234002	Navy	Male
167164	Marine Corps	Male
206734	Air Force	Male
29374	Coast Guard	Male
59672	Army	Female
41294	Navy	Female
11049	Marine Corps	Female
51361	Air Force	Female
3854	Coast Guard	Female

How to do it...

The following steps will compare the proportion of enlisted male and female personnel in the US armed services using a Chi-Square test:

1. Go to the **Stat** menu, click on **Tables**, and select **Cross Tabulation and Chi-Square**.

2. Enter **Service** in the field For **rows:** column.

3. Enter **Gender** in the field **For columns:** column.

4. Enter **Enlisted** in the field **Frequencies are in:** column.

5. Select the **Chi-Square...** button.

6. Check the options for **Chi-square test**, **Expected cell counts**, and **Each cell's contribution to the Chi-Square statistics**.

7. Click on **OK** twice.

How it works...

The Cross Tabulation and Chi-Square tools are a great way to build a table of frequencies. We have used rows and columns in this example, but we could also use layers to split the table by a third factor. The default view is to display the counts within the table.

The null hypothesis for this test is that the Chi-Square score is zero; the alternative is that it is not zero.

We can find the expected cell count for women in the services using this formula: (total number of females/total number of personnel) * number of personnel in that service.

The same can be run for the number of males in each service.

The contribution to Chi-Square for a cell is found from this formula: (Observed-Expected)^2/Expected.

Pearsons Chi-Square is the sum of the contributions.

There's more...

Bar charts would be a great way to present the results of this Chi-Square test. Read about bar charts in *Chapter 2, Tables and Graphs*. Use **Values from a table bar chart**, **One column of values** and select the **Stacked** graph. Graph options can be used to show the percentages; set these options within columns that are at level 1.

Using equivalence tests to prove zero difference between the mean and a target

Equivalence tests are new in Minitab v17. We will use an equivalence test to determine if the mean of a sample can be found to be equivalent for a target value.

These tests are similar to t-tests, but where the t-test null hypothesis is no difference, an equivalence test uses a null hypothesis of there is a difference.

The example dataset here is fill volumes of syringes. The target fill volume is 15 ml; we would like to know if the fill volumes of this process are equivalent to the goal of 15 to within +/- .25 ml around the target.

Getting ready

Open the `equivalence 1 sample.mtw` worksheet from the support files.

How to do it...

The following steps compare the measured volumes to the target of 15:

1. Navigate to **Stat | Equivalence Tests | 1 Sample...**.
2. Enter **Volume** for the **Sample:** column.
3. Enter `15` as **Target:**.
4. For **Lower limit:**, enter `-.25`.
5. For **Upper limit:**, enter `.25`.
6. Click on **OK**.

How it works...

Equivalence tests are also known as two one-Sided t-tests. The 1-Sample equivalence test uses two 1-Sample t-tests. The first null hypothesis is that the *mean - target* is less than equal to lower limit, with an alternative of greater than.

The second null hypothesis is that the *mean - target* is greater than or equal to upper limit with an alternative of less than.

When both null hypotheses can be rejected, we can prove that the *mean - target* is greater than the lower limit, and lesser than the upper limit, proving that the *mean-target* is within the equivalence limits.

If one null hypothesis cannot be rejected, then the *mean - target* is outside the equivalence region.

This is the opposite of a t-test. With a t-test, we can only prove a difference between a target or between means. With the equivalence test, we swap the null hypothesis to be a difference so that we can then look for evidence of no difference.

This becomes useful when we would like to prove that a process is on target.

T-tests cannot be used to prove that we are on target. This is because we never prove the null hypothesis. A t-test can show us that we cannot prove a difference, but this may be because we didn't take enough data to be able to observe that difference.

Equivalence tests, unlike t-tests, look for evidence to prove that there is no difference. If we do not have enough data to prove no difference, then we would fail to reject the null hypothesis that there is a difference.

There's more...

Like t-tests, Minitab has power and sample size tools for the equivalence tests, tests for 2 samples, and paired equivalence. See the *Calculating the sample size for a 1-Sample equivalence test* recipe.

It is also possible to set a limit based on a multiplication around the target instead of a difference. Setting a lower limit at -0.1 and the upper at +0.1 will put the equivalence limits at -1.5 or +1.5 around the target of 15. This can be useful if specifying equivalence to a stated percentage of the target.

See also

- ▸ The *Calculating the sample size for a 1-Sample equivalence test* recipe

Calculating the sample size for a 1-Sample equivalence test

The power and sample size tools enable us to calculate the number of samples we require to prove that a test sample is equivalent to a target or another sample.

Here, we check the number of samples required to prove that a batch of syringes have a fill volume with a mean of 15 ml. To be equivalent, the mean fill volume should be within +/- 0.25 of the target. The goal is to be able to identify that the mean is less than 0.1 different to the target, with at least 80 percent or 90 percent power.

We will use a standard deviation of 0.27 for this study.

Getting Ready

We will not open a dataset for this study. This example follows the previous recipe, *Using equivalence tests to prove zero difference between the mean and a target*.

How to do it...

The following steps will calculate a sample size required to check for equivalence with at least 80 percent power:

1. Navigate to **Stat | Power and Sample Size | Equivalence Tests | 1-Sample...**.
2. Set **Lower limit:** to -0.25 and **Upper limit:** to 0.25.
3. Enter **Differences (within the limits):** as 0.1.
4. Enter **Power values:** as .8 .9.
5. Enter **Standard deviation:** of 0.27.
6. Click on **OK**.

How it works...

The difference within the limits is the size of difference that we want to be able to declare is equivalent 80 percent or 90 percent. For example, if the mean is .1 different to the target, we will want to know how many samples are required to prove that this result is equivalent with 80 percent or 90 percent power.

The equivalent limits are the range within which the confidence interval must fall to be able to prove that the mean is no further away than the equivalence limit.

See also

▸ The *Using equivalence tests to prove zero difference between the mean and a target* recipe

4
Using Analysis of Variance

In this chapter, we will cover the following recipes:

- ▸ Using a one-way ANOVA with unstacked columns
- ▸ Calculating power for the one-way ANOVA
- ▸ Using Assistant to run a one-way ANOVA
- ▸ Testing for equal variances
- ▸ Analyzing a balanced design
- ▸ Entering random effects model
- ▸ Using GLM for unbalanced designs
- ▸ Analyzing covariance
- ▸ Analyzing a fully nested design
- ▸ The repeated measures ANOVA – using a mixed effects model
- ▸ Finding the critical F-statistic

Introduction

The **Analysis of Variance** (**ANOVA**) tools generalize the ideas of T-tests by checking the difference across means of many groups of data. Most of the tools used in this section are found in the ANOVA section, under the **Stat** menu. The following screenshot shows the route to the tools that we will use:

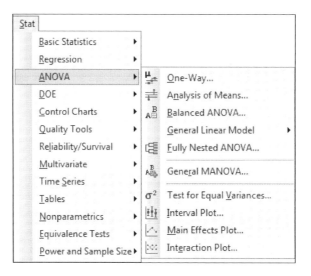

Most of the recipes here use the **General Linear Model** option. This option can use 31 factors, 50 covariates, and up to 50 response variables, making this a quick one-stop shop for use. The **General Linear Model** option can run a one-way ANOVA, two-way, balanced ANOVA, and fully nested ANOVA.

In the Minitab Version 17, the **General Linear Model** tools have been updated to store fitted models back into the worksheet. The fitted models then allow the use of contour plots, surface plots, response optimizer, and more.

One-way ANOVA tools offer the use of data in an unstacked format and can be found in the assistant as well.

The options for interval plots, main effects plots, and interactions plots offer useful graphical tools to display the results after analysis.

The datasets used in this chapter come from a number of sources. We will copy data and in some examples, the data can be typed into the worksheet.

Using a one-way ANOVA with unstacked columns

In the first activity, we will use the one-way ANOVA to check the differences between population means across several groups of data. We will be using atmospheric data for the **North Atlantic Oscillation** (**NAO**). The NAO is an important climatic phenomenon that affects the North Atlantic. Variations in the NAO affect the weather across Europe. Measurements of the pressure difference between the northern weather station in Iceland and more southerly stations are an important measure of this phenomenon.

Here, we will use the one-way ANOVA to investigate the effect of the pressure difference across months.

This data was obtained from the Climactic Research Unit and is located at `http://www.cru.uea.ac.uk/cru/data/nao/`; this can be opened in Minitab by opening the DAT file using **Open Worksheet** or by can copying and pasting the results directly. Within the DAT file, missing data is indicated as -99. These will need to be converted to a * symbol for Minitab to recognize as missing values.

We will open the data into Minitab, identify missing values in the worksheet, and then use the one-way ANOVA to study the pressure difference by month.

Getting ready

Either open the `nao.dat` file using the **Open Worksheet** option in Minitab or copy the data to Minitab from the NAO website. On opening the worksheet, set the file type to ***.dat**. Then use the **Options** file to set **Variable Names** to **None** and **Field Definition** to **Free format**.

This file is available on the Packt Publishing website.

How to do it...

The following steps will recode the value -99 as missing data, and then study the effect of a month of the year on pressure difference:

1. With the data in Minitab, we need to rename the columns. Enter the column names for C1 to C14 as Year, Jan, Feb, Mar, Apr, May, Jun, Jul, Aug, Sep, Oct, Nov, Dec, Annual.

2. Next, go to the **Editor** menu and click on **Replace**. Enter -99.99 in the section for **Find what:** and in the **Replace with:** section, enter *. Click on **Replace All**.

3. Navigate to **Stat | ANOVA** and then click on **One-Way...**.

4. From the drop-down selection, change the option for the data setup to **Response data are in a separate column for each factor level**.

5. Select the columns for the monthly results and enter **Responses:** as shown in the following screenshot. They can be entered in one group by highlighting the columns in the left-hand selection and then clicking on the **Select** button.

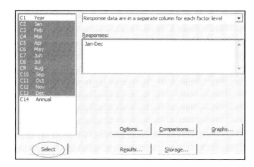

6. Click on the **Graphs** button; choose **Boxplots of data** and **Three in one** residual plots.
7. Click on **OK** in each dialog box.

How it works...

Rather than needing to stack the columns of data, we can use the unstacked one-way ANOVA. The same results could be obtained using the general linear model but we would need to stack the data first. For more on stacking columns, see the *Stacking several columns together* recipe in *Chapter 1, Worksheet, Data Management, and the Calculator*.

The one-way ANOVA options have changed slightly in Minitab v17, compared to previous releases. The separate dialog boxes for unstacked or stacked data have been combined into one selection. The one-way ANOVA can also run Welch's test now. Under **Options**, there is a tick box to select **Assume equal variances**. When this is unselected, we would run Welch's ANOVA.

Another change for Minitab v17 is the move of the character graph that displays means and confidence intervals into an interval plot.

Multiple columns can be selected in the dialog boxes by left-clicking and selecting the top item and dragging it down in the list. Using *Shift* or *Ctrl* for selection will work too. When selecting multiple columns, they will be identified in the column list as C1-C5—where the dash indicates the range of columns between the first and last.

The comparison options allow the use of Tukey's, Fisher's, Dunnett's, Hsu's multiple comparisons. Also included is the Games-Howell comparison for when we cannot assume equal variances.

The output from the one-way ANOVA will generate the sum of square values for the months, F-statistics, and the p-value for the test. The null hypothesis for the one-way ANOVA means that there is no difference between means or has no effect on the variation.

The three-in-one residual plots that are generated allow us to check the assumptions of normality of the residuals and homoscedasticity, equal variance, or the residual error. If the residuals show unequal variances, then the p-value of the one-way ANOVA test can be inaccurate. When we cannot assume equal variances, we can choose to use Welch's ANOVA as indicated previously.

The **Assistant** menu also provides a one-way ANOVA test. This will always use Welch's ANOVA for unequal variance.

Residuals over time are not produced for unstacked data as the results may not follow a logical time order. With the results of pressure difference, we do have a time component and this should be checked with time series plots to look for any patterns in the results.

See also

▸ The *Stacking several columns together* recipe in *Chapter 1, Worksheet, Data Management, and the Calculator*

▸ The *Testing for equal variances* recipe

▸ The *Calculating power for the one-way ANOVA* recipe

▸ The *Using Assistant to run a one-way ANOVA* recipe

Calculating power for the one-way ANOVA

Here, we will look at the number of samples needed in a one-way ANOVA to detect differences of 1, 2, or 3 standard deviations in size for 80 or 90 percent power. When we do not have a historical standard deviation, we can use a figure of one in the dialog box. The differences are then referred to as multiples of the standard deviation.

How to do it...

The following steps will generate the sample sizes required to find differences of 1, 2, or 3 standard deviations with at least 80 or 90 percent power:

1. Navigate to **Stat | Power and Sample Size**. Then click on **One Way ANOVA**.

2. In the **Number of levels:** field, enter 12.

3. In **Values of the maximum difference between means:**, enter 1 2 3.

4. In **Power values:**, enter .8 .9.

5. In **Standard deviation:**, enter 1. The dialog box should look like the following screenshot:

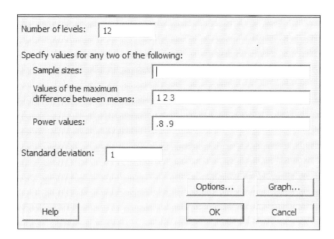

6. Click on **OK**.

How it works...

Most typically, we would use this tool to assess the power of results where we have a known standard deviation. This could then be run after a study to verify if the results have enough power to identify a difference of interest for us.

When the historical standard deviation is unknown to us and we are planning on samples to take, we can refer to the differences as a ratio of the standard deviations. We should note that we will obtain the same sample sizes when using a standard deviation of 2 and differences of 2, 4, and 6.

The results here indicate that in a study with 12 groups, we need 10 samples per group to have an 80 percent chance of identifying a difference of a two-standard deviation between the means of the levels. If this is a study looking at differences across 12 months of the year, we would need 10 samples from each month to achieve the power stated previously.

As a general note on the entry of values into dialogs, Minitab uses spaces to identify separate values. Entering the differences as 1 2 3 with a space will tell the software to find sample sizes for each difference. Entering multiple power values will give us sample sizes for each difference and power. This is presented on a power curve and in the session window.

See also

▶ The *Using a one-way ANOVA with unstacked columns* recipe

▶ The *Using Assistant to run a one-way ANOVA* recipe

Using Assistant to run a one-way ANOVA

The **Assistant** tools will also run a one-way ANOVA. This provides a simpler route to generate the test and is presented as a series of graphical report pages.

For this recipe, we will compare the different mean times between failures of pressure sensors. The response is the number of weeks in service; the category is the failure mode of the circuit. The dataset we will open is `circuit.mtw` and is one of the example datasets that are installed with Minitab.

How to do it...

The following steps will run a one-way ANOVA and display the graphical reports:

1. Go to the **File** menu and click on **Open Worksheet**.
2. Click on the button for **Look in Minitab Sample Data folder**.
3. Open the `circuit.mtw` file.
4. Go to the **Assistant** menu and then click on **Hypothesis tests**.
5. From the **Compare more than two samples** heading, select **One-Way ANOVA**.
6. From the drop-down box, make sure that the choice for data is selected as **Y data are in one column, X values are in another column**.
7. In **Y data column:**, enter `Weeks`.
8. In **X values column:**, enter `Failure`.
9. Click on **OK**.

How it works...

The assistant tools are a great way to obtain guidance on the test to run and the results of that test. They give the user a simpler dialog box by limiting the options available.

We can select a tool directly from the objective's screen or use the **Help Me Choose** option. The following screenshot shows the three objectives that we can select. By clicking on the **Compare more than two samples** title, we are taken to a decision tree to choose between **One-Way ANOVA**, **Standard Deviations Test**, or **Chi-Square Test for Association**:

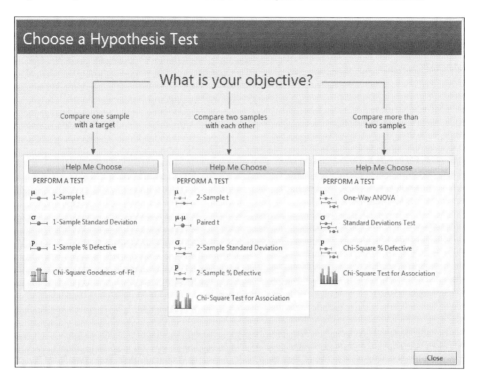

The results from the one-way ANOVA will generate four graphical report pages.

The first page is the report card; here, we will find information or warnings about outliers, normality, and sample size. This will also inform us if the test has enough power to detect the difference that can be specified in the dialog power.

The second page is a power report of the study. When entering a value for the difference between the means, then we would obtain the power for that difference; this page will also provide alternative sample sizes or the differences that can be detected for a given power value.

The third page is a diagnostic report on the results. Time series plots are shown for each level, and outliers will be highlighted in red. The distribution of the results in each level will also be given as boxplots, individual value plots, or histograms. The type of chart that is displayed depends on the number of levels and the number of subgroups.

The last page is the summary report. This shows the p-value of the ANOVA. To help make the interpretation of the results easier, the null hypothesis is rephrased as the question. Do the means differ? The results of the p-value are plotted on a decision bar underneath. A means comparison chart is plotted to help identify the means that differ from each other, and comments are completed for us as well.

It is worth noting that the **Assistant** menu uses Welch's one-way ANOVA. Welch's method provides a correction for unequal variances across groups. It is used in the **Assistant** menu to provide a more conservative estimate of the p-value.

See also

▶   The *Using a one-way ANOVA with unstacked columns* recipe

Testing for equal variances

In this recipe, we will return to the topic of atmospheric pressure data. The data was obtained from the Climactic Research Unit. We will look at the atmospheric pressure recorded at the Gibraltar weather station. The test for equal variances will be used to check for differences in variance by month.

As with the data for the pressure difference used in the example, using the one-way ANOVA with unstacked columns' missing values is coded as -10. We will recode these to *. We will also need to stack the data before checking for differences in variation between the months.

Getting ready

Either open the file nao_gib.dat using the **Open Worksheet** command in Minitab or copy the data to Minitab from the NAO website. If opening the worksheet, set the file type to ***.dat**. Then use the **Options** file to set the **Variable Names** option to **None** and the **Field Definition** option to **Free Format**.

This nao_gib.dat file is also available on the Packt Publishing website.

How to do it...

The following steps will recode the value -10 to * and then stack the results before running a test for equal variance:

1.   Name the columns C1 to C14 as Year, Jan, Feb, Mar, Apr, May, Jun, Jul, Aug, Sep, Oct, Nov, Dec, Annual.

2.   Next, go to the **Editor** menu and click on **Replace**. Enter -10 in the **Find what:** field and in **Replace with:**, enter *. Click on **Replace All**.

3. Navigate to **Data | Stack**, and click on **Stack columns**.

4. Select the month columns to stack the data by highlighting them and clicking on the **Select** button. In the **Store stacked data in:** field, enter the name for the **New worksheet** field as `Stacked Data`. The dialog should appear as shown in the following screenshot:

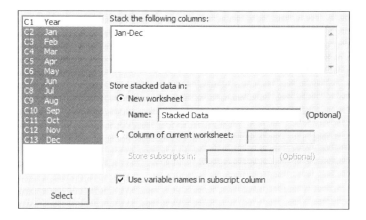

5. Name the datasets in the new worksheet: column 1 as `Month` and column 2 as `Pressure`.

6. Navigate to **Stat | ANOVA** and then click on **Test for Equal Variances**.

7. Enter `Pressure` in the **Response** field.

8. Enter `Month` in the **Factors** field.

9. Click on **OK.**

How it works...

We could also have used the data without stacking the results. In Minitab v17, we can choose between the data in separate columns or in stacked ones. If we are using a previous version, we need to use the stack data command to put the results into one column.

The stack data commands will quickly create one column with all the numeric responses and a subscript column. Here, this subscript column identifies the month based on the column names of the unstacked data.

As stacked columns will not keep the information about a year in the new worksheet, there are two options to ensure that we keep this information. Use **Stack Blocks of Columns** or alternatively, we could create a new column for the year using the calculator tools of **Make Patterned Data**.

The results that we have generated plot the standard deviations of pressure for each month. They also include a confidence interval for the value of the population standard deviation—sigma. The degree of overlap between confidence intervals can give us an indication of how similar sigma is between categories. Note that it is not always the case that intervals which overlap the standard deviation of another category are similar.

On the right-hand side of the chart, we obtain the results of Bartlett's test and Levene's test. We will use the p-value for Bartlett's test when we expect each category to be distributed normally. Levene's test is not as sensitive to departures from a normal distribution and may be used for any continuous distribution. The results of Levene's test do not provide as accurate a figure for the p-value when the data is normal.

There's more...

The **Assistant** option can also be used to run a standard deviations test. This can accept results as stacked or unstacked. The assistant output will give only the p-value for Levene's test, and it can be used only for one factor.

See also

- The *Using a one-way ANOVA with unstacked columns* recipe
- The *Using Assistant to run a one-way ANOVA* recipe
- The *Stacking several columns together* recipe in *Chapter 1, Worksheet, Data Management, and the Calculator*
- The *Stacking blocks of columns at the same time* recipe in *Chapter 1, Worksheet, Data Management, and the Calculator*

Analyzing a balanced design

A balanced ANOVA is one where all combinations of factors have the same number of observed results.

Here, we will look at the analysis of a designed experiment. The study is on an automobile filter to reduce pollution. This study looks at the noise properties of the filter. The response of the noise level is in decibels. The factors include vehicle size—1 2 3, representing small to large, type of filter—1 representing standard and 2 representing octel, and side—1 representing right and 2 representing left.

We will use a balanced ANOVA to study the effect on the results as all treatment conditions have the same number of observations. The terms in the model will be checked for significance using an alpha of 0.05. All main effects and interactions will be included in the model and we will produce residual plots to check the assumptions of using ANOVA.

Getting ready

The data and story behind this example are available from StatLib at
`http://lib.stat.cmu.edu/DASL/Stories/airpollutionfilters.html`.

Copy the data into Minitab and label the columns appropriately.

The `filter noise.mtw` file is also provided on the Packt Publishing website.

How to do it...

The following steps will run the balanced ANOVA with all the main effects and interactions:

1. Navigate to **Stat | ANOVA** and click on **Balanced ANOVA**.

2. Enter `Noise` into the **Responses** field and `Size`, `Type`, and `Side` as **Factors**. Place the pipe symbol (|) between the factors, as indicated in the following screenshot:

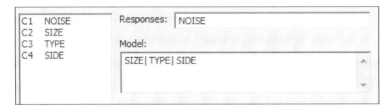

3. Click on **OK** to run the analysis.

4. Go to the results in the session window. From the analysis of the variance table, check the terms that are significant. Use a decision of 0.05 for the p-value.

5. The three-way interaction term `Size*Type*Side` is significant. The model must be hierarchical, therefore we need to include all the two-way and main effects terms to calculate the model. Use Ctrl + *E* to return to the last dialog box to select the residual plots.

6. Click on the **Graphs** button.

7. Click on the radio button for **Four in One residuals**.

8. Click on **OK** in each dialog.

How it works...

The balanced ANOVA and general linear model tools can be used with up to 31 factors. The model must be hierarchical; this means that the inclusion of the three-way `Size*Type*Side` interaction needs to include all the two-way interactions between `Size`, `Type`, and `Side`.

The residual plots can be generated as individual pages or as the **Four in one** option, as used here. This produces the four residuals on one page as a diagnostic plot. This allows us to check the assumptions of the residual error, which are normally distribution and homoscedasticity.

If we include random factors, these must be entered into the model and then declared as a random factor in the section for **Random Factors:**. They must be included in both sections for the model to work.

The following information illustrates the use of the notation of pipe, exclamation, and star to specify the model terms. The pipe symbol or exclamation mark can be used as a shortcut to run all interactions between the factors. The | and ! marks can be used interchangeably.

For example, if we use factors of A, B, and C, then enter the factors as A!B!C into the design, this will specify a model using the A B C AB AC BC ABC terms. If we had just used A!B C, the model would be A B C AB.

Interactions can be entered with the use of a * symbol between factors. Entering A B C A*B B*C will generate a model of A B C AB BC.

Terms can be excluded in a model by the use of a minus sign. By specifying the model as A|B|C - A*B*C, we would have a model of A B C AB AC BC.

The general linear model tool from ANOVA can also be used for balanced designs, one-way ANOVA, two-way ANOVA, and to define nested designs. The only option that balanced designs offer us over the general linear model is the option to run a restricted model. The restricted model can be used when both fixed and random terms are included in the design.

See also

▸   The *Using GLM for unbalanced designs* recipe

Entering random effects model

In the random effects model, both factors are declared as random factors. This recipe looks at a study on taste from a panel of professional taste testers. Different batches of a food product are tested to check the consistency of taste. Each appraiser tastes each batch twice. This way we can observe the consistency of scores from within the appraiser.

As the product is a selection of batches from a much larger population of batches, the samples represent a random selection from all product batches. The taste testers are a sample of appraisers from a group of tasters, representing a random selection as well; we will use the appraiser as a random factor to represent the variation across appraisers.

The scores are a mean figure from four attributes: taste, aroma, texture, and appearance.

The data will be provided later to type into Minitab; for ease of entry, it is set out as a table. We will stack this into columns to run the general linear model with both factors defined as random factors.

Getting ready

Enter the data shown in the following screenshot into Minitab:

Appraiser	Batch1	Batch2	Batch3	Batch4
A	7.75	7.25	8.75	7.50
A	7.50	7.25	8.50	7.50
B	8.00	7.50	8.00	6.75
B	7.50	6.75	8.25	7.00
C	7.25	7.00	8.50	7.25
C	7.00	7.50	8.25	7.00
D	7.50	6.25	8.00	6.75
D	7.75	6.50	8.50	7.00

How to do it...

The following steps will stack the data into a new worksheet. After renaming the stacked data, we will look at the effects of the batch and the appraiser on the taste scores using a general linear model:

1. Navigate to **Data** | **Stack** and click on **Blocks of Columns**.
2. Enter the columns into the dialog as shown in the following screenshot:

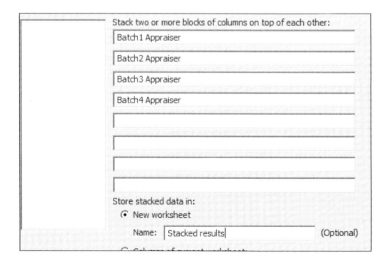

3. Click on **OK** to create a new worksheet with the stacked data.

4. Rename column 1 as `Batch`, column 2 as `Score`, and column 3 as `Appraiser`.

5. Navigate to **Stat | ANOVA** and click on **Fit General Linear Model**.

6. Enter `Score` in the **Responses:** field and in the **Factors:** field, enter `Batch Appraiser`.

7. Select the **Random/Nest...** button.

8. Change **Factor type:** to **Random** for both the **Batch** and **Appraiser** columns, as shown in the following screenshot:

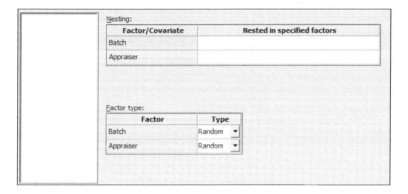

9. Click on **OK**.

10. Next, click on the **Model...** button.

11. Highlight **Batch** and **Appraiser** in the **Factors and covariates:** section and then click on the **Add** button next to the **Interactions through order:** field. As shown in the following screenshot, add the interaction of `Batch` and `Appraiser` to the model:

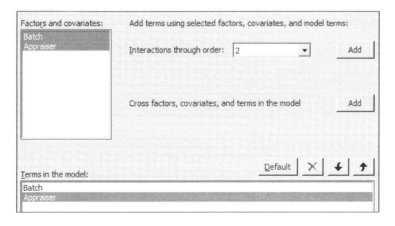

12. Click on **OK** in each dialog box to run the analysis.

13. Check the results in the session window. Use a decision level of 0.05 for the p-value.

14. As the interaction between `Batch` and `Appraiser` is significant, we will leave all terms in the model. To check the assumptions of using the general linear model, we will generate residual plots. Press *Ctrl + E* to return to the last dialog box.

15. Click on the **Graphs** button and select the **Four in one** option.

16. Click on **OK** in each dialog box to run the study.

How it works...

The random effects model from the general linear model will find the F-statistics for the factors of `Batch` and `Appraiser` from the following expression: $F = MS_{batch} / MS_{Batch*Appraiser}$. As both factors are random, the error for these terms is found from the interaction term.

To define the model that we are fitting, we enter all the factors into the factors section within Minitab, and any covariates would be entered into the separate covariate section. Then we use the **Random/Nest...** button to identify nesting and random factors in the design.

The **Terms...** button gives us the options to identify the terms to be included in the model. We select the factors from the **Factors and covariates:** section and then by selecting the **Interactions through order:** field, all interactions for the highlighted factors up to the stated order would be included.

For example, if we have the three factors A B C and the D covariate, we could highlight A and B and select interactions up through order 2 to include the A*B interaction. Alternatively, we could highlight A through D and select order 3 and then we could include the interactions AB AC AD BC BD CD and the three-way interactions.

Quadratic or cubic effects on covariates can be included in the **Terms through order:** option. Note that this will be available only when covariates are included in the model.

This change for Minitab v17 makes the inclusion and removal of terms much simpler than it previously was. When reducing a model, we only need to highlight the terms that would be removed from the model and click on the X button to remove them.

The data supplied here was provided in a tabular format. Instructions 1 to 3 stack the data to be used in the general linear model tools. If our data was provided in this format, then we could skip these steps.

The GLM is run first with all the terms included. We check the results of the p-values and if the interaction cannot be proved as significant, then we would remove this term. At this point, we would return to the GLM and remove the interaction from the study. Without any interactions in a study with random factors, then the F-statistic for the main effects returns to mean square divided by the mean square error.

Finally, when only the significant terms are left in the model, we include the residual plots in the response, so we can verify the assumptions of using the analysis of variance. With the results of this study, we should notice an odd effect on the probability plot of the residuals. This is because the results are very discrete in nature.

The general linear model tool in Minitab will fit the unrestricted form of the ANOVA. For the restricted model, use the balanced ANOVA and select the restricted model from options.

There's more...

For more on random effects models, see, *Applied Linear Statistical Models, Fourth Edition*, by *Neter, Kutner, Nachtsheim*, and *Wasserman*, page 1005.

The GLM tools have changed a lot for Minitab v17. With the previous version of Minitab, the dialog box will follow the same setup as the balanced ANOVA tools. This has changed how we enter terms into the model and also how we define nested or random factors.

The **Fit General Linear Model** option also stores the model in the response column of the worksheet. When returning to the worksheet, there will be a green tick in the `Score` column to indicate that we have a model fitted to `Score`.

This model can be used to run multiple comparisons and generate plots based on predicted values of the model.

Users of previous versions of Minitab will also notice that the output of the GLM tools has been greatly expanded. The **Results...** button gives us a lot of control over the amount of output we can choose to display. Everything from the model summaries, regression equations, variance components, and much more can be expanded from here.

Other new options for GLM with Minitab v17 include the ability to standardize the covariates. We have five options to help standardize the covariates:

- Low and high levels standardized to -1, +1
- Subtract the mean and divide by the standard deviation
- Subtract the mean
- Divide by standard deviation
- Subtract by a value and divide by another specified value

See also

- The *Analyzing a balanced design* recipe
- The *Stacking blocks of columns at the same time* recipe in *Chapter 1, Worksheet, Data Management, and the Calculator*
- The *Using GLM for unbalanced designs* recipe

Using GLM for unbalanced designs

GLM or General Linear Model is a general tool for ANOVA. As such, we see that it will run studies from factors 1 to 31, and can include nesting or random factors.

For this example, we will look at a larger dataset. The data is for crash test dummies that have been used to look at forces in controlled crash environments. The National Transportation Safety Board collected data from crashing vehicles into a wall at 35 mph. Columns contain information on the make and model of the car. Head injury criterion, chest deceleration, left femur load, right femur load, D/P (whether the dummy was in the driver or passenger seat), protection, doors, year of the car, weight in pounds, and size of the vehicle.

We will look at a few of the factors to study the effect on chest deceleration. It is not possible to investigate all interactions in the data. This is due to some missing values in the results, and not all combinations of levels are possible. We will start by focusing on just a few.

The instructions will reduce the model step-by-step, removing the interactions in the model. Alpha for the decision level is used as 0.05 in this data.

As a note, the recipe is meant to be indicative of how such a study can be run and is not an exclusive study into a full model. We should build on these instructions and use the example as a base for a more in-depth study. We should also be careful of associations as a cause until we can discount other reasons. This data was also used in support of legal arguments over safety.

Getting ready

The crash test data can be found at the following link:

`http://lib.stat.cmu.edu/DASL/Datafiles/Crash.html`

The results can be copied and pasted directly into Minitab.

How to do it...

The following instructions will specify a model with several interactions and then reduce the design by removing steps highest p-values:

1. Navigate to **Stat | ANOVA | General Linear Model** and click on **Fit General Linear Model**.

2. Enter `'Chest decel'` in the **Responses:** field and enter `'D/P' Protection Doors` and `Size` into the **Factors:** field as shown in the following screenshot:

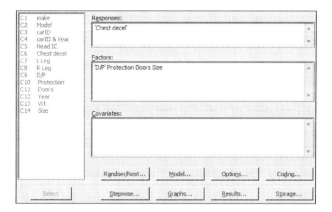

3. To enter interactions for the factors, click on the **Model...** button.

4. Highlight the factors within the **Factors and covariates:** section and click on the **Add** button next to **Interactions through order:**, as shown in the following screenshot:

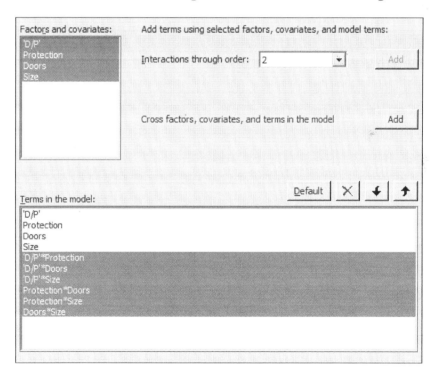

5. Click on **OK** and return to the session window to check the results. Look for interactions with a p-value above the decision level.

6. Check for the interaction with the highest p-value. From the results shown in the following screenshot, **D/P*Size** has the highest p-value. Press *Ctrl + E* to return to the last dialog box: .

```
Analysis of Variance

Source              DF    Adj SS   Adj MS   F-Value   P-Value
   D/P               1     458.1   458.06      7.67     0.006
   Protection        4     538.3   134.57      2.25     0.064
   Doors             1     659.6   659.60     11.04     0.001
   Size              5    3243.9   648.79     10.86     0.000
   D/P*Protection    4      96.6    24.15      0.40     0.806
   D/P*Doors         1     130.2   130.15      2.18     0.141
   D/P*Size          5      95.5    19.10      0.32     0.901
   Doors*Size        5     203.0    40.60      0.68     0.639
Error               248   14818.2    59.75
   Lack-of-Fit       35    2234.6    63.85      1.08     0.358
   Pure Error       213   12583.6    59.08
Total               274   22757.9
```

7. Click on the **Model...** button. Then, select the interaction of **'D/P'*Size** from the **Terms in the model:** field and click on the red **X** to remove this term. Also, remove the terms of **Protection*Doors** and **Protection*Size**. These cannot be estimated, as indicated in the session window.

 Double-clicking on a term in the list will remove it from the model as well. Click on **OK** in each dialog to rerun the model.

8. Return to the session window and look for interactions with a p-value greater than 0.05. As in the previous step, look for the interaction with the highest p-value. Press *Ctrl + E* to return to the GLM and remove this term from the dialog.

9. Repeat steps 6 and 7 until only the interactions with p-values below 0.05 remain in the model.

10. Steps 6 and 7 should then be repeated for the main effects, removing each term one by one. Main effects must be included, which are part of an interaction or have a p-value less than 0.05.

11. When only the significant terms are left in the model, return to the **Fit General Linear Model** dialog box and run residual plots. Click on the **Graphs** button and select the **Four in one** residuals.

12. Click on **OK** in each dialog box.

13. To create main effects plots, navigate to **Stat | ANOVA | General Linear Model** and click on **Factorial Plots**.

14. The **Response:** field of Chest decel should already have been included and to create charts of the terms included in the model, click on **OK**.

How it works...

The data has several missing values in different columns and is unbalanced due to incomplete cells of the study having the same number of results. For example, there are 59 results with two-door vehicles and 84 results with four-door vehicles. The number of doors for vans and pickup trucks are not recorded and are shown as missing. We should be careful of these missing results as they will be left out of the model.

Using the descriptive statistics tables under the **Tables** menu, we can show the number of observations for each level within each factor. Entering Protection and Size columns in this tool would show us that the driver and passenger airbags are present only in the size group hev, and driver airbags are not present in mini, mpv, pu, and van. This prevents us from looking at interactions between Protection and Size.

As the design is not balanced, the values of the sequential sum of squares and the adjusted sum of squares will be different. The order of the data in the results could change the estimation of the sequential sum of squares. By default, the adjusted sums of squares are used to calculate the significance of the terms. The button for options allows us to change the calculations to use the sequential sum of squares, if required.

We reduce the model one term at a time, starting with the highest order interactions due to the design being unbalanced. At each step, we look for the term with the highest p-value and remove that term. When all two-way interactions are removed or we are left with interactions that are significant, we move to reducing main effects in the same manner. Main effects must still be included even if they are not significant when they are used in an interaction.

The final model that we should reduce down to when using a p-value of 0.05 as a decision is D/P (Doors and Size), as shown in the following screenshot:

```
Analysis of Variance

Source          DF    Adj SS   Adj MS   F-Value   P-Value
  D/P            1    2487.4   2487.37    41.94     0.000
  Doors          1     851.0    851.00    14.35     0.000
  Size           5    3600.6    720.11    12.14     0.000
Error          267   15836.9     59.31
  Lack-of-Fit   54    3253.3     60.25     1.02     0.447
  Pure Error   213   12583.6     59.08
Total          274   22757.9
```

Differences between the levels can be investigated with the use of the comparisons tool in GLM. Pairwise comparisons, or comparisons versus control can be selected. In Minitab v16, this is found within the GLM dialog box.

In Minitab v17, this is accessed from the **General Linear Model** menu and is available after we have fitted a model.

There's more...

The results here have only investigated the effects of the factors. The weight of the vehicle will be found as significant when entered as a covariate. In Minitab v17, to identify a covariate, this is added into the **Covariates:** section of the general linear model dialog box. Interactions with covariates, quadratic or cubic terms for the covariates can be included from the **Model** section of the **General Linear Model** dialog box.

The worksheet can be subset to focus on a few results rather than the total. This is useful when a level for a factor is creating a lot of missing cells in the design. For example, removing the vans and pickup trucks from the dataset will mean that we can look at the interaction for Doors*Size for the size of vehicles that we have left in the worksheet.

We should check the residual plots after the study has focused on the significant terms. This is to verify the assumptions of using the analysis of variance on the final model. In this example, a couple of results appear to have high residuals. See the graph in the following screenshot:

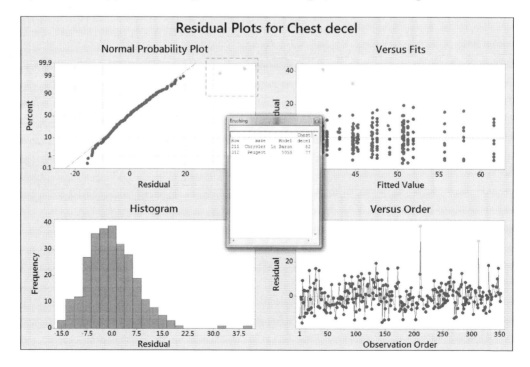

This graph uses the brushing tool to highlight the high values on the probability plot. Its make and model is included to identify the cars associated with these results.

To use the brushing tool, right-click on the chart and select brush from the right-click menu. Highlight the two high residual points by dragging a box around them. Right-click on the graph again and click on **Set ID Variables**. Enter the make and model columns into the brushing variables to add this information into the **Brushing** box.

The residuals for the chest deceleration appear to show a slight right-hand skew. The assumptions to run an analysis of variance are that the residuals are distributed normally. For an underlying distribution that is expected to not be distributed normally, the response can be transformed. A lognormal transformation of the results can be used in some cases. The calculator tool in the **Calc** menu can be used to find the lognormal transformation of chest deceleration. The function is `Ln(column)` and can be found in the function list of the calculator.

You should take care with transformation of the data to ensure that the reasons for transformation are justified and a logical explanation exists for the shape of the data. Note that in this recipe, using a lognormal transformation of the chest deceleration force will result in residuals that appear more normally distributed. The resultant model from the lognormal results will not be appreciably better than using the untransformed data.

The residuals are produced as regular by default and there are options for standardized or deleted residuals as well.

See also

> ▶ The *Finding correlation between multiple variables* recipe in *Chapter 3, Basic Statistical Tools*

> ▶ The *Analyzing covariance* recipe

> ▶ The *Calculator - basic functions* recipe in *Chapter 1, Worksheet, Data Management, and the Calculator*

Analyzing covariance

With the analysis of covariance, we are going to investigate the effect of a continuous variable alongside a categorical response. The dataset used in this example is of the average salary paid to teachers and expenditures per pupil in the U.S.. We will look for effects on pupil expenditure by state and by average salary of teachers.

Getting ready

The data is available at the data and story library. Copy the data in the following link into Minitab: `http://lib.stat.cmu.edu/DASL/Datafiles/EducationalSpending.html`.

How to do it...

The following steps will use `Pay` as a covariate in a general linear model and reduce the model by removing terms with a p-value above 0.05:

1. Navigate to **Stat | ANOVA | General Linear Model** and select **Fit General Linear Model...**.

2. In the **Responses:** field, enter `Spend`.

3. In the **Factors:** field, enter `Region` and in **Covariates:**, enter `Pay`.

4. Click on the **Model...** button and then highlight both `Region` and `Pay` and select the **Add** button next to **Interactions through order:**.

5. Click on **OK** in each dialog box.

6. Go to the session window and check the **Analysis of Variance** table:

```
Analysis of Variance

Source         DF   Adj SS   Adj MS   F-Value   P-Value
  Pay           1   6.8875   6.88753    24.09     0.000
  Region        8   3.0162   0.37702     1.32     0.269
  Pay*Region    8   3.1138   0.38922     1.36     0.249
Error          33   9.4356   0.28593
  Lack-of-Fit  31   9.2775   0.29927     3.79     0.230
  Pure Error    2   0.1581   0.07903
Total          50  55.6447
```

7. The p-value for the interaction of `Region*Pay` is above our decision of 0.05. Press *Ctrl + E* to return to the last dialog box. Go to the **Model...** section and double-click on the term of `Pay*Region` to remove the interaction from the **Terms in the model:** field.

8. Click on the **Graph** button and select the **Four in one** residual plots.

9. Click on **OK** in each dialog.

How it works...

We could run the same data as a one-way ANOVA without including `Pay` as a covariate. Just using region as the factor and `Spend` as the response, we will obtain a significant effect for `Region` on `Spend`. This is because the regions that pay higher wages to teachers also spend more per pupil on education. The effect of region on `Pay` and `Spend` can be visualized using boxplots. Use `Pay` and `Spend` as variables and `Region` as the grouping variable.

By viewing the data with a scatterplot, we can show the correlation between `Pay` and `Spend`. Using the scatterplot **With Regression and Groups**, we can display the relationship between `Pay` and `Spend` alongside the differences between regions.

Covariates can also include quadratic and cubic terms. These are specified in the **Model** section of **Fit General Linear Model** using the **Terms through order:** selection.

Four in one residual plots produce a normal probability plot, histogram of residuals, residuals versus fitted values, and residuals versus order of the data on one page. They can be generated on separate graphs by checking the boxes for each one individually.

There's more...

The same study on `Pay` and `Spend` could be run from the **General Regression** tool. General regression and general linear model tools are very similar in approach. General regression can be used to display variance inflation factors for the terms. After running the **Fit General Linear Model** tool, we can use **Comparisons** from inside the **General Linear Model** menus to use tests such as Tukey's pairwise comparisons.

Minitab v17 also includes a **Predict** tool from the **General Linear Model** menu. The **Predict** dialog box allows a simple method to generate fitted values, confidence intervals, and prediction intervals for stated levels of factors and values of the covariates. The following screenshot shows us the setup of the dialog box. We can enter values for the predictors individually or as columns in the worksheet:

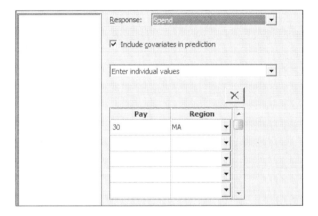

The **Main Effects Plot** and **Interactions Plot** options can be generated from the ANOVA menu or from **Factorial plots** within the **General Linear Model** submenu. The **Factorials Plot** option will generate graphs based on the fitted model values. Main effects and interaction plots from the **ANOVA** menu will generate charts based on the data means in the worksheet.

See also

- ▶ The *Analyzing a balanced design* recipe
- ▶ The *Using the Assistant tool to run a regression* recipe in *Chapter 5, Regression and Modeling the Relationship between X and Y*

> ▶ The *Creating a scatterplot of two variables* recipe in *Chapter 2, Tables and Graphs*
>
> ▶ The *Generating a paneled boxplot* recipe in *Chapter 2, Tables and Graphs*

Analyzing a fully nested design

With this recipe, we will look at the readability advertisement in different magazines. The data was collected from nine magazines covering different reader demographics. The responses include the number of words, number of sentences, and number of three plus-syllable words in the advertising copy. The first factor is the selected magazine. The second factor, group, is an educational level of the magazines readers, 1 being the highest and 3 being the lowest.

Magazines are randomly selected from a group of magazines at each readership educational level. The magazines in the study are nested under the group.

Getting ready

The data is from the magazine dataset at The Data and Story Library. Copy the data from the following link into Minitab:

`http://lib.stat.cmu.edu/DASL/Datafiles/magadsdat.html`

When copying the data in to Minitab, there is a blank line under the column headers. This can cause the column names to copy incorrectly. Copy just the **Data** section in to Minitab and then rename the columns. In the following instructions, the columns have been named `Words`, `Sentences`, `3+Syllables`, `Magazine`, and `Group`.

How to do it...

1. Navigate to **Stat | ANOVA | General Linear Model** and click on **Fit General Linear Model**.

2. Enter `3+ Syllables` in the **Responses** field.

3. Enter `Group` and `Magazine` as the **Factors**, as shown in the following screenshot:

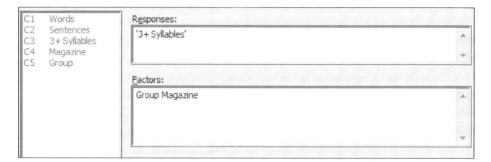

Chapter 4

4. Click on the **Random/Nest** button. In the **Factor type:** section, change **Magazine** to **Random**. Then, in the **Nesting:** section, enter Group in the row for **Magazine**. Click on **OK**.

5. Click on the **Graphs** button and choose **Four in one** residuals.

6. Click on **OK** in each dialog to run the study.

How it works...

The results of the nested design should show us that the main component of variation is the magazine rather than the group the magazine belongs to. This asks some interesting questions about the grouping by education level and what this means.

The **Random/Nest...** section of the **General Linear Model** menu allows us to define factors as either **Fixed** or **Random** and the nesting structure of the factors.

Magazine is defined as a random factor as the magazines are selected at random from a larger population of publications within each group.

The **Fully Nested ANOVA** tool can also be used to run the same results. The order of factors being entered into the model defines the nesting structure. For instance, A B would nest B within factor A. All factors within the **Fully Nested ANOVA** tool would be considered random.

The repeated measures ANOVA – using a mixed effects model

These studies use repeated measurements on a subject. Typically, they are used to assess the change over time, or the same observation under different conditions. In this recipe, the results of a blind wine tasting are studied. Three types of wine are tested by three judges; a third factor is included for the type of glass the wine is being tested in. The score is accumulated across several responses and the maximum score is 40.

We will stack the data first before using the general linear model to study the effect of Judge, Wine, and Glass type on the score. The Judge factor can be considered a random factor in the design. Wine and Glass become our fixed factors.

We will use a decision level of 0.05 for the p-value.

Getting ready

Type the data into Minitab from the following screenshot:

Judge	Wine1	Wine2	Wine3	Glass Type
A	23	18	26	1
A	20	16	23	2
A	22	19	25	1
B	25	22	28	1
B	23	19	25	2
B	22	19	25	2
C	20	17	23	2
C	23	19	25	1
C	23	19	27	2

How to do it...

The following steps will stack the data in one column before using the general linear model. We then reduce the model by removing the terms by hierarchy and p-value:

1. Navigate to **Data | Stack** and click on **Blocks of Columns**.

2. Enter the columns in the dialog box as shown in the following screenshot. Uncheck the **Use variable names in subscript column** option.

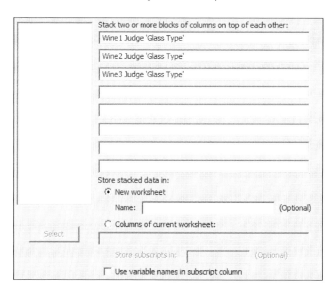

3. Click on **Ok** to create the new worksheet.

4. Name the new columns as `Wine, Score, Judge, Glass type`.

5. Navigate to **Stat | ANOVA | General Linear Model** and click on **Fit General Linear Model**.

6. Enter `Score` in the **Responses:** field.

7. In the **Factors:** field, enter `Wine Judge 'Glass type'`.

8. Click on the **Random/Nest...** button and in the section for **Factor type:**, change **Judge** to **Random**.

9. Click on **OK** and click on the **Model...** button.

10. Highlight all three factors in the **Factors and covariates:** section and change **Interactions through order:** to **3**. Then click on the **Add** button to add all two-way interactions and the three-way interaction to the model terms. Click on **OK** in each dialog box to run the analysis.

11. Check the p-value of the three-way interaction. As this is above 0.05, press *Ctrl + E* to return to the **General linear Model** tool.

12. Click on the **Model...** button and double-click on the three-way interaction in the **Terms in the model:** section to remove it from the study. Click on **OK** in each dialog to rerun the study.

13. Return to the session window and check the results. Check the interactions for significance. Look for p-values less than 0.05; press *Ctrl + E* to return to the last dialog box.

14. As all two-way interactions are not significant, remove these by clicking on the **Model...** button. Highlight the two-way interactions as shown and click on the red **X** to remove these from the model. Click on **OK** in each dialog to rerun the study.

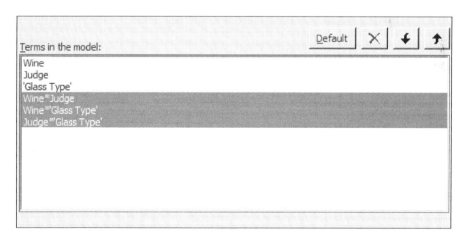

15. Return to the session window and check the main effects for their significance. Use the decision level of 0.05 for the p-value.

16. As all the terms are significant, press *Ctrl + E* to return to the last dialog and click on the **Graphs...** button. Select the **Four in one** residual plots. Click on **OK** in each dialog.

17. To run comparisons of the wines on each other, navigate to **Stat | ANOVA | General Linear Model** and click on **Comparisons**. Double-click on **Wine** in the list under **Choose terms for comparisons:**. Wine should now be noted with C to indicate that this is selected.

18. Click on the **Results...** button and check the **Tests and confidence intervals** box.

19. Click on **OK** in each dialog to generate the Tukey pairwise comparisons.

20. To generate factor plots, navigate to **Stat | ANOVA | General Linear Model** and click on **Factorials Plot**.

21. Click on **OK** to generate the main effects plots.

How it works...

Judge is identified as a random factor as it is a random selection of Judge from a population of Wine tasters. The Wine column is a fixed factor as we wish to assess which wine has the greatest or lowest score. The glass type in the trial forms a fixed factor because we want to know how the glass type affects the score.

The section within the **Fit General Linear Model** tool for **Random/Nest...** allows us to identify factors as random, fixed, or nesting in the model. The **Model...** section gives us the ability to quickly add interaction terms to a study.

When entering columns, they can be typed in by name or column number, double-clicked to move across, or highlighted and then moved across by clicking on **Select**. If we are typing the names of the columns, we must use ' ' to identify any column name with spaces or special characters, a in 'Glass type'. Double-clicking or selecting columns into the model will automatically place single quotes where appropriate.

We specified a pairwise comparison of the wine results. Without changing the options, we obtain a grouping information table. This identifies the comparison levels by placing them into separate letter groups. This is generated for the selected comparison method. By selecting the option for **Tests and confidence intervals**, we output the results of the comparison as tables of t-values and p-values.

The interval plot for comparisons shows us the 95 percent confidence intervals for the differences between each pair of groups. Here, we should see that as all wine differences do not overlap the zero; we can prove a difference in score by wine.

The interval plot shows comparisons between pairs of wines. The x-axis displays the differences between the means of each pair of wines. A line at 0 is drawn to indicate 0 differences. `Wine2` to `Wine1` for instance shows a mean difference of -3.66 and a 95 percent confidence interval of -4.9 to -2.4. A confidence interval that crosses the zero line would indicate that there could be no difference between the means of that pair. Here none of the confidence intervals cross the zero line and all wines can be proved to be different to each other.

Finding the critical F-statistic

The critical F-statistic is the point at which the F-statistic has a proportion in the tails of the distribution equal to the decision level of the test. Usually, these figures are referred to in tables. Such a table can be found in the *Index* of *Applied Linear Statistical Models, Fourth Edition,* by *Neter, Kutner, Wasserman*, and *Nachtsheim*.

Here we will use a significance level of 0.05, and find the critical F-statistic for 8 df in the numerator and 33 df in the denominator. These figures come from the example of Teacher Pay in the analysis of covariance in the model with the included interactions. We will derive this graphically from the probability distribution plot and from the probability distributions from the **Calc** menu.

How to do it...

The following steps will graphically plot the F-distribution shading the right-hand tail for an area of 0.05:

1. Go to the **Graph** menu and select **Probability distribution plot**.

2. Select the **View probability** option.

3. Change the distribution to **F** and complete the dialog as shown in the following screenshot:

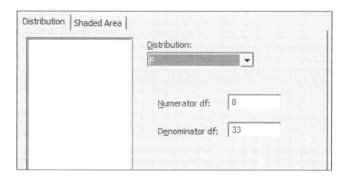

4. Click on the tab for **Shaded Area**.

5. Make sure that the choice for **Probability** is selected and **Right Tail** is chosen from the graphs, as shown in the following screenshot:

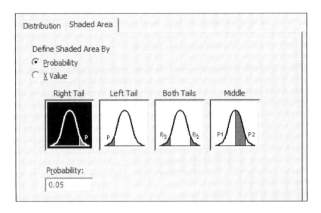

6. Click on **OK** in each dialog.

7. To calculate the critical F-statistic from the calculator tools, navigate to **Calc | Probability distributions | F...**.

8. Complete the dialog as shown in the following screenshot:

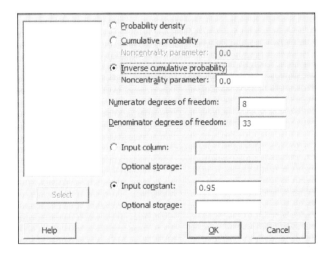

9. Click on **OK**.

How it works...

The chart that is created will show us the right-hand tail with an area of 0.05. This occurs at 2.235 for the numerator and denominator degrees of the specified freedom. This is then our critical F-statistic, the point at which the p-value for the analysis of variance would equal 0.05.

The probability distribution plot can be used to shade areas of distribution curves as well as to plot the distribution curve. By selecting the right tail of the distribution and 0.05 in the tail of the curve, we ask Minitab to shade the right 0.05 proportion of the distribution, our critical F-statistic.

We could also have found the p-value for a result using the X-value instead of probability and entering the F-statistic that was calculated.

Probability distribution from the **Calc** menu can be used to return values for probability density, cumulative, or inverse cumulative probability for different distributions. Using the inverse cumulative probability to 0.95, we find the point at which we cover 95 percent of the F-distribution—again, the critical F-statistic.

The p-value can be found from the cumulative probability using the F-statistic obtained as the input value. The result is the cumulative probability up to the entered value. The p-value is 1.

See also

▶ The *Analyzing covariance* recipe

5
Regression and Modeling the Relationship between X and Y

In this chapter, we will cover the following recipes:

- ▸ Visualizing simple regressions with fitted line plots
- ▸ Using the Assistant tool to run a regression
- ▸ Multiple regressions with linear predictors
- ▸ Model selection tools – the best subsets regression
- ▸ Model selection tools – the stepwise regression
- ▸ Binary logistic regression
- ▸ Fitting a nonlinear regression

Introduction

The regression tools in Minitab cover the very simple studies with a single predictor, fitted line plot, or the assistant regression tools, up to the very complex ones, such as nonlinear regression. This chapter starts with a fitted line plot and works through multiple regressions, logistic regression, and finally, nonlinear regression tools.

Minitab v17 has added new features to regression, compared to previous versions. The regression tools are now expanded to store fitted regression models in the response column. We can fit models for continuous data, binary, and poisson responses. Once a model has been analyzed, we can use it to predict responses, display contour plots of the response, find optimal values from the response optimizer, and more.

Majority of the steps in this chapter will take place in the **Regression** menu, which is found under the **Stat** menu, as shown in the following screenshot:

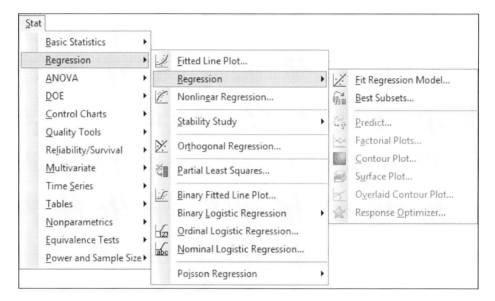

Similar to other menus, **Regression** is divided into subsections. The first group of tools are used to fit a numeric response and cover tools for single predictors, multiple regression, and model-fitting techniques. Orthogonal regression is held in its own group as this tool considers the errors to be in both the x and y coordinates. Here we would estimate the ratio of the y/x variance to estimate the regression model.

Partial least square regression covers a multivariate regression technique. The next group is for logistic regression models where the predictor is categorical.

Another new feature in the regression tools for Minitab v17 is **Poisson Regression** at the end of the menu.

Visualizing simple regressions with fitted line plots

The fitted line plot is a simple regression tool in Minitab that produces a scatterplot with a least square regression line fitted to the data. It provides additional output to the regression fits that are provided under scatterplot tools, such as the analysis of variance and R-squared statistics.

This will only use a single predictor; multiple predictors are best used with **Regression...** or **General Regression...**.

We will use the data from the Oxford weather station to investigate the relationship between the mean maximum temperature and hours of sunlight per month.

Getting ready

We will use the data from the Oxford weather station in this example. This data is from the Met Office website and is found at the following location:

`http://www.metoffice.gov.uk/climate/uk/stationdata/`

Select the Oxford station. The data is also made available in the `Oxford data.txt` files, which preserve the format from the website. Also, the `Oxford weather (Cleaned).MTW` Minitab file will be correctly imported into Minitab for us.

How to do it...

The following steps will plot the relationship between the hours of sunlight and mean maximum temperature. This will fit a least squares regression line and generate the analysis of variance statistics.

1. Follow the given link to the Met Office weather station site.
2. Choose the Oxford station.
3. In your web browser, save the file as a text file.
4. In Minitab, go to **File** and select **Open Worksheet...**.
5. Change **Files of type:** to **Text (*.txt)**.
6. Select the file that we have just saved or the provided `Oxford Data.txt` file.
7. Go to the **Stat** menu, then go to **Regression** and select **Fitted Line Plot...**.
8. In the **Response(Y):** section, enter the column for the maximum temperature.
9. In the **Predictor(X):** section, enter the column for Sun(hours).

10. Select **Options...** and check the boxes for confidence and prediction intervals.

11. Click on **OK**.

12. Select **Graphs...** and select the **Four in one** residual plots.

13. Click on **OK** in each dialog box.

How it works...

The results of the fitted line plot are generated as a graphical page, displaying the scatterplot and least squares regression line. There is also an **Analysis of Variance** table in the session window. This output will give us the regression model and the R-squared and R-squared adjusted values. We should be careful with R-squared values. They are not a measure of the quality of the model; they report the amount of variation that we have explained in the data. We should observe in the study that 67 percent of the variation in the mean maximum temperature is accounted for by the hours of sunlight. Rather than looking for R-squared values of 80 or 90 percent, we should consider the implications on the results.

We have accounted for over two-thirds of the variation with a metric of the hours of sunlight, and its result seems quite high.

We should also be careful of correlation and causation. Are hours of sunlight really the cause? Hours of sunlight will be affected by the time of the year and weather conditions.

Selecting the options for prediction intervals and confidence intervals will place 95 percent CI and 95 percent PI lines around the fitted line.

Residual plots are an important diagnostic in informing us of problems related to the fit of the data. The four in one residuals generate a page displaying **Normal Probability Plot**, **Histogram**, **Versus Fits**, and **Versus Order** of the data to check the assumptions of the regression model. These should be used to check the assumptions of the normality of the residual error, homoscedasticity, and check patterns over time.

Here, the residuals versus order of the data will show a gap at the start of the results. This relates to the data for only the hours of sunlight being collected after 1929.

There's more...

Quadratic and Cubic models can be easily selected from the main dialog box. When selecting either of these models, we generate the sequential sum of squares in the session window. The sequential output will show us the amount of the sum of squares accounted for by the linear term, and then the amount the quadratic term that has been added to the model. If we include the cubic term, this will show the additional sum of squares accounted for by the cubic term over the quadratic term.

See also

▸ The *Using the Assistant tool to run a regression* recipe

Using the Assistant tool to run a regression

The **Assistant** tool provides us with two methods of regression and a response optimizer for multiple regression. As with all the assistant tools, guidance is offered on the setup of the study and on the output. There are less options to choose from but the dialog box is simpler to use.

Here, we will use the **Assistant** tool to run a fitted line plot and then pick between Linear, Quadratic, and Cubic models for data on Hubble's constant.

Hubble's law describes the relationship between the distance of a galaxy and the velocity at which it is moving away from us. The greater the distance, the greater the velocity of recession. The data comes from observations on recession velocity of Nebula and its distance from the Earth.

Getting ready

The data can be obtained from the Data and Story Library. The following link will take us to the Hubble results:

```
http://lib.stat.cmu.edu/DASL/Datafiles/Hubble.html
```

The data can be copied and pasted directly into Minitab.

How to do it...

The following steps will use the **Assistant** menu to generate a fitted line plot.

1. Go to the **Assistant** menu and select **Simple Regression** from the decision tree.

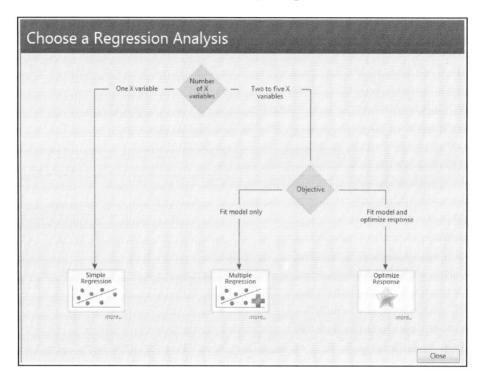

2. In **Y column:**, enter Recession Velocity.

3. In **X column:**, enter distance.

4. Ensure that the **Choose for me** option is selected for the type of regression model and then click on **OK**.

How it works...

The assistant regression model will output several graphical report pages. The first page is a report card with many notes or warnings on the analysis. This will check the number of samples in the study and unusual data, and will contain notes about the normality of the residuals.

The second page, that is, the prediction report, contains the fitted regression model and prediction intervals. Also included on this output are prediction intervals for a table of x values and their predicted y values.

Unusual data points are highlighted for values that are more than two standard errors from the predicted values. In this example, the result in row 16 is flagged up as unusually high.

The residual plots will indicate the types of patterns that may indicate problems with the fitted model under the residual plots. By default, only the residuals versus fitted values is generated. If we know that the data is in a time order, then we would tick the option within the dialog box stating that data is in the time order. This would then generate the residuals versus order of the data.

The fourth page, that is, the model selection report, shows the model fitted. It will pick between the Linear, Quadratic and Cubic models by using the R-squared adjusted term. Should we wish to pick a different model to the one fitted we would select the relevant option directly from the dialog box.

The last page, that is, the summary report, presents the results of the regression. The P-value for the study is listed and the null hypothesis is restated as the question "Is there a relationship between Y and X?", which can make interpretation of the P-value easier. When a linear regression model is fitted, the correlation score is also produced. Comments are automatically completed for the data and can be edited.

There's more...

Strictly speaking, Hubble's law is stated as *Recession velocity = HO*Distance*, where HO refers to Hubble's constant. The recession velocity at 0 distance should be 0. Both the fitted line plot and the assistant regression will fit the data for a nonzero intercept. To fit a regression model without an intercept, we would use the **Regression** or **General Regression** tools. We can remove the fit for the intercept from the option's subdialog.

See also

- ▶ The *Multiple regression with linear predictors* recipe

Multiple regression with linear predictors

This recipe will look at studying a multiple regression on determining the sleep duration of mammals. The dataset is available at `StatSci.org`.

We will run the study with all predictors included for the initial model and then remove the terms in the model step-by-step. Our goal is to reduce the terms until only the significant ones are left. As this data does have a degree of correlation among the predictors, we will use matrix plots, correlation, and variance inflation factors to highlight the degree of multicollinearity.

We will initially produce the matrix plots and the correlation scores before moving on to the analysis of the regression.

After reducing the model to only significant terms, we will then produce the residual plots to gradually verify assumptions on the analysis.

The value of alpha for the decision level used here will be 0.05.

Getting ready

The data is available at the following link from `StatSci.org`:

`http://www.statsci.org/data/general/sleep.html`

The data is tab delimited and can be copied directly into the worksheet.

How to do it...

The following steps will run a regression that studies the sleep duration. We will produce a matrix plot and correlation scores to check for multicollinearity before using regression to gradually reduce the model until only the significant terms remain included:

1. Go to the **Graph** menu and select **Matrix Plot...**.
2. From the selection, choose the **Simple** matrix plot.
3. Enter the columns `BodyWt`, `BrainWt`, `TotalSleep`, `Lifespan`, `Gestation`, `Predation`, `Exposure`, and `Danger` as **Graph variables:**.
4. Click on **Matrix Options...** and then select the option to display **Lower left** of **Matrix Display**.

5. Click on **OK** in each dialog box to produce a matrix of scatterplots.

6. Display the correlation scores by going to **Stat**, then **Basic Statistics**, and then **Correlation...**.

7. Enter the same columns as before into the **Variables:** section and click on **OK** to generate the correlation scores.

8. Navigate to **Stat | Regression | Regression...** and select **Fit Regression Model...**.

9. Enter `TotalSleep` as the column for **Response**.

10. In the section for **Continuous predictors:**, enter the columns for `BodyWt`, `BrainWt`, `Lifespan`, `Gestation`, `Predation`, `Exposure`, and `Danger`.

11. Click on **OK** to run the regression.

12. Return to the session window and check the results for the regression. Check the terms for the highest P-value, as shown in the following screenshot:

```
Coefficients

Term           Coef  SE Coef  T-Value  P-Value    VIF
Constant      16.60     1.08    15.40    0.000
BodyWt     -0.00160  0.00146    -1.09    0.280  12.93
BrainWt     0.00232  0.00161     1.44    0.158  16.70
LifeSpan    -0.0398   0.0354    -1.13    0.266   2.80
Gestation  -0.01647  0.00621    -2.65    0.011   4.84
Predation     2.393    0.971     2.46    0.018  12.90
Exposure      0.633    0.559     1.13    0.263   4.80
Danger        -4.51     1.19    -3.80    0.000  17.71
```

13. Press *Ctrl+E* to return to the last dialog box and remove the term with the highest P-value, **BodyWt**, from the **Continuous predictors**.

14. Return to the session window and look for the term with the highest P-value.

15. Repeat steps 12 to 14 until only the terms with a P-value below **0.05** are included.

16. With only those terms included for the final results, go back to the **Regression** dialog box by pressing *Ctrl+E* and then go to the **Graphs...** button. Select the **Normal** plot of residuals and **Residuals vs fits**.

17. Click on **OK** in each dialog box.

How it works...

The model is reduced sequentially to minimize the problems of multicollinearity in the predictors. The reason for generating the matrix plots and correlation scores is to observe the relationships in the predictors that we have to be careful of. We should observe strong correlations between body weight and brain weight, predation and danger, exposure and danger, among others. We will find it difficult to isolate the effects of highly correlated predictors.

Variance inflation factors (**VIF**) in the output also identifies strong correlations between predictors. The variance inflation factor is a measure of how the variance of the coefficients is inflated by multicollinearity. High VIF scores can indicate that terms in the model are difficult to interpret. Predation and danger, as observed in the correlation scores and the matrix plots, will show a high VIF. Values of 1 will indicate no inflation of the variance and values above 5 will indicate high correlations. As such, we should be careful of any terms with high VIF scores such as predation and danger, as these are strongly correlated.

Residual plots for order of the data are not needed as the worksheet is ordered alphabetically. When our results do not appear to follow a logical order in the dataset, we should not run the versus order charts. The residual versus fits for this study may seem to indicate a degree of funneling, as shown the following screenshot:

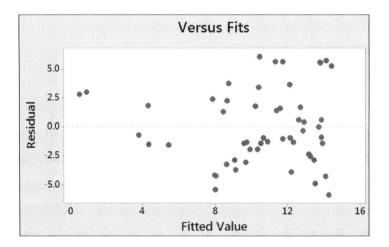

Funneling is an indicator that the response does not possess equal variance across the fitted values and that we are observing heteroscedasticity.

The assumptions for a regression analysis include normally distributed residuals and homoscedasticity. When we are concerned about unequal variance in the residuals, a transformation of the response may be used. Here, a natural log of the sleep duration can be used to return the residuals to show equal variance.

The effect of unequal variance on the results can be to calculate coefficients and variance figures incorrectly. Transformations on the response can help find the values of the variance and coefficients with a better precision. However, we must be careful that we understand the reasons behind transformation of the data. Transformation of the data is not a technique to fix outliers or special causes in our results.

We can run a transformation on the response directly from the regression options. Minitab can be allowed to pick an optimal lambda for the transformation or it can be specified directly. Try running the same regression with the **Box-Cox...** options. You should obtain a similar model with transformed and untransformed data.

Interactions, Quadratic, and Cubic terms can be easily specified from within the **Model...** options of the **Fit Regression Model...** dialog box.

Predictors can be standardized as well. Standardizing the predictors can be a useful method to reduce multicollinearity between predictors. The **Coding...** options give us five methods to standardize predictors.

The **Stepwise...** options allow us to use a stepwise model fitting technique. Here, we can choose between stepwise, forward, or backward selection.

There's more...

The session window is 93 characters wide by default. With large correlation tables or long column names in a study, this can cause a table to be presented across several lines, with the last columns spilling over into a new table.

The options for Minitab, found in the **Tools** menu, can expand the session window's width to 132 characters.

See also

▸ The *Model selection tools – the best subsets regression* recipe
▸ The *Model selection tools – the stepwise regression* recipe

Model selection tools – the best subsets regression

We will use the sleep duration dataset to illustrate the use of best subsets regression as a model reduction tool. The best subsets will check through all possible linear models and display the best models at each step.

When running the regression of sleep duration in the *Multiple regression with linear predictors* recipe, we observed that the residuals showed unequal variance. Initially, we will transform the data by taking the lognormal of the sleep duration response. The transformed response will show homoscedasticity.

We will use best subsets regression to show only the best model at each number of variables to include from 1 to all predictors. After identifying the model, we will enter the results into the general regression study.

Getting ready

The data is available at the following link from `StatSci.org`:

`http://www.statsci.org/data/general/sleep.html`

The data is tab delimited and can be copied directly into the worksheet.

How to do it...

The following steps will transform the sleep duration response by taking the natural log of the results. Then, best subsets regression is used to identify a regression model to use.

1. Go to the **Calc** menu and select **Calculator...**.

2. Enter a column name of `Ln(Sleep)` in the section for **Store result in variable:** to create the transformed data.

3. Enter the expression as shown in the following screenshot:

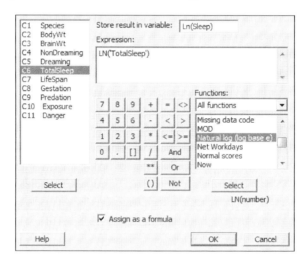

4. Check the **Assign as a formula** option and click on **OK**.

5. Navigate to **Stat | Regression | Regression** and select **Best Subsets Regression...**.

6. Enter the `Ln(Sleep)` column in the **Response:** section.

7. Enter the following columns as **Free Predictors:**, as shown in the following screenshot:

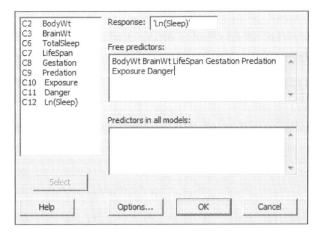

8. Click on **Options...** and change the **Models of each size to print:** section from 2 to 1.

9. Click on **OK** in each dialog box.

10. Check the results in the session window, as shown in the following screenshot:

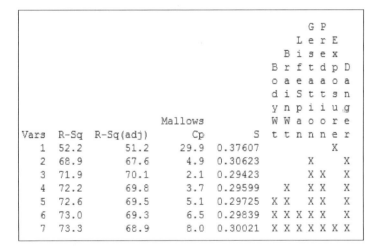

Vars	R-Sq	R-Sq(adj)	Mallows Cp	S	BodyWt	BrainWt	LifeSpan	Gestation	Predation	Exposure	Danger
1	52.2	51.2	29.9	0.37607							X
2	68.9	67.6	4.9	0.30623					X		X
3	71.9	70.1	2.1	0.29423					X X		X
4	72.2	69.8	3.7	0.29599	X				X X		X
5	72.6	69.5	5.1	0.29725	X X				X X		X
6	73.0	69.3	6.5	0.29839	X X X X						X
7	73.3	68.9	8.0	0.30021	X X X X X X X						

11. Compare the results for highest **R-Sq(adj)**, lowest standard deviation, and **Mallows Cp** for a score close to the number of predictors. Find the row that corresponds to that result.

12. Navigate to **Stat | Regression | Regression** and then select **Fit Regression Model...**.

13. Enter the Ln(sleep) column as the response.

14. In the **Model:** section, enter the columns for our chosen predictors as selected from the best subset results, which are Gestation, Predation, and Danger.

15. To check the assumptions of running a regression, create residual plots by clicking on the **Graphs...** button and selecting **Normal plot of residuals** and **Residuals versus fits**.

16. Click on **OK** in each dialog box to run the regression.

How it works...

In the previous recipe, we obtained residual plots that appear to show the funneling of the residuals versus fits. This seems to indicate that the variance is changing with the predicted values. By taking the natural log of the recorded sleep duration, we can ensure that the variances of the natural log of sleep durations remains roughly constant across fitted values. The following screenshot shows the results of the regression coefficients in Minitab:

```
Analysis of Variance

Source        DF   Adj SS   Adj MS  F-Value  P-Value
Regression     3  10.5249  3.50829    40.23    0.000
  Gestation    1   1.9890  1.98897    22.81    0.000
  Predation    1   0.4688  0.46884     5.38    0.025
  Danger       1   1.5108  1.51078    17.32    0.000
Error         50   4.3606  0.08721
  Lack-of-Fit 49   4.3547  0.08887    14.91    0.203
  Pure Error   1   0.0060  0.00596
Total         53  14.8855


Model Summary

       S    R-sq  R-sq(adj)  R-sq(pred)
0.295318  70.71%     68.95%      65.70%
```

The following chart shows the comparison of the residuals using the **TotalSleep** results and the natural log of **TotalSleep**. We should also notice that the use of the natural log of the sleep durations results in a slightly improved fit to the results from measures such as **R-Sq(pred)** and **R-sq(adj)**.

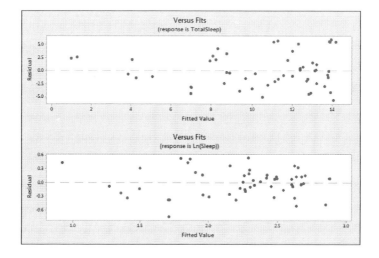

Fit Regression Model... can use a Box-Cox transformation on the original data as part of the analysis. This is found inside the **Options...** section. As the best subsets regression does not have this option, we will need to use the calculator to transform the results.

The best subsets procedure will identify models that produce the highest R-squared terms and display these in the session window. The options for this tool allow us to pick how many R-squared terms at each number of variables are displayed. The default options will display the two best models with a 1 predictor, then 2, and then 3, until we reach the full model.

Entering columns as **Free Predictors** allows these variables to be included or excluded from the model. Entering a variable into the **Predictors in all models:** section will force the best subsets regression to always include this variable.

Best subsets will only look for linear model terms. Interactions or quadratics cannot be specified in this dialog box.

See also

▶   The *Model selection tools – the stepwise regression* recipe

▶   The *Multiple regression with linear predictors* recipe

Model selection tools – the stepwise regression

The stepwise regression has been changed in Minitab v17. In the previous versions, this was its own tool. Now, stepwise regression is an option within the **Fit Regression Model...** tools. This includes the fit regression models for binary logistic regression and poisson regression. The same options for stepwise regression are used in all three of the fit regression model tools.

We will use the sleep dataset with stepwise regression to select predictors for a regression model.

We will use the total sleep column for the study and specify using the Box-Cox transformation on the response before running the stepwise regression on all two-way interactions.

Getting ready

The data is available at the following link from StatSci.org:

http://www.statsci.org/data/general/sleep.html

The data is tab delimited and can be copied directly into the worksheet. Once the data is in Minitab, calculate the natural log of total sleep. See steps 1 to 5 in the *Model Selection, best subsets* recipe.

How to do it...

The following steps will use a stepwise regression to identify a regression model within the **Fit General Linear Model** function:

1. Navigate to **Stat | Regression | Regression** and select **Fit Regression Model...**.

2. Enter `TotalSleep` in the **Responses:** section.

3. In **Continuous predictors:**, enter `BodyWt`, `BrainWt`, `Lifespan`, `Gestation`, `Predation`, `Exposure`, and `Danger`.

4. To add interactions to the study, click on the **Model...** button and highlight **Predictors:** in the top-left section of the dialog box. Then click on the **Add** button next to **Interactions through order: 2**.

5. Click on **OK** and then select the **Stepwise...** button.

6. From the **Method:** drop down, select **Stepwise** and click on **OK**.

7. Go to the **Graphs...** button and select the **Four in one** residual plots and click on **OK** in each dialog box to run the model.

8. Check the results in the session window to observe the fitted model, as shown in the following screenshot:

```
Coefficients
|
Term                 Coef     SE Coef   T-Value   P-Value     VIF
Constant            2.359       0.197     11.97     0.000
Gestation       -0.002109    0.000409    -5.16     0.000    2.29
Predation           0.421       0.110      3.81     0.000   18.26
Danger             -0.174       0.135     -1.29     0.204   25.06
Exposure           0.0953      0.0568      1.68     0.101    5.44
Predation*Danger  -0.0868      0.0276     -3.15     0.003   37.37
```

9. From the results of the preceding stepwise regression, we should observe that the model converged on a solution of **Gestation, Predation, Danger, Exposure**, and **Predation*Danger**.

10. To observe predicted responses, navigate to **Stat | Regression | Regression** and select **Factorial Plots**.

11. Select all available predictors to put them in the plots and click on **OK**.

 Use the **>>** arrow to move everything into the charts.

12. To observe the interaction of `Predation` and `Danger`, generate a contour plot. Navigate to **Stat | Regression | Regression** and select **Contour Plot**.

13. Change the **X Axis:** section to `Danger` and click on **OK**.

How it works...

The stepwise regression will initially run forwards, including terms in the regression model. The first round is to select the predictor with the lowest P-value. The second round continues in the same way, looking to add the predictor that would be the best addition to the model. This continues round by round until no more terms can be added.

The default stepwise method will work forwards and backwards. If a term that was added on a previous round has an increase in P-value above the decision level, it will be removed during the next round. Because of this selection method, we do not study all possible models, unlike the **Best Subsets...** tool.

If the results here show exposure at round three with a P-value of 0.815, then the fourth round will remove this term.

The stepwise selection method can be changed to forward selection, where terms are added but cannot be removed; or, it can be changed to backwards elimination, where all variables are included in round 1; each subsequent round uses the P-value to exclude a term.

With the steps here, we do not see the decision at each step in the regression; we see only the final fitted model. The **Stepwise** options can be selected to include the details for each step in the session window. This will reveal the terms included or removed at each point in the model. This will also display **R-sq**, **R-sq(adj)**, **R-sq(pred)**, and **Mallows' Cp** for each step as well.

The decision method is based on the alpha risk or the decision for the P-value. The default can be changed along with the method to allow model hierarchy to be calculated as well.

See also

▸ The *Model selection tools – the best subsets regression* recipe
▸ The *Multiple regression with linear predictors* recipe

Binary logistic regression

Logistic regression models allow us to fit a regression model to categorical data. Here, we will look at the survival rates of passengers on the Titanic. This data is binomial in that we list the survivors or casualties of the disaster.

We will initially recode the Survival columns to state 1 as survived and 0 as casualty. Then, we study the effects of age, class, and gender on the chances of survival. This isn't essential but can be a useful aid to the interpretation of the results.

The final steps will store the event probability calculated from the fitted model to plot the results in a scatterplot.

Getting ready

The data is contained in test format at the StatSci website. The direct link to the Titanic data is as follows:

`http://www.statsci.org/data/general/titanic.txt`

The data will copy and paste directly into Minitab. The data columns are listed as `Passenger class`, `Age`, `Gender`, and `Survival`.

Do make sure that you check the dataset, as a couple of passenger details are shuffled into the wrong columns; for example, rows `296` and `307` need to be corrected manually.

Not all the passengers' ages are listed in this dataset and it is possible to find a listing of this data in other formats with a quick web search.

The Titanic data is available in different formats; performing a search on the Internet will reveal other datasets.

The data at the American statistical association lists passengers as child or adult rather than listing them by age.

How to do it...

The following steps recode the results from numeric values to categorical ones. Then, we fit a binary logistic regression to find how the age, gender, and class affected survival chances. We will then use factorial plots to visualize the fitted model.

1. Navigate to **Data | Code** and select **Numeric to Text...**.

2. Enter `Survived` into the **Code data from columns:** and the **Store coded data in columns:** sections.

3. Enter the original values and the new values as shown in the following screenshot:

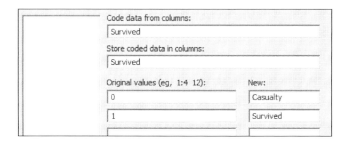

4. Click on **OK**.

5. Navigate to **Stat | Regression | Binary logistic Regression** and select **Fit Binary Logistic Regression**.

6. Enter `Survived` in the **Response:** section, then enter `Age` in the **Continuous predictors:** section, and `PClass` and `Sex` as **Categorical predictors:**, as shown in the following screenshot:

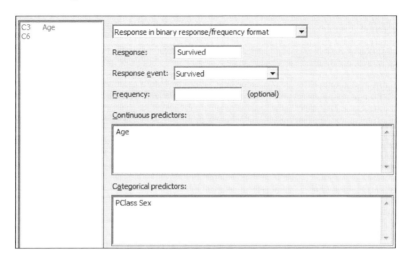

7. Select the **Model...** button and highlight `Age`, `PClass`, and `Sex` in the **Predictors:** section; in the **Interactions through order:** section, enter 2, then click on the **Add** button. Click on **OK** in each dialog box.

8. Return to the session window and check the results, as shown in the following screenshot.

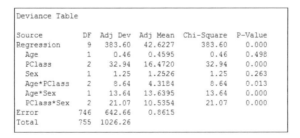

9. Use the regression table to look for interactions with a P-value above 0.05, or the Chi-square for interactions with low values.

10. As all interactions are significant, we will not reduce the model. To produce diagnostic plots, return to the last dialog box by pressing *Ctrl+E*.

11. Click the **Graphs...** button and select the **Three in one** residuals. Click on **OK** in each dialog box.

12. To plot the calculated event probabilities, we will use the factor plots. Navigate to **Stat | Regression | Binary logistic Regression** and select **Factorial Plots...**.

13. Move Age from the **Available factors:** section to the **Selected:** section by double-clicking on Age. Then click on **OK**.

How it works...

The code tool used in steps 1 to 4 works in a way that is similar to an IF statement in the calculator. Although we cannot use this to create a formula in the worksheet, it is a very visual way to recode the data. Ranges of numbers can be coded using a colon as the range separator. For example, 1:10 would specify a range from 1 to 10.

By default, the Binary logistic regression model uses a logit transform with a probability of 0 to 1. The regression is then fitted to the logit transform, which is shown as follows:

$$Y = \ln\left(\frac{\pi}{1-\pi}\right)$$

Normit and Gompit transformations are also available to be selected from options within Binary Logistic Regression. The Normit transformation uses the inverse CDF of the standard normal distribution to map the probability. For example, a result at +2.326 from 0 has a 99 percent probability of occurring and -2.326 from 0 has a 1 percent probability of occurring.

The Gompit or log model is useful in growth models of biological data as the curve of the function is not symmetric like the Logit or Normit functions.

Minitab has picked the event for the regression model as Survived. The model then calculates the probability of survival. The event is indicated at the start of the analysis. The default event is picked reverse alphabetically. We can change **Response event:** from the main dialog box to **Fit Binary Logistic Regression**. This drop down can be used to change between the two possible outcomes.

The **Coding...** options allow us to choose the reference level of the categorical predictors. Also, here we can change the increment used in calculating the odds ratios for the continuous predictors.

Minitab provides residual plots for either Pearson or Deviance residuals. The residuals can be used to check for outliers or patterns over time in the results, as shown in the following example:

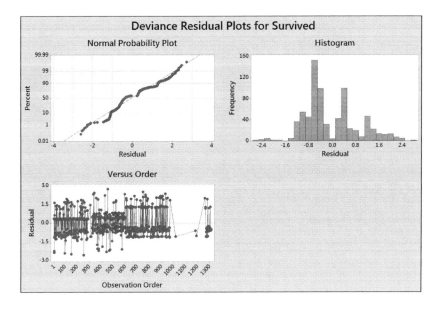

Factorial plots are used to help visualize the result of the logistic regression. Main effects and interaction plots of the fitted probabilities are generated for the three sets of interactions, as shown in the following screenshot:

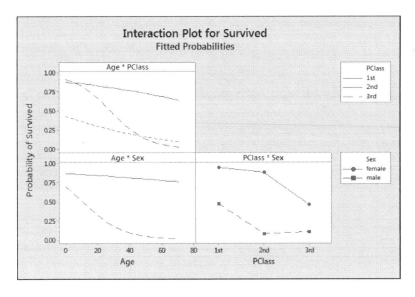

The results show some dramatic interactions between the three predictors used in the model.

We can also generate predicted probabilities with confidence intervals and prediction intervals from the **Predict...** tool. This has the same options as the predict tool for **Regression** and **Poisson regression**.

The **Fit Binary Logistic Regression** tool can also run a stepwise analysis for us. The options are the same as **Fit Regression Model...**.

See also

▶ The *Coding a numeric column to text values* recipe in *Chapter 1, Worksheet, Data Management, and the Calculator*

Fitting a nonlinear regression

Nonlinear regression tools give us the ability to specify an expectation function that goes beyond the Linear, Quadratic, or Cubic models. Applications of nonlinear regression are present where the Linear models fail to fit very well. Models for exponential growth and decay rates are good examples, where the nonlinear tools will provide a better fit to the data. The use of nonlinear regression tools is more complicated than the Linear models, and initial estimates of the coefficients must be provided.

Here we will use the data from the Oxford weather station to define our own expectation function, set the initial parameters of the function, and find the parameters of the coefficients. We will concentrate on the results from 2000 onwards, hence the initial steps will be to subset the worksheet.

From these results, we will define a regression model to predict the mean maximum monthly temperature from the month of the year.

Getting ready

The data for this example can be found on the Met Office website at the following link:

`http://www.metoffice.gov.uk/climate/uk/stationdata/oxforddata.txt`

Follow steps 1 to 12 from *the Generating a paneled boxplot recipe in Chapter 2, Tables and Graphs*, to import the results.

The data is also made available in the `Oxford data.txt` files; this preserves the format from the website. Also, the `Oxford weather (Cleaned).MTW` Minitab file is correctly imported into Minitab for us.

How to do it...

The following steps will create a subset of the worksheet using just the data from 2000 onwards. Then, we will use a Sine function to fit the mean maximum temperature by month:

1. First, we will subset the data; use the **Data** menu and **Subset Worksheet....**

2. Enter the name of the new worksheet as `Year 2000 onwards`.

3. Select the **Condition...** button and enter the condition as `'Year' >= 2000`.

4. Click on **OK** in each dialog box to create the new worksheet.

5. To view the shape of the results, we will use a time series plot. Go to **Graph** and then select **Time Series Plot....**

6. Select the **Simple** time series.

7. Enter the column for mean maximum temperature in the **Series:** section.

8. Click on the **Time/Scale...** button.

9. Select the **Stamp** option and then select month and year as the stamp columns, as shown in the following screenshot:

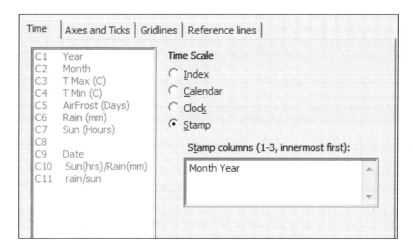

10. Click on **OK** in each dialog box.

11. The results should generate a regular pattern as shown in the following screenshot:

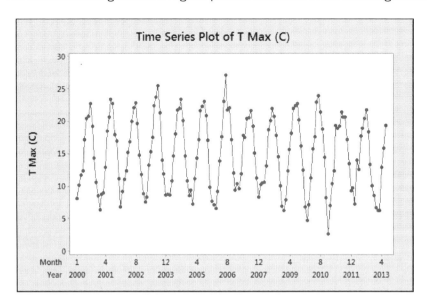

Gaps in the chart will correspond to estimated temperatures. The table on the Met Office website marks these as values with a * symbol at the end. For example, 13.6* is an estimated temperature. Minitab will replace these values with a * symbol for the missing data when copying into the worksheet. These values can be corrected manually.

12. We need to estimate an expectation function for temperature. The results follow a sinusoidal repeating pattern, with a range from minimum to maximum of roughly 20 degrees. The frequency of the Sine wave is every 12 months, with a mean value of roughly 15 degrees.

13. A suitable form for the expectation function would be *Mean + Magnitude *Sine(months)*. This can be written as follows:

$$\theta_0 + \theta_1 * \sin\left(\theta_2 * Month + \theta_3\right)$$

The respective parameters are explained as follows:

$$\theta_0 = \text{Mean temperature}$$

$$\theta_1 = \text{Magnitude of the sine wave}$$

$$\theta_2 = 2 * \pi / 12$$

$$\theta_3 = \text{Offset for the start of the sine wave}$$

14. To fit the model, navigate to **Stat | Regression** and select **Non Linear Regression**.
15. In the **Response:** section, enter TMax for mean maximum temperature.
16. Click on the **Use Calculator...** button to specify your expectation function.
17. Enter values in the **Expectation function:** section, as shown in the following screenshot:

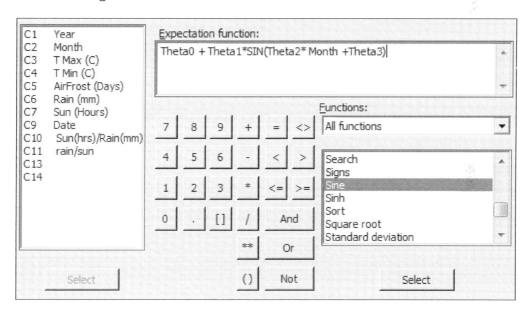

18. Click on **OK** and then select the **Parameters...** button.

19. Set the parameters with the following values as the starting points of the coefficients. **Theta0** corresponds roughly to the mean temperature of 15 degrees. **Theta1** is placed roughly at the magnitude of the wave at 10 degrees. **Theta2** becomes 2*Pi/12 and **Theta3** will be the start position of the sine wave that can be estimated at 0, as shown in the following screenshot:

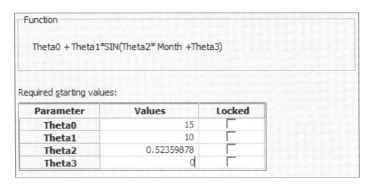

20. Click on **OK** and select the **Options...** button. Change **Algorithm** to **Levenberg-Marquardt**.

21. Click on **OK** and select the **Graphs...** button.

22. To check the assumptions of running the regression, select the **Four in one** residuals and click on **OK** in each dialog box.

How it works...

Theta is traditionally used as our coefficient in nonlinear regression rather than beta, although it does not matter what name is used for the coefficients. Any text that is not recognized as a function, a column, or a constant is defined as a coefficient.

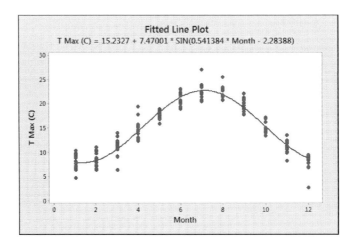

With the nonlinear regression, finding coefficients is not as simple as linear regression. We have to start with an estimate for the values of the coefficients. These starting points are then searched around with either the Gauss-Newton or Levenberg-Marquardt algorithms. Options within the main dialog box allow us to choose between the two search algorithms and specify the maximum number of iterations to find a solution.

If we are very wrong with the initial estimates, then the search algorithms may fail to converge on a solution. The session window will indicate whether this has happened. We could then expand the number of iterations, change the search algorithm, or recheck the estimates of the coefficients.

We have set the coefficients in this example as the mean temperature for Theta0; Theta1 is defined by the range/2 and Theta2 becomes 2*Pi/12; they give us the full number of radians in 12 months. Theta3 is defined as the offset to start the Sine function. Its parameters can be locked to fix the values of Theta. In this example, we may wish to lock Theta2 to 2*Pi/12.

Nonlinear regression has the same assumptions for the residuals and we should check the residuals for normality, equal variance, and independence over time.

This tool also contains a catalogue of predefined functions. We could select a number of these based on our knowledge of the process being studied or by the shape of the function.

As we define our own functions, these are saved within the catalogue as well. They are saved within the drop down under **My functions**. They can also be renamed and given a category.

There's More...

With the study here, we looked at the relationship of month and temperature for the results after 2000. We could run the same study for all data from 1853 onwards. When running these results, try looking at the residual plots and see if there is anything unusual.

The benefit of the nonlinear regression tools is their ability to fit models where the standard Linear models do not quite work. Linear models also refer to Quadratic or Cubic models, which can be slightly confusing.

We could compare the results of this nonlinear regression using the Sine function to fit the month to a Quadratic model. We would obtain a result that seems to fit reasonably well; you should notice that around July and August and towards January and December, the data deviates appreciably from the fitted quadratic. The use of residual plots will reveal that the residuals versus fits still has a curved pattern, indicating poor fits across the line.

The use of the Sine function gives us a closer-fitting model over the results and a better predictive model. The simple sine function doesn't account for other random weather patterns, but still keeps a good fit for expected temperatures by month. The inclusion of terms to fit to trends over years or other predictors can help reveal more structure in the results.

A trend component can be added by including $\theta_4 * Year$.

If we analyze this data using **General Linear Model** (**GLM**) or a one-way ANOVA, we will obtain a similar result. GLM will find the mean response for each month, rather than the equation obtained here.

See also

> ▸ The *Using one-way ANOVA with unstacked columns* recipe in *Chapter 4, Using Analysis of Variance*

> ▸ The *Using GLM for unbalanced designs* recipe in *Chapter 4, Using Analysis of Variance*

6
Understanding Process Variation with Control Charts

In this chapter, we will cover the following recipes:

- ▸ Xbar-R charts and applying stages to a control chart
- ▸ Using an Xbar-S chart
- ▸ Using I-MR charts
- ▸ Using the Assistant tool to create control charts
- ▸ Attribute charts' P (proportion) chart
- ▸ Testing for overdispersion and Laney P' chart
- ▸ Creating a u-chart
- ▸ Testing for overdispersion and Laney U' chart
- ▸ Using CUSUM charts
- ▸ Finding small shifts with EWMA
- ▸ Control charts for rare events – T charts
- ▸ Rare event charts – G charts

Introduction

Control charts are very simple graphical tools which show us if measurements/results are stable over time. They look at the mean and variation of the data and check to see whether the observed data shows any patterns that would not be expected to occur if the data was purely random. This special cause variation is indicated by tests that look for these patterns. They are based on there being a low probability of these patterns occurring randomly.

Minitab provides a wide range of control charts for different scenarios. These include the standard control charts for monitoring a process over time such as Xbar-R or I-MR charts as well as multivariate control charts and charts to plot rare events. Now, we will look at using some of the more traditional charts, but also show the use of some of the newer charts in Minitab.

The **Control Charts** menu is separated into different submenus to make it easier for the user to select the correct chart. The following screenshot shows us where to find the **Control Charts** section within the **Stat** menu and the choices presented by the sub menus:

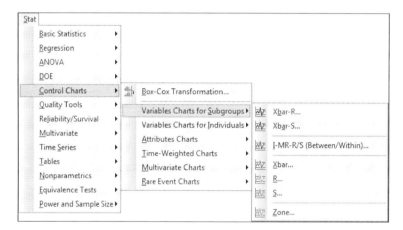

Xbar-R charts and applying stages to a control chart

As with all control charts, the Xbar-R charts are used to monitor process stability. Apart from generating the basic control chart, we will look at how we can control the output with a few options within the dialog boxes. Xbar-R stands for means and ranges; we use the means chart to estimate the population mean of a process and the range chart to observe how the population variation changes.

For more information on control charts, see *Understanding Statistical Process Control* by *Donald J. Wheeler* and *David S. Chambers*.

As an example, we will study the fill volumes of syringes. Five syringes are sampled from the process at hourly intervals; these are used to represent the mean and variation of that process over time.

We will plot the means and ranges of the fill volumes across 50 subgroups. The data also includes a process change. This will be displayed on the chart by dividing the data into two stages.

The charts for subgrouped data can use a worksheet set up in two formats. Here the data is recorded such that each row represents a subgroup. The columns are the sample points. The Xbar-S chart will use data in the other format where all the results are recorded in one column.

The following screenshot shows the data with subgroups across the rows on the left, and the same data with subgroups stacked on the right:

Subgroup	Measure1	Measure2	Measure3	Measure4	Measure5		Stacked Data	Stacked Subgroup
1	15.84	15.55	15.39	15.45	15.75		15.84	1
2	15.79	15.09	14.72	15.20	14.74		15.55	1
3	15.73	15.35	15.06	15.40	15.52		15.39	1
							15.45	1
							15.75	1
							15.79	2
							15.09	2
							14.72	2
							15.20	2
							14.74	2
							15.73	3
							15.35	3
							15.06	3
							15.40	3
							15.52	3

How to do it...

The following steps will create an Xbar-R chart staged by the `Adjustment` column with all eight of the tests for special causes:

1. Use the **Open Worksheet** command from the **File** menu to open the `Volume.mtw` worksheet.

2. Navigate to **Stat | Control Charts | Variables charts for subgroups**. Then click on **Xbar-R...**.

3. Change the drop down at the top of the dialog to **Observations for a subgroup are in one row of columns:**.

4. Enter the columns `Measure1` to `Measure5` into the dialog box by highlighting all the measure columns in the left selection box and clicking on **Select**.

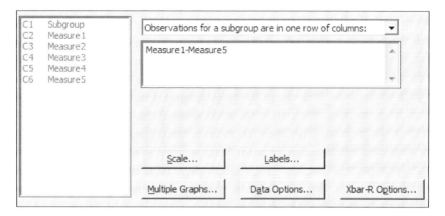

5. Click on **Xbar-R Options** and navigate to the tab for **Tests**.
6. Select all the tests for special causes.
7. Select the **Stages** tab.
8. Enter `Adjustment` in the **Define Stages** section.
9. Click on **OK** in each dialog box.

How it works...

The R or range chart displays the variation over time in the data by plotting the range of measurements in a subgroup. The Xbar chart plots the means of the subgroups.

The choice of layout of the worksheet is picked from the drop-down box in the main dialog box. The **All observations for a chart are in one column:** field is used for data stacked into columns. Means of subgroups and ranges are found from subgroups indicated in the worksheet. The **Observations for a subgroup are in one row of columns:** field will find means and ranges from the worksheet rows.

The Xbar-S chart example shows us how to use the dialog box when the data is in a single column. The dialog boxes for both Xbar-R and Xbar-S work the same way.

Tests for special causes are used to check the data for nonrandom events. The Xbar-R chart options give us control over the tests that will be used. The values of the tests can be changed from these options as well. The options from the **Tools** menu of Minitab can be used to set the default values and tests to use in any control chart.

By using the option under **Stages**, we are able to recalculate the means and standard deviations for the pre and post change groups in the worksheet. Stages can be used to recalculate the control chart parameters on each change in a column or on specific values. A date column can be used to define stages by entering the date at which a stage should be started.

There's more...

Xbar-R charts are also available under the **Assistant** menu. For more on how to use the **Assistant** menu to generate a control chart, see the *Using the Assistant tool to create control charts* recipe.

The default display option for a staged control chart is to show only the mean and control limits for the final stage. Should we want to see the values for all stages, we would use the **Xbar-R Options** and **Display** tab. To place these values on the chart for all stages, check the **Display control limit / center line labels for all stages** box. See Xbar-S charts for a description of all the tabs within the **Control Charts** options.

For more information on changing the values of the tests for special causes, see the *Using I-MR charts* recipe.

See also

- ▶ The *Using an Xbar-S chart* recipe
- ▶ The *Using I-MR charts* recipe
- ▶ The *Using the Assistant tool to create control charts* recipe

Using an Xbar-S chart

Xbar-S charts are similar in use to Xbar-R. The main difference is that the variation chart uses standard deviation from the subgroups instead of the range. The choice between using Xbar-R or Xbar-S is usually made based on the number of samples in each subgroup. With smaller subgroups, the standard deviation estimated from these can be inflated. Typically, with less than nine results per subgroup, we see them inflating the standard deviation, and which increases the width of the control limits on the charts. **Automotive Industry Action Group (AIAG)** suggests using the Xbar-R, which is greater than or equal to nine times the Xbar-S.

Now, we will apply an Xbar-S chart to a slightly different scenario. Japan sits above several active fault lines. Because of this, minor earthquakes are felt in the region quite regularly. There may be several minor seismic events on any given day. For this example, we are going to use seismic data from the Advanced National Seismic System. All seismic events from January 1, 2013 to July 12, 2013 from the region that covers latitudes 31.128 to 45.275 and longitudes 129.799 to 145.269 are included in this dataset. This corresponds to an area that roughly encompasses Japan.

The dataset is provided for us already but we could gather more up-to-date results from the following link:

```
http://earthquake.usgs.gov/monitoring/anss/
```

To search the catalog yourself, use the following link:

```
http://www.ncedc.org/anss/catalog-search.html
```

We will look at seismic events by week that create Xbar-S charts of magnitude and depth. In the initial steps, we will use the date to generate a column that identifies the week of the year. This column is then used as the subgroup identifier.

How to do it...

The following steps will create an Xbar-S chart for the depth and magnitude of earthquakes. This will display the mean and standard deviation of the events by week:

1. Use the **Open Worksheet** command from the **File** menu to open the `earthquake.mtw` file.

2. Go to the **Data** menu, click on **Extract from Date/Time**, and then click on **To Text**.

3. Enter `Date` in the **Extract from Date/time column:** section.

4. Type `Week` in the **Store text column in:** section.

5. Check the selection for **Week** and click on **OK** to create the new column.

6. Navigate to **Stat | Control Charts | Variable charts for Subgroups** and click on **Xbar-S**.

7. Enter `Depth` and `Mag` into the dialog box as shown in the following screenshot and `Week` into the **Subgroup sizes:** field.

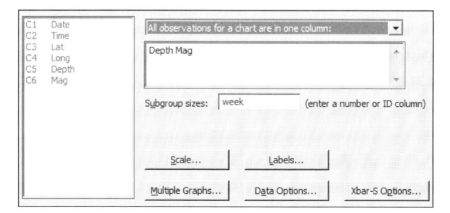

8. Click on the **Scale** button, and select the option for **Stamp**.

9. Enter `Date` in the **Stamp columns** section.

10. Click on **OK**.

11. Click on **Xbar-S Options** and then navigate to the **Tests** tab.

12. Select all tests for special causes.

13. Click on **OK** in each dialog box.

How it works...

Steps 1 to 4 build the `Week` column that we use as the subgroup. The extracts from the date/time options are fantastic for quickly generating columns based on dates. Days of the week, week of the year, month, or even minutes or seconds can all be separated from the date.

Multiple columns can be entered into the control chart dialog box just as we have done here. Each column is then used to create a new Xbar-S chart. This lets us quickly create charts for several dimensions that are recorded at the same time. The use of the week column as the subgroup size will generate the control chart with mean depth and magnitude for each week.

The scale options within control charts are used to change the display on the chart scales. By default, the x axis displays the subgroup number; changing this to display the date can be more informative when identifying the results that are out of control. Options to add axes, tick marks, gridlines, and additional reference lines are also available. We can also edit the axis of the chart after we have generated it by double-clicking on the x axis.

The Xbar-S options are similar for all control charts; the tabs within **Options** give us control over a number of items for the chart. The following list shows us the tabs and the options found within each tab:

▶ **Parameters**: This sets the historical means and standard deviations; if using multiple columns, enter the first column mean, leave a space, and enter the second column mean

▶ **Estimate**: This allows us to specify subgroups to include or exclude in the calculations and change the method of estimating sigma

▶ **Limits**: This can be used to change where sigma limits are displayed or place on the control limits

▶ **Tests**: This allows us to choose the tests for special causes of the data and change the default values. The *Using I-MR charts* recipe details the options for the **Tests** tab.

▶ **Stages**: This allows the chart to be subdivided and will recalculate center lines and control limits for each stage

▶ **Box Cox**: This can be used to transform the data, if necessary

▶ **Display**: This has settings to choose how much of the chart to display. We can limit the chart to show only the last section of the data or split a larger dataset into separate segments. There is also an option to display the control limits and center lines for all stages of a chart in this option.

▶ **Storage**: This can be used to store parameters of the chart, such as means, standard deviations, plotted values, and test results

There's more...

The control limits for the graphs that are produced vary as the subgroup sizes are not constant; this is because the number of earthquakes varies each week. In most practical applications, we may expect to collect the same number of samples or items in a subgroup and hence have flat control limits.

If we wanted to see the number of earthquakes in each week, we could use **Tally** from inside the **Tables** menu. This will display a result of counts per week. We could also store this tally back into the worksheet.

The result of this tally could be used with a c-chart to display a count of earthquake events per week.

If we wanted to import the data directly from the Advanced National Seismic System, then the following steps will obtain the data and prepare the worksheet for us:

1. Follow the link to the ANSS catalog search at `http://www.ncedc.org/anss/catalog-search.html`.

2. Enter `2013/01/01` in the **Start date, time:** field.

3. Enter `2013/06/12` in the **End date, time:** field.

4. Enter `3` in the **Min magnitude:** field.

5. Enter `31.128` in the **Min latitude** field and `45.275` in the **Max latitude** field.

6. Enter `129.799` in the **Min longitude** field and `145.269` in the **Max longitude** filed.

7. Copy the data from the search results, excluding the headers, and paste it into a Minitab worksheet.

8. Change the names of the columns to, `C1 Date, C2 Time, C3 Lat, C4 Long, C5 Depth, C6 Mag`. The other columns, `C7` to `C13`, can then be deleted.

9. The `Date` column will have copied itself into Minitab as text; to convert this back to a date, navigate to **Data | Change Data Type | Text to Date/Time**.

10. Enter `Date` in both the **Change text columns:** and **Store date/time columns in:** sections.

11. In the **Format of text columns:** section, enter `yyyy/mm/dd`.

12. Click on **OK**.

13. To extract the week from the `Date` column, navigate to **Data | Date/Time | Extract to Text**.

14. Enter `'Date'` in the **Extract from date/time column:** section.

15. Enter `'Week'` in the **Store text column in:** field.

16. Check the box for **Week** and click on **OK**.

See also

▸ The *Using I-MR charts* recipe

▸ The *Xbar-R charts and applying stages to a control chart* recipe

▸ The *Using the Assistant tool to create control charts* recipe

Using I-MR charts

I-MR charts are used to plot single values over time. Individuals charts are typically used when we have single measurements at a point of time or at every result. Examples might include be related to the production of smaller volumes such as aircraft or perhaps aircraft engines. Other scenarios might include situations where data collection is automated and all results are captured. The individual values are plotted against the overall mean and the moving range tracks variation by looking at differences between the results. Unlike Xbar-R or Xbar-S, which use a sample or subgroup to estimate the mean and variation, an I-MR chart estimates the short term variation from the average moving range. This is based on the successive differences between the individual values.

Here, we will use the values of temperature from the Oxford weather station to check the stability of temperature. Temperature is a seasonal value and we will look at the measurements separately by month. As the temperature data has been given to us in the form of the mean maximum daily temperature for each month, there are no logical subgroups into which to divide the data. We will therefore plot the temperature as individual values.

As temperatures show a high degree of seasonality across the year, it would not be sensible to plot all of the original temperature data as a control chart. Therefore, we will plot the temperature for a single month instead. In this recipe, we will plot the temperature for January from every year from the start of record keeping to the present day..

We will first split the worksheet by month, before running the I-MR chart on the results for January.

Getting ready

The data for this example can be found on the MET office website at the following address:

`http://www.metoffice.gov.uk/climate/uk/stationdata/oxforddata.txt`

Copy the data into Minitab and label the columns `Year`, `Month`, `T Max`, `T Min`, `AirFrost(days)`, `Rain(mm)`, and `Sun(Hours)`.

This data is also available from the `Oxford weather.txt` file or the `Oxford Weather (Cleaned).mtw` file.

How to do it...

The following steps will create a new worksheet for each month and then generate an I-MR chart for mean maximum and minimum January temperatures:

1. Go to the **Data** menu and click on **Split Worksheet**.
2. Enter the `Month` column as **By variables:**.
3. Click on **OK**.
4. Select the worksheet for **Month = 1** for the January temperatures.
5. Navigate to **Stat | Control Charts | Variables Charts for Individuals** and click on **I-MR**.
6. Enter the columns for `'T Max'` and `'T Min'` as **Variables**.
7. Click on the **Scale** button and enter `Year` in the **Stamp columns** field by selecting the options as shown in the following screenshot:

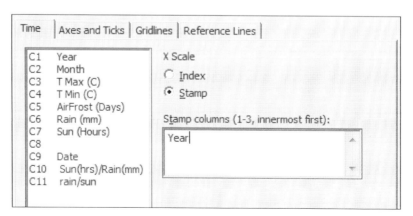

8. Click on **OK**.

9. Select the **I-MR options** button, then choose the tab labeled **Tests**, and select **Perform all tests for Special causes**.

10. Click on **OK** in each dialog box.

How it works...

Each column entered into the variables section for I-MR charts will create a separate control chart. We have created charts for both the mean maximum temperatures and the mean minimum temperatures for January from the start of the data in 1853.

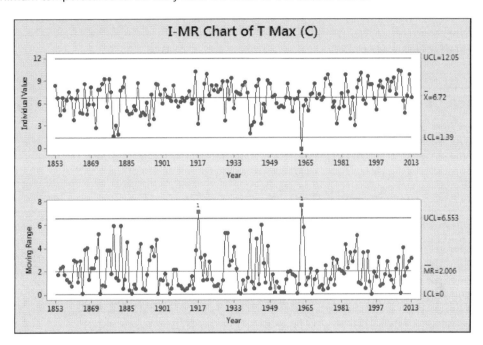

Results that break the rules for identifying special causes or unusual variation are flagged in red with the test that has been broken. In the results shown in the preceding screenshot, Test 1 is flagged up for years 1917 and 1963 on the moving range chart. This seems to indicate a large change in temperatures from 1916 to 1917 and 1962 to 1963. Notice the result in the individuals' chart for 1963. This corresponds to one of the coldest winters in the UK since records began.

Some care should be taken with the interpretation of the previous results as adjacent points are one year apart.

The use of the **Scale** option, **Stamp**, allows us to use a column in the worksheet for the x axis labels. By displaying the year instead of the row number as the index, we can identify the years which contain unusual results. If the graph is the active window pop up, text highlighting the year will be displayed when we hover the cursor over a point.

I-MR charts, like most control charts, are an updating graph within Minitab. We can right-click on the chart and click on **Update Graph Now** when new data is entered or click on **Update Graph Automatically**.

Time-weighted charts are more appropriate than I-MR charts if we are interested in observing small changes. Advanced charts such as CUSUM or EWMA can be used to pick up on these smaller shifts in the process. See the example of the EWMA chart later as a comparison.

There's more...

As the dialog boxes in Minitab remember previous settings, we can easily generate the charts for the other months by selecting one of the other worksheets. Go back to the previous dialog box using *Ctrl + E*, and all we need to do is click on **OK** to run the same settings on the new worksheet. This can be automated by the use of macros. The macro command `Worksheet` can be used to specify a worksheet to make it active.

Defaults for the tests used in control charts can be specified from **Tools** and **Options**, as shown in the following screenshot:

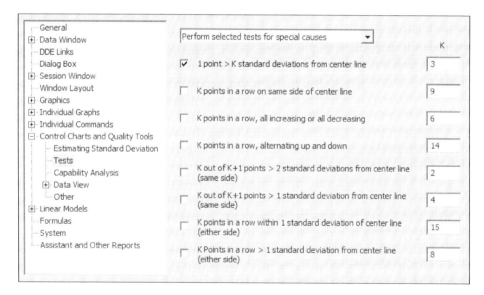

The preceding screenshot shows the location of the options. Here it is possible to pick the tests to be used by default and the values of those tests. While Minitab uses the most common values of these tests, often test 2 is set at 7 or 8 points in a row rather than 9. This would make the test more sensitive to a process shift at the cost of increasing the risk of a false alarm.

An alternative method of selecting the results of January for the I-MR chart would be to use the **Data Options** button from the dialog box.

Here we can specify which rows to include or exclude from the study in the same manner as in the **Subset Worksheet** option.

See also

▶ The *Using CUSUM charts* recipe

▶ The *Finding small shifts with EWMA* recipe

Using the Assistant tool to create control charts

The **Assistant** menu first appeared in Minitab v16 to make the use of statistics and their interpretation more accessible. As such, this menu helps us select a control chart, before giving us some advice on our results. The **Assistant** menu does not offer all the control charts that are found under the **Stat** menu; it offers us only the most commonly used ones.

We will not look at any data but we will step through the decisions offered by the assistant in selecting a chart. Try the steps with your own data. The steps here follow the choices for an Xbar-R chart. This is to illustrate the choices given at each step of the **Assistant** menu.

How to do it...

The following steps will guide us through the **Assistant** tool decision tree to an Xbar-R chart:

1. Go to the **Assistant** menu and select **Control Charts...**.

2. From the decision tree, select the top decision diamond **Data type** as shown in the following screenshot:

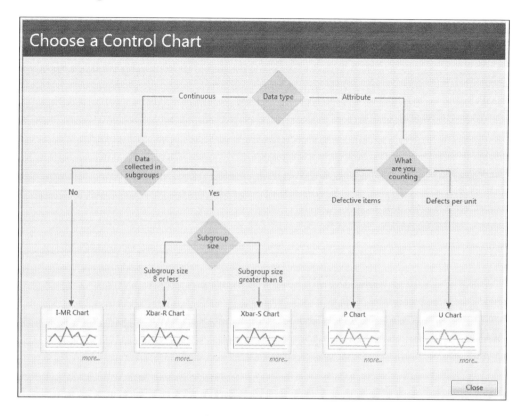

3. Read the description about the data type choice and then click on **Back**.

4. Read the description for **Data collected in Subgroups** then, click on **Back** to continue.

5. Click on the **more...** label beneath **Xbar-R Chart**.

6. We are presented with guidelines on collecting data for an Xbar-R chart and guidelines on using the chart. Select the section about collecting data in rational subgroups.

7. After reading the guidelines, click on the **Back** button and select an appropriate chart.

8. If you have data to be used with this recipe, enter the column and subgroup size.

9. Under **Control limits and center line**, choose from **Estimate from the data** or **Use known values**.

10. Click on **OK** to generate the reports.

How it works...

The **Assistant** tool control charts will generate three report cards. The first report card will inform us about stability, the amount of data, and check for correlated data in the response. The second page will present the control chart, highlighting out of control points. The third page is a summary report with comments. This is shown in the following screenshot:

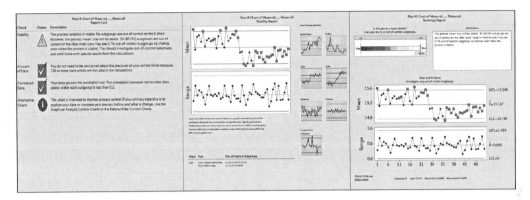

Each page gives us useful information, helping us build conclusions about the study.

All the assistant tools present us with a simpler-to-use dialog box to make it easier to run the study. They also give us guidance to help direct us to the correct tool to be used.

To make the use of the tools and interpretation of the output easier, Minitab does not have all the options available under the **Stat** menu. If we wanted to change the scale on the axis from an index or subgroup number to a date column, we would need to use the control charts in the **Stat** menu.

Not all tests for special causes are used. The Assistant will use Test 1, which is one point more than three standard deviations from the center line. Test 2 is nine points in a row on one side of the center line and Test 7 is 15 points in a row that are within +/- 1 standard deviation. For ease of use and interpretation of the results, we cannot change these rules. If we wanted to specify other tests for special causes or change the values used, we would need to go back to the control charts under the **Stat** menu.

Minitab can be a powerful aid for many users and is excellent for presentations to any audience, because of its assistant tools and the clarity with which it presents data. It is worth pointing out that although the **Assistant** menu provides a very quick and powerful start to using control charts, it does not have as many options as the **Stat** menu control charts. More advanced use of control charts can only be run from the **Stat** menu.

As an example, the **Assistant** tool will allow us to stage control charts from the **Before/After Control Charts** tool; if we wish to plot more than two stages, we need to use the control charts in the **Stat** menu.

 Before/After control charts are new to the **Assistant** menu in release 17.

See also

▸ The *Xbar-R charts and applying stages to a control chart* recipe

▸ The *Using an Xbar-S chart* recipe

▸ The *Using I-MR charts* recipe

▸ The *Creating a u-chart* recipe

▸ The *Attribute charts' P (proportion) chart* recipe

Attribute charts' P (proportion) chart

In this recipe, we will use a proportion chart to track events or defective items out of a total.

This data looks at the number of breaches within an accident and emergency department. The hospital has a target, according to which patients arriving at the accident and emergency ward must be seen by a doctor within four hours. A breach is classified as a patient who has not been attended to within this time. The dataset that we are using is organized into columns for ease of entry. Total attendance at accident and emergency is listed in row 1 and breaches are listed in row 2.

We will need to transpose the data into a new worksheet to put it back into a column format, before generating the P chart.

Getting ready

Enter the data in the following screenshot into a worksheet in Minitab. Label the columns of the data as 1 through to 9.

	1	2	3	4	5	6	7	8	9	10	11	12	13
A&E attendance	101	98	90	91	91	109	110	102	93	92	97	104	113
Breaches	10	10	9	5	7	9	7	17	5	5	6	10	7

How to do it...

The following steps will transpose the data into a new worksheet before generating a P chart:

1. Go to the **Data** menu and click on **Transpose columns...**.

2. Highlight the columns 1 to 13 and click on the **Select** button to move them into the top section and enter C1 into the space for creating variable names, as shown in the following screenshot:

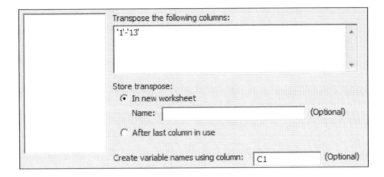

3. Click on **OK**.

4. Navigate to **Stat | Control charts | Attributes Charts** and then select the **P...** chart.

5. Enter Breaches in the **Variables**: field.

6. Enter 'A&E attendance' in the **Subgroup sizes:** field.

7. Click on the **P Chart Options...** button.

8. Select the tab labeled **Tests**.

9. Select **Perform all tests for special causes** in the drop down.

10. Click on **OK** in each dialog box.

How it works...

The proportion chart plots the mean proportion of all of the data data and the proportion for each subgroup. The control limits are set based on the binomial distribution at +/- 3 standard deviations.

$$p \pm 3 \sqrt{\frac{p(1-p)}{n_i}}$$

Lower control limits that are calculated as negative are fixed at 0 and by the same token, limits that exceed one are fixed at 1. As the control limits depend on the subgroup sample size, n_i, we will observe control limits that vary in width for this result as the number of occupied beds differs per month. For the data plotted here, they appear as shown in the following screenshot:

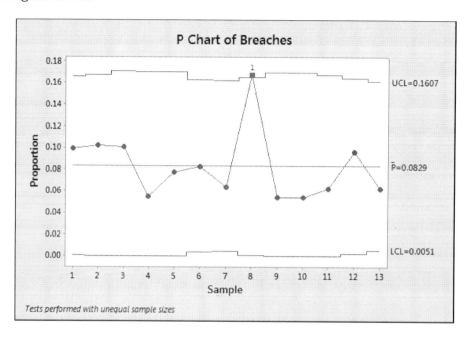

We can set the control limits for the P chart to a constant value using the **S Limits** tab within the **P Chart options...**. The following screenshot shows where to fix the control limits to use an assumed subgroup size:

AIAG suggests that the mean subgroup size can be used for the control limits as long as the minimum subgroup size is no more than 0.75 of the maximum subgroup size.

There's more...

The P chart sets control limits based on the data following a binomial distribution. This can be a problem as subgroup sizes increase. When subgroups become larger, it is possible that group variation can be seen as different from the binomial variation. This is known as overdispersion. See Laney P' charts for correcting group variation in the P chart.

When selecting multiple columns for dialog boxes, we can drag down the list of available columns and click on the **Select** button. All selected columns are entered into the dialog box. A range of columns is indicated by a hyphen between them. `C1-C10` would indicate all columns from 1 to 10.

See also

▶ The *Testing for overdispersion and Laney P' chart* recipe

Testing for overdispersion and Laney P' chart

We will use a Laney P' chart to correct the overdispersion in our data. The P chart in the previous example calculates the control limits on the binomial distribution. If the process being studied has a natural variation in the proportion that has a variation larger than the binomial distribution, then a P chart can show many more out of control points than it should. The P chart uses the variation between groups to estimate the position of the control limits.

Minitab has a P chart diagnostic tool to look for overdispersion or underdispersion in the data.

Initially, we will run the P chart diagnostic to check our data and then run the P' chart.

How to do it...

The following steps will check for overdispersion in the data and then generate a P' chart:

1. Use **Open Worksheet...** from the **File** menu to open the `Calls Lost.mtw` worksheet.
2. Navigate to **Stat | Control Charts | Attributes Charts** and select **P Chart Diagnostic**.
3. Enter `Hung up` in the **Variables:** field.
4. In **Subgroup sizes:** field, enter `Calls`.
5. Click on **OK**.

6. Check the results of the P chart diagnostic to see if there is evidence of overdispersion.

7. Navigate to **Stat | Control Charts | Attribute Charts** and click on **Laney P'**, as suggested from the diagnostic tool.

8. Enter `Hung up` in the **Variables:** field.

9. Enter `Calls` in the **Subgroups sizes** field.

10. Click on **P' Chart Options**.

11. Navigate to the tab for **Tests** and select **Perform all tests for special causes**.

12. Click on **OK** in each dialog box.

How it works...

The traditional P chart assumes that the variation exhibited in the process is all part of the within variation or rather the variation from a binomial distribution. In most cases, the variation in P over time and the variation between groups is usually smaller than the variation that is observed due to the within variation. If the subgroup sizes are very large, then the between variation can be a significant component of the variation in the study.

This results in overdispersion—a P chart where the control limits are too narrow. As the control limits are too narrow, they cause an elevated false alarm rate. The Laney P' charts account for the variation between groups and use it to plot the control limits.

The diagnostic charts for P and U check to see if the variation observed in the proportion or per-unit values is higher or lower than expected from a binomial or Poisson distribution. The diagnostic tool will then tell us if we need to use the P' chart instead of the traditional P chart.

The results here can be checked for comparison against the P chart.

There's more...

The traditional approach to overdispersion is to use I-MR charts. The problem with individual charts is that while they plot the variation between groups, they do not see the subgroup size for the proportion. The control limits remain flat and do not vary with the subgroup size. The P' chart allows for variable control limits with subgroup size.

When subgroup sizes are constant, the P' chart will be the same as the I-MR chart. Also, P' charts will be the same as P charts when the data follows a binomial distribution.

For more on Laney control charts see the paper *Improved Control Charts for Attributes, David B. Laney.*

- ▶ The _Attribute charts' P (proportion) chart_ recipe
- ▶ The _Creating a u-chart_ recipe
- ▶ The _Testing for overdispersion and Laney U' chart_ recipe

Creating a u-chart

U-charts and c-charts are used for Poisson data rather than binomial. U is for defects per unit and c for counts. While similar to the P or NP charts, the control limits are based on a Poisson distribution.

In this recipe, we will type data for falls and beds occupied per month at a hospital into the worksheet. We will then use the u-chart to plot the number of falls in a hospital per occupied bed. The results are displayed as a per-unit figure.

This data is loosely based on an example discussed in the paper, _Plotting basic control charts: tutorial notes for healthcare practitioners_, by _M.A. Mohammed, P. Worthington_, and _W. H. Woodall_.

This paper is available at the following location:

```
http://medqi.bsd.uchicago.edu/documents/
ControlchartsmohammedQSHC4_08.pdf
```

The data is given with monthly results in separate columns for ease of data entry. We will first transpose the data before plotting it on a u-chart. As the minimum number of occupied beds is within 75 percent of the maximum number occupied, we can use options to set the limits to use the mean value.

Getting ready

Enter the data shown in the following screenshot into a new worksheet within Minitab:

	Month1	Month2	Month3	Month4	Month5	Month6	Month7	Month8	Month9	Month10	Month11	Month12	Month13
Falls	1	4	3	4	2	3	5	2	0	2	6	2	5
Beds Occupied	1048	996	918	995	866	896	876	930	832	830	829	822	912

How to do it...

The following steps will transpose the worksheet before generating a u-chart.

1. Go to the **Data** menu and click on **Transpose Columns...**.

2. Enter the results into the dialog box, as shown in the following screenshot:

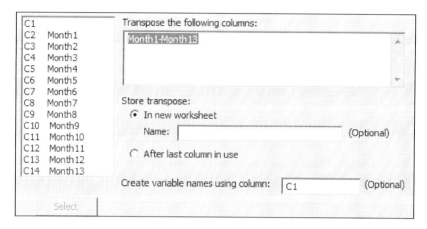

3. Click on **OK**.

4. Navigate to **Stat | Control Charts | Attributes Charts** and select the **U...** option.

5. Enter the column for falls into the **Variables:** field.

6. Enter the column for the occupied beds into the **Subgroup sizes:** field.

7. Click on **U Chart Options....**

8. Select the **S Limits** tab.

9. In the **When subgroup sizes are unequal, calculate control limits** section, select the **Assuming all subgroups have size:** option and enter 904 for the mean number of occupied beds.

10. Click on **OK** in each dialog box.

How it works...

The control limits for the u-chart are based on the Poisson distribution and use the following formula:

$$u \pm 3 \sqrt{\frac{\mu}{n_i}}$$

The control limits are set by default at the value of +/- 3 around the mean. As with the P chart, values of the control limit that are less than zero will be fixed to 0.

By setting the option to use the mean number of beds occupied we fix the control limits to be constant. The default will generate a chart with control limits that vary with the subgroup size.

As long as the minimum subgroup size is greater than 75 percent of the maximum subgroup size it is reasonable to fix the control limits to be constant. This will not affect the per-unit figure.

The **Display Descriptive Statistics** option in the **Basic statistics** menu can be used to generate the mean, maximum and minimum values of the Beds Occupied column.

Four tests for special causes can be used with attribute control charts: tests 1, 2, 3, and 4. By default, only test 1 is selected. The other tests can be selected from within the u-chart options and the tab for tests.

Using the options for Minitab under the **Tools** menu, the default tests and rules for the tests can be chosen.

See the I-MR charts for more details of where to find these settings.

See also

▶   The *Using I-MR charts* recipe
▶   The *Testing for overdispersion and Laney U' chart* recipe

Testing for overdispersion and Laney U' chart

The Laney U' chart is similar to the Laney P' chart in its use. We use this chart when we have the Poisson data that shows evidence of overdispersion or underdispersion. As the steps for use of the Laney U' chart are very similar to the P' chart, we will not use an example dataset.

How to do it...

The following steps will show us how to check for overdispersion, after which we will use a Laney U' chart:

1. Navigate to **Stat | Control Charts | Attributes Charts** and select **U Chart Diagnostic...**.

2. Enter the data from the column containing the counts of events in the **Variables:** field.

3. Enter the data from the subgroup size column in the **Subgroups sizes:** field.

4. Click on **OK**.

5. Check the results of the **U Chart Diagnostic...** option. If the u-chart diagnostic indicates overdispersion or underdispersion, proceed to step 6. If not, use the u-chart (see the previous example).

6. Navigate to **Stat | Control Charts | Attributes charts** and select **Laney U' Chart**.
7. Enter the column containing the counts of events in the **Variables:** field.
8. Enter the column containing the subgroups sizes in the **Subgroup sizes:** field.
9. Click on **U' Chart Options**.
10. Select the **Tests** tab.
11. Select **All tests for special causes**.
12. Click on **OK** in each dialog box.

How it works...

The U' chart works in a manner that is similar to the P' chart. Control limits are set based on variation between groups.

See also

  ▶ The *Testing for overdispersion and Laney P' chart* recipe
  ▶ The *Creating a u-chart* recipe
  ▶ The *Using I-MR charts* recipe

Using CUSUM charts

A CUSUM chart is used to look for small shifts from a target. There are two types of CUSUM chart that Minitab will generate: One-sided CUSUM charts, which we will use here, or the two-sided or V-mask CUSUM.

CUSUM charts like EWMA charts can be useful when subgrouping of the data for an Xbar chart is not feasible and the I-MR chart is not sensitive enough. These may include scenarios where we have low production volumes, or where sampling can be prohibitively expensive or potentially destructive.

The data in this example looks at the fill volumes of syringes. There is a target volume of 15 ml. We will plot the CUSUM using a subgroup size of one to identify deviations from this target.

How to do it...

The following steps will generate a CUSUM for a target of 15 and a subgroup size of 1:

1. Use **Open Worksheet...** from the **File** menu to open the `Volume2.mtw` worksheet.
2. Navigate to **Stat | Control Charts | Time-Weighted Charts** and select **CUSUM...**.
3. Enter `Volume` and enter **Subgroup size:** as `1` and the target as `15`.
4. Click on **OK** to create the CUSUM.

How it works...

The default plan type is the one-sided CUSUM. This plots two lines. The top line detects upwards shifts from the target and the lower CUSUM detects downward shifts. The type of CUSUM can be changed in **CUSUM Options** and the **Plan/Type** tab.

The values of h and k for the CUSUM plan affect the sensitivity of the CUSUM. In a one-sided CUSUM, h, the decision interval is the number of standard deviations between the center line and the control limits. The value of k affects the drift to be detected. Default figures of h and k are 4 and 0.5.

The **Plan/Type** tab also has options to select Fast Initial Response (FIR) and the two-sided CUSUM can be centered on a given subgroup.

The results can be compared with an I-MR chart using a historical mean of 15. By looking at the cumulative sum away from target, the CUSUM becomes more sensitive at identifying the small shifts away from target.

See also

▶   The *Using I-MR charts* recipe

Finding small shifts with EWMA

Exponentially weighted moving average charts are useful for finding small shifts in the mean in a process. Here, we will use the EWMA chart to study the temperature data from the Oxford weather station. We will look at the results for January to investigate whether we have a change in mean monthly maximum and minimum temperatures across the data from 1853.

Both EWMA and CUSUM charts are useful in scenarios where we cannot collect rational subgroups for an Xbar chart. As with the temperature data from the Oxford weather station, we have a mean maximum temperature for a month; there are no subgroups. We can use the EWMA to be more sensitive to smaller scale shifts than the I-MR chart.

We will start by splitting the worksheet into months, selecting the worksheet for January, and then plotting the EWMA for maximum and minimum temperatures.

Getting ready

The data for this example can be found on the MET office website at the following address:

```
http://www.metoffice.gov.uk/climate/uk/stationdata/oxforddata.txt
```

Copy the data into Minitab but do not copy the headers or column names. The text file uses two rows of headers: name and units. Minitab will only accept one column header; copying and pasting both headers will convert all columns to text.

Label the columns `Year`, `Month`, `T Max`, `T Min`, `AirFrost(days)`, `Rain (mm)`, and `Sun(Hours)`.

This data is also available from the `Oxford Weather.txt` file or the `Oxford Weather (Cleaned).mtw` file.

How to do it...

1. Go to the **Data** menu and select **Split Worksheet**.

2. Enter `Month` in the **By Variables:** field.

3. Click on **OK**.

4. Select the worksheet for `Month = 1` for the January temperatures.

5. Navigate to **Stat | control charts | Time weighted charts** and select **EWMA...**.

6. Enter the columns for temperature into the dialog box, as shown in the following screenshot:

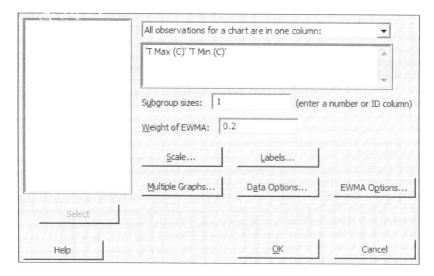

7. Click on the **Scale** button and select the **Stamp** option.

8. Enter `Year` in the section labeled **Stamp Columns**.

9. Click on **OK** in each dialog box.

How it works...

EWMA charts plot the value of the EWMA of a subgroup at time *i* as $Z_i = w\bar{x}_i + (1-w)Z_{i-1}$, where *w* is the weight of the exponentially weighted moving average and $\bar{x}_i$ is the mean of the *ith* subgroup. A value of *w* can be selected to tune the graph to detect shifts of different sizes. Lower values of the weight place less emphasis on the current result and more emphasis on previous values; higher values will mean that the graph can react more quickly to changes in the data.

Subgroup sizes for this data are 1 as each value indicates the results for one year. We could, as an alternative, run the same chart for a study looking at mean yearly temperatures rather than the temperatures from a month. To run this, return to the complete data worksheet. Use the Year column to specify the subgroup. The chart will then plot the EWMA of mean yearly temperatures.

The data that we obtain from the MET office website may generate an error when using it. The following error indicates that data is missing in the worksheet and a subgroup has no data. The EWMA chart cannot be produced with a subgroup that has no values or consists only of missing values:

```
EWMAChart 'T Max (C)' 1.
NOTE *** Closed graph:  Graph4

* ERROR * Could not process command with missing subgroup mean.
```

Some of the data from the MET office may be given as provisional or estimated. This is indicated by the use of * in the source document at the MET office website. When copying this data into Minitab, a value of 21.8* will be pasted into Minitab as a missing value, *. need to correct these figures manually. The latest results are indicated as provisional; when copied into Minitab, we will see that these are missing. Also notice that in 1860, there was no recorded mean minimum temperature for December.

The Oxford weather (cleaned).mtw worksheet provides a set of data with all the provisional figures entered.

See also

▶ The *Using CUSUM charts* recipe
▶ The *Using I-MR charts* recipe

Control charts for rare events – T charts

Rare event charts are used to plot intervals between events. Time between events tends to follow a Weibull distribution. The T chart is used to track whether the intervals between events are changing or remain stable.

If we were to plot the number of events in a day or week, it may be possible to use this data as a c-chart that displays a count of events. The problem with this technique is that rare events tend to have a rate that is very close to zero. Any event that occurs will be flagged up as unusually high.

Here we use the T chart to plot the time between eruptions of Vesuvius. Vesuvius is historically a very active and dangerous volcano, which was responsible for the destruction of Pompeii and Herculaneum in 79 AD. The dataset that we are using tracks the start dates of the eruptions from the year 1000 onwards.

How to do it...

The following steps open the dataset for the eruptions of Vesuvius and then produce the T chart of days between eruptions:

1. The data is in the `Vesuvius eruptions.mtw` worksheet. Use **File** and **Open Worksheet...** to navigate to the `vesuvius eruptions.mtw` file.

2. Navigate to **Stat | Control Charts | Rare Event Charts** and click on **T...**.

3. Enter `Year` in the **Variables:** field.

4. Click on **T Chart Options...** and navigate to the tab labeled **Tests**.

5. Select **Perform all the tests for special causes**.

6. Click on **OK**.

7. Click on the **Scale...** button.

8. Select the **Stamp** option and enter `Year` in the **Stamp columns** field.

9. Click on **OK** in each dialog box.

How it works...

The T chart plots the number of days between events and uses a Weibull distribution for the time between events. The plotted data points are the time between events or in this case, eruptions. High values equate to more time between events, and in the case of Vesuvius, a long quiet time between eruptions. Lower values indicate shorter times between events. See the following chart where we get long intervals around 1500 AD.

Tests 1, 5, 6, 7, and 8 use probability zones on the Weibull distribution instead of the usual rules for an Xbar-R or individuals chart.

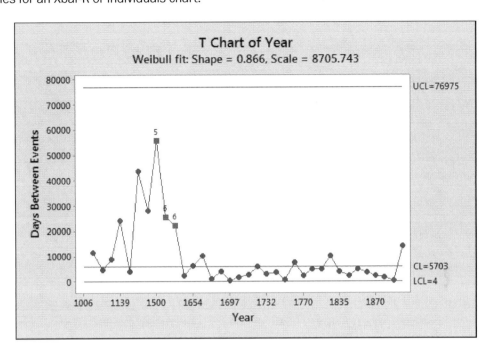

The results of the T chart should reveal a larger interval between eruptions flagged up at 1500. This interval has a value of 55882 days or roughly 153 years between the eruption in 1347 and the eruption in 1500.

The data was plotted only for the years in which an eruption occurred. This could also be constructed as a number of intervals, days, or hours between events. For this option, we would record the number of days between eruptions in the worksheet and then set the form of data in the dialog box as the number of intervals between events. See the example for G charts for data in this format.

There's more...

T charts are very similar to G charts. The G chart in the next recipe uses a geometric distribution. The choice between T and G charts is made on whether the data represents the time between occurrence of events or the number of opportunities between events.

The **T Chart Options** will also allow us to choose between using the Weibull or the exponential distribution.

See also

▸ The *Rare event charts – G charts* recipe

Rare event charts – G charts

G charts, like T charts, are used to plot rare events. The G chart uses the geometric distribution of the number of opportunities between events.

The data for this recipe uses the number of days between incidents at a factory. The worksheet lists this information as days until an incident has occurred. We will plot the number of days between accidents to look for unusually high or low numbers of days.

How to do it...

The following steps will create a G chart of the number of days between accidents at a factory:

1. Open the `Accidents.mtw` worksheet using **Open Worksheet...** from the **File** menu.
2. Navigate to **Stat | Control Charts | Rare Event Charts** and select the **G...** option.
3. Change the drop down for **Form of data** to **Number of opportunities** and the **Method of counting opportunities** drop down to **Opportunities between events**.
4. In the **Variables:** field, enter `Days`.
5. Select **G Chart Options...** and navigate to the **Tests** tab.
6. Select **Perform all tests for special causes**.
7. Click on **OK** in each dialog box.

How it works...

The G chart is named for the geometric distribution. This produces a chart that is similar to the T chart. T charts are typically used for time between events where a Weibull distribution would be fitted to the data. The G chart plots discrete intervals or the number of opportunities until an event. It would be more accurate to plot the total number of employee days between events but in most cases, it is simpler to list the number of actual days.

Other examples of when a G chart might be used could include the number of days at a hospital until an infection in a patient is observed. Again, while it would be more accurate to give out the total number of beds occupied until an infection, this would more typically be replaced by days.

Like the T chart, higher values on the chart indicate an increase in the number of opportunities until an event occurs. In the used data here for incidents at a factory, higher results are better.

The first test for special causes has an interesting problem with this chart. The lower control limit often sits at 0. Test 1 looks for data that falls outside the control limits to indicate a result that is unusually high or low. As negative days between events can never happen, we would not cross the lower control limit. This makes it difficult to find events that show unusually short days between events.

The Benneyan test is used for test 1 on the lower control limit. This looks for a number of consecutive plotted points that lie on the lower control limit. The number of points that will be highlighted as unusual is based on the mean of the data.

See also

▶   The *Control charts for rare events – T charts* recipe

7

Capability, Process Variation, and Specifications

This chapter contains the following recipes:

- ▶ A capability and control chart report using the capability analysis sixpack
- ▶ Capability analysis for normally distributed data
- ▶ Capability analysis for nonnormal distributions
- ▶ Using a Box-Cox transformation for capability
- ▶ Using a Johnson transformation for capability
- ▶ Using the Assistant tool for short-run capability analysis
- ▶ Comparing the capability of two processes using the Assistant tool
- ▶ Creating an acceptance sampling plan for variable data
- ▶ Creating an acceptance sampling plan for attribute data
- ▶ Comparing a previously defined sampling plan – C = 0 plans
- ▶ Generating run charts
- ▶ Generating tolerance intervals for summarized data
- ▶ Datasets that do not transform or fit any distribution

Introduction

This chapter looks at some of the quality tools found within Minitab. The majority of the functions used here are of the different *capability analysis* available. We will look at both normal and nonnormal distributions. Also, we take a look at a couple of the **Assistant** tools for capability as **Assistant** offers some great options for capability and presentation of data.

The final recipe in this chapter is more a note for a typical scenario that occurs with the data, namely, the problem that occurs when our data does not fit a distribution or a transformation comfortably.

It should be noted that capability analysis should only be run after we can establish that the process is stable. The results of capability, when a process is varying over time with trends or shifts in the mean or variation, will give an inaccurate estimate of capability. It should also be mentioned that the measurement systems are also expected to be verified as precise and accurate. For more on checking measurement systems, see *Chapter 8, Measurement Systems Analysis*. For control charts and checking for stability, see *Chapter 6, Understanding Process Variation with Control Charts*.

Along with the capability tools, we also look at acceptance sampling plans. These are shown for creating acceptance plans and a way to look at acceptance plans when the acceptance number is 0; these are known as **C = 0 plans**. The acceptance on 0 or C = 0 plans are popular in pharmaceutical applications.

For this chapter, the tools we are using are found in the **Stat** menu and **Quality Tools** as shown in the following screenshot. The relevant tools are found in the **Capability Analysis** option.

Gage R&R and other measurement systems analysis tools are also found in the **Quality Tools** menu. We will investigate these in the next chapter.

A capability and control chart report using the capability analysis sixpack

The sixpack function lets us generate six charts to give the control charts and capability in a single page. This forms a useful overview of the stability of our process and how well we fit to customer specifications. It also helps to avoid the common error of trying to fit specifications to control charts.

The example we will be using looks at the fill volumes of syringes. We check the capability of the fill volumes against a target fill volume of 15 ml and specifications of 14.25 ml and 15.75 ml.

Within the worksheet, 40 results are collected per day, taken at the rate of five samples per hour. The data is presented as these subgroups across rows; each row representing the results of the five samples within that hour.

How to do it...

The following steps will generate Xbar-R charts, normality tests, capability histograms, and Cpk and Ppk, all on a six-panel graph page:

1. Open the worksheet `Volume3.mtw` by using **Open Worksheet** from the **File** menu.
2. Navigate to **Stat | Quality tools | Capability Sixpack** and then select **Normal**.
3. Select the option **Subgroups across rows of** from the drop-down menu at the top. Insert columns `C2` to `C6` into the section under the section **Subgroups across rows of**.
4. In **Lower spec**, enter `14.25`.
5. In **Upper Spec**, enter `15.75`.
6. Click on the **Options** button.
7. Enter `15` in the **Target** field.
8. Click on **OK** in each dialog box.

How it works...

The **Capability Sixpack** option produces a page of six charts. These give an overview of the process from control charts, capability histograms, and a normality test on the data. This creates a very visual summary page.

The control chart displayed for the sixpack will be chosen from I-MR, Xbar-R, or Xbar-S charts, based on the subgroup size.

Results that can be used are either listed in one column or where the data is laid out in the worksheet with subgroups across rows. Each row has the five samples measured every hour. The drop-down selection at the top of the dialog box is used to specify the layout of the data. See the *Capability analysis for normally distributed data* recipe for data used in one column.

There are four sets of tools that we can use on capability studies. They are as follows:

▸ **Transform**: This option allows a Box-Cox or Johnson transformation to be used on the data.

   Using a normal distribution to fit to nonnormal data will give us an incorrect estimate of capability. Depending on the nature of the results, the direction they are skewed in can cause the capability to be over or underestimated. One method of finding a more accurate estimate of capability is to apply a transform to return the data to a normal distribution.

   Transformation of data should only be used if we understand why the data is not normally distributed and we are confident that the natural shape of the data is not normal. See the examples on Box-Cox or Johnson transformation. Transformations are only found in the capability tools for normal distributions.

▸ **Tests**: This allows us to specify the tests for special causes used in the control charts. The **Tests** option is only used in the sixpack charts.

▸ **Estimate**: This gives options on the methods of estimating within a subgroup variation.

▸ **Options**: This gives us the choice to add a target or change the tolerance for capability statistics. We can also choose between **Cpk/Ppk** or **Benchmark Z's**.

There's more...

The **Capability Sixpack** can also be run on nonnormal data and as a between within study as well. These are not covered here, but the instructions are similar to those here and the capability analysis for data that does not fit a normal distribution.

See also

- ▸ The *Capability analysis for normally distributed data* recipe
- ▸ The *Capability analysis for nonnormal distributions* recipe
- ▸ The *Using a Box-Cox transformation for capability* recipe
- ▸ The *Using a Johnson transformation for capability* recipe

Capability analysis for normally distributed data

The **Normal** tool in **Capability Analysis** fits a normal distribution to the data before calculating its capability. The sixpack in the previous recipe provides an overview page with control charts, whereas here, we focus on using just the capability histogram. We obtain a more detailed capability metrics output compared to the sixpack without the control charts or distribution plot.

Just like the previous recipe, we will use the study on the fill volume of syringes. The target fill volume is 15 ml with specifications of 14.25 ml and 15.75 ml.

Within the worksheet, 40 results are collected per day at the rate of five samples per hour. The data is presented as subgroups across rows, each row representing the results of the five samples within that hour.

We will generate a capability analysis and add confidence limits to the capability calculations.

How to do it...

The following steps will generate a histogram of the data with specification limits and capability metrics to assess how well the results meet customer specifications:

1. Open the worksheet `Volume3.mtw` by using **Open Worksheet** from the **File** menu.
2. Navigate to **Stat | Quality Tools | Capability analysis** and select **Normal**.
3. Select the radio button for **Subgroups across rows of**.
4. Insert the first five measure columns by selecting `Measure1` and dragging down to highlight all the columns till `Measure5`. Click on **Select** to move the columns to the section **Subgroups across rows of:**.

5. Enter the **Lower spec:** as 14.25 and the **Upper spec:** as 15.75. The dialog box should look as the following screenshot:

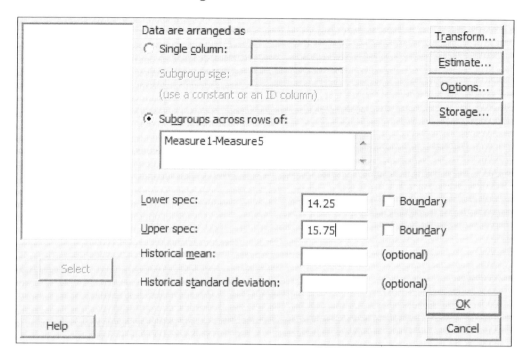

6. Click on the **Options** button, and enter 15 in **Target**.
7. Check the box **Include confidence intervals** and click on **OK** in each dialog box.

How it works...

The following screenshot shows the histogram of the data and the two normal distribution curves for the within and overall standard deviation. As with the six pack example in the previous recipe, we use the option for subgroups across rows. For an example of data used in a single column, refer to the *Capability analysis for nonnormal distributions* recipe.

Process Capability Report for Measure1, ..., Measure5
(using 95.0% confidence)

LSL	Target	USL

Process Data

LSL	14.25
Target	15
USL	15.75
Sample Mean	15.2972
Sample N	250
StDev(Overall)	0.304343
StDev(Within)	0.291146

Overall
Within

Overall Capability

Pp	0.82
CI for Pp	(0.75, 0.89)
PPL	1.15
PPU	0.50
Ppk	0.50
CI for Ppk	(0.44, 0.56)
Cpm	0.59
LB for Cpm	0.55

Potential (Within) Capability

Cp	0.86
CI for Cp	(0.77, 0.94)
CPL	1.20
CPU	0.52
Cpk	0.52
CI for Cpk	(0.45, 0.58)

14.4   14.7   15.0   15.3   15.6   15.9

Performance

	Observed	Expected Overall	Expected Within
PPM < LSL	0.00	290.08	161.15
PPM > USL	88000.00	68384.90	59929.17
PPM Total	88000.00	68674.98	60090.32

The capability metrics of Cpk and Ppk are calculated as follows:

▸ Cpk is found from the smaller of the $Cpl = \dfrac{\bar{x} - LCL}{3\sigma_{Within}}$ and $Cpu = \dfrac{UCL - \bar{x}}{3\sigma_{Within}}$ quantities.

▸ Ppk is found by substituting the overall standard deviation for the within standard deviation.

The calculations for within standard deviation use the pooled standard deviation when the subgroup size is greater than one. We could change this to use either Rbar or Sbar by navigating to **Capability Analysis | Normal | Options**.

When the subgroup size is one, the default option for within standard deviation is the average moving range. This can be changed to use the median moving range or the square root of MSSD instead.

Along with changing the calculation for within standard deviation, **Options** allows us to choose between displaying parts per million out of spec, percentage figures for the performance, confidence intervals, and Zbench figures.

Zbench is a capability metric derived from Z LSL and Z USL. **Z LSL** is a measure of the number of standard deviations from the mean to the lower specification limit, while **Z USL** is a measure of the the upper specification limit. Z bench takes the area of the normal distribution curve outside both limits and combines the two values to give an overall sigma level.

Confidence intervals are selected to give us a 95 percent confidence interval for the Cpk and the Ppk values.

When we have only one specification limit, the fill volume must only be above 14.25 ml. Then we need to enter only the single specification. The other specification limit must be left blank.

The **Boundary** checkbox is used to identify a hard limit for the data that cannot be crossed. In most situations, this need not be specified; it could be used when we have a hard limit at zero. We could identify this as a boundary to ignore the results below this figure. As the boundaries indicate that it is impossible to have a value outside this region, we will only calculate the capability to nonboundary limits.

There's more...

The two measures of capability, Cpk or Ppk, can be confusing. Cpk is calculated based on the within variation of the process. This variation is found from the average range of the subgroups, the average standard deviation of the subgroups, or the pooled standard deviation.

Ppk is calculated from the standard deviation across all the data that are considered as individual values.

The effect is that, the within standard deviation should typically be smaller than the overall. The within standard deviation can be considered as an estimate of the variation when the subgroups have the same mean value. The larger the variation between the subgroups, the greater the difference between the within and overall standard deviation.

We can consider Cpk as an estimate of the capability if our process is stable and Ppk as an estimate of the process performance.

See also

▸ The *A capability and control chart report using the capability analysis sixpack* recipe
▸ The *Capability analysis for nonnormal distributions* recipe

Capability analysis for nonnormal distributions

In the previous recipes, we used normal distribution to estimate capability. When data is not distributed normally, the normal distribution will incorrectly estimate the amount of the results that we find outside of the specifications, and it makes the calculation of the capability inaccurate. Here, we will look to find an appropriate nonnormal distribution or transformation to fit to the data.

It is vital to indicate that before looking at transformations or nonnormal distributions, we must understand the process that we are investigating. We must consider the reasons for the data not being normal. An unstable process can fail the normality test because the mean or variation is moving over time. There may be trends or process shifts. With this data, we should investigate the issues of the unstable process before using transformations as a fix.

Other issues may be that we have several distributions within the block of data. Different machines produce the parts at different means, each machine makes items with a normal distribution, but combined together, we get a bimodal or multimodal distribution.

Measurement systems can also cause nonnormal data. If the measurement device is not accurate across the whole measurement range, a linearity problem may cause kurtosis. Resolution problems may mean that the results come from a discrete scale instead of a continuous scale.

Even a human error or intervention can cause data that is not normal. Specifications and deadlines can drive operators to behavior that places results just inside specification.

Lastly, if we are using an alpha risk of 0.05— the decision for the P-value—then there is still a 5 percent chance that normally distributed continuous data may fail the normality test just through random variation.

There should be a physical reason why our data follows a given distribution, and we would want to satisfy ourselves that the process is stable, the measurement system is verified, and that we have a single distribution. Finally, we understand why such data may not follow a normal distribution before we really look for the distribution that it does follow.

A good example of nonnormal distributions would be the process times. These typically follow a lognormal or a similar distribution due to there being a boundary at 0 time. To fit a nonnormal distribution, we will look at the waiting time experienced at an accident and emergency ward by all the patients across a day. The data set contains two columns of wait times reported at 1-minute intervals, and the same wait times reported at 5-minute intervals. The goal is that patients arriving at the A&E unit should be seen by a doctor within four hours (240 minutes).

We will initially use Distribution ID plots for the reported 1-minute wait times to find a distribution that fits the data. Then, we use capability analysis with the appropriate distribution and an upper specification limit of 240 minutes. See the example at the end of this chapter where we use the same data reported to the nearest 5-minute interval.

How to do it...

The following steps will identify a distribution that fits the wait time data before using a capability analysis with a lognormal distribution:

1. Go to the **File** menu and click on **Open Worksheet**.

2. Open the worksheet `Wait time.mtw`.

3. Navigate to **Stat | Quality tools | Individual Distribution Identification**.

4. Enter the `Wait time (1 Mins)` column in the **Single column** field and the **Subgroup size** as 1, as shown in the following screenshot:

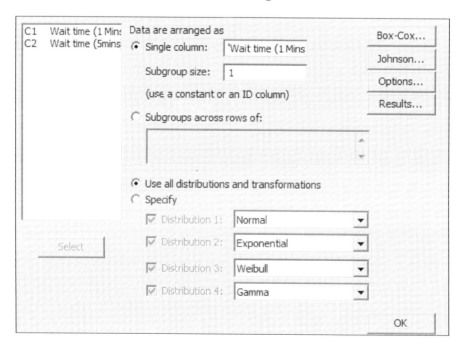

5. Click on **OK** to generate the ID plots.

6. Scan through each page, looking at the closeness of the fitted data looking graphically, the AD scores, and P-values for each distribution. An example of a distribution is shown in the following screenshot:

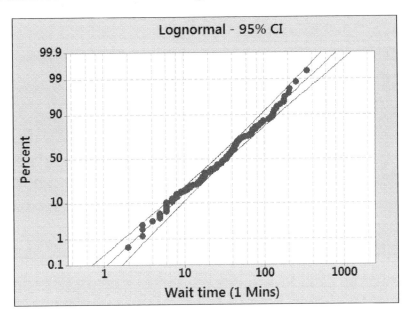

7. We will use the lognormal distribution, as the data seems to fit the distribution. The Anderson-Darling test has low values and a P-value greater than 0.05.

8. Navigate to **Stat | Quality Tools | Capability Analysis** and select **Nonnormal**.

9. Insert the column `Wait time (1Mins)` into the section **Single column**.

10. From the section **Fit Distribution**, select **Lognormal**.

11. In **Upper spec** field, enter `240`.

12. Select **Options**.

13. In the **Display** section, select **Percents**.

14. Click on **OK** in each dialog box.

How it works...

The distribution ID plot generates probability plots for 14 different distributions and two transformations to find a fit to the data. We will use a visual inspection of the probability plots to identify which distributions give us a close fit to our results. Each probability plot will also run the Anderson-Darling statistics and generate a P-value.

Goodness of fit tests are generated in the session window. This allows a quick comparison across all the options. For the results here, we can see that several of the possible distributions may work for the wait times.

```
Goodness of Fit Test

Distribution                   AD         P  LRT P
Normal                     10.511    <0.005
Box-Cox Transformation      0.394     0.371
Lognormal                   0.394     0.371
3-Parameter Lognormal       0.420         *  0.857
Exponential                 1.110     0.087
2-Parameter Exponential     0.906     0.141  0.003
Weibull                     1.124    <0.010
3-Parameter Weibull         0.632     0.103  0.001
Smallest Extreme Value     17.844    <0.010
Largest Extreme Value       4.453    <0.010
Gamma                       1.226    <0.005
3-Parameter Gamma           0.765         *  0.003
Logistic                    6.810    <0.005
Loglogistic                 0.455     0.217
3-Parameter Loglogistic     0.548         *  0.235
Johnson Transformation      0.306     0.562
```

Some of the 3-parameter distributions do not have a P-value calculated; it can not be calculated easily and will show a missing value. In such instances, the LRT P value generated by the likelihood ratio test is a good test to use.

LRT P is generated for the 3- or 2-parameter extensions to a distribution. For example, the Weibull distribution with a threshold as the third parameter. LRT P tests the likelihood of whether the 3-parameter Weibull fits better than the standard Weibull distribution. In the above results, we can see that the 3-parameter Weibull has an LRT P of less than 0.05 and will give a different fit compared to the Weibull test.

The aim is to find the distribution to fit to the population. We should also consider what distribution is expected to fit the distribution. As we are dealing with times in this example, we can expect that the population of wait times will follow a lognormal distribution. As the P-value for the lognormal is above 0.05, we cannot prove that it does not fit this distribution. When selecting a distribution, we would want to preferentially use the expected or historically observed distribution. In practice, distributions that fit in similar ways will give similar results.

We used the nonnormal capability analysis here to use the lognormal distribution. If we had wanted to apply a transformation to the data, we would use the normal capability analysis. See the Box-Cox and Johnson transformation subjects.

There is no calculation of within group variation with nonnormal distributions. Due of this, only Ppk for the overall capability is calculated. Within capability is only calculated for a normal distribution. To obtain an estimate of Cpk, we would need to use a Box-Cox transformation. Also, without Cpk and within variation, there is no requirement to enter the subgroup size for the nonnormal capability.

We could run a similar sixpack on nonnormal capability, as illustrated in the normal capability sixpack. This will require a subgroup size only to be used with the control charts.

As we only have an upper specification, we will only obtain Ppu, the capability to the upper specification. There will be no estimate of Pp.

There's more...

Strictly speaking, capability is calculated as the number of standard deviations to a specification from the mean divided by 3. As the data is not normally distributed, this is not an accurate technique to use. There are two methods that Minitab can use to calculate capability for nonnormal data.

The ISO method uses the distance from the 50th percentile to the upper or lower specification divided by the distance from the 50th percentile to the 99.865th or 0.135th percentile.

For the example here with only an upper specification, we have the Ppk calculated from the PpU by using the formula

$$PpU = \frac{UCL - X_{0.5}}{X_{0.99865} - X_{0.5}}$$

Here, X0.5 refers to the 50th percentile and X0.99865 refers to the 99.865th percentile.

This formula uses the equivalent positions of the +/-3 standard deviation point of a normal distribution. It does not always give the same capability indices like a transformed data set using the normal capability formula. The proportion outside the specification will be similar throughout. See the Box-Cox transformation in Minitab for more information.

An alternative is to use the Minitab method. It can be selected from the options for Minitab under the **Tools** menu, which is in **Quality tools** under **Control Charts**.

This method finds the proportion of the distribution outside the specification. Then, it finds the equivalent position on a standard normal distribution. This equivalent position for Z is divided by 3 to give the capability.

We should also look at the data for waiting times that has been recorded to the nearest five minutes. When used with the distribution ID plots, notice what happens to our results. For more on this, see the datasets that do not transform or fit any distribution.

See also

▶   The *A capability and control chart report using the capability analysis sixpack* recipe
▶   The *Capability analysis for normally distributed data* recipe

> ▸ The *Using a Box-Cox transformation for capability* recipe
>
> ▸ The *Using a Johnson transformation for capability* recipe

Using a Box-Cox transformation for capability

Box-Cox transformations are used to transform a dataset that is not normally distributed. The transformed data is then fitted to a normal distribution and used to find a value for the capability of the process.

Nonnormal distributions in continuous data are typically associated with some form of boundary condition. Limits restrict the distribution in one direction. Good scenarios are where we have the boundary at 0. An example may include a measure of particle contamination in a packaging. The ultimate goal for medical devices would be to achieve zero particles; negative particle counts are not possible, and the closer we get to achieving the goal of zero, the more skewed our data can become.

Process times, again, are restricted to the 0 boundary; for example, we could study telephone answer times at a call centre. The time taken for an operator to pick up a call that is coming through to their phone cannot be negative; the phone must ring for them to answer the call.

We will use the example from the previous recipe for nonnormal distribution. The data is for patient waiting times at an accident and emergency ward. Patients should wait no more than 240 minutes before being seen by a doctor.

In the previous example, we used a distribution ID plot to find a distribution to fit to the data. Just like the lognormal distribution, the Box-Cox transformation also provided a reasonable fit.

Here, we will check the fit using the Box-Cox transformation under control charts before analyzing the capability with the normal distribution tools.

How to do it...

The following steps will check to see if the Box-Cox transformation will work on our data and then use the **Capability Analysis** tool's normal distribution with the transformation:

1. Open the worksheet `Wait time.mtw` by using **Open Worksheet** from the **File** menu.
2. Navigate to **Stat | Control charts** and select **Box-Cox Transformation**.
3. Enter the column `Wait time (1Mins)` in the section under the drop-down list and select **All observations for a chart are in one column** in the list.
4. Enter **Subgroup sizes** as `1`.
5. Click on **OK**.

6. The Box-Cox results indicate the use of **Lambda** for the transformation of 0. To use this with the capability analysis, navigate to **Stat | Quality Tools | Capability Analysis** and select **Normal**.

7. Enter `Wait time (1 Mins)` in the **single column** field and 1 in the **Subgroup size**.

8. Enter `240` in the **Upper spec** field.

9. Click on the **Transform** button and select the **Box-Cox power transformation** radio button.

10. Click on **OK**; then click on the button **Options**. Check the box **Include confidence intervals**. Change the **Display** section to **percents**.

11. Click on **OK** in each dialog box.

How it works...

The use of the **Box-Cox Transformation** tool in steps 1 to 4 is not necessary to run the capability. By using the distribution ID plots as in the previous recipe, we will see that the Box-Cox transformation will work on our results. The **Box-Cox Transformation** tool can show us the potential range of Lambda and can be used to store the transformed results back into the worksheet. The following screenshot shows the range of Lambda that would work for this data:

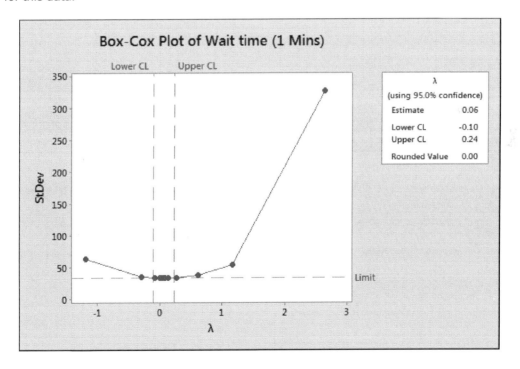

Box-Cox transformations are simple power transforms. The response Y is transformed by the function Y^λ. When Lambda is 0, we use the natural log of the data. While the Box-Cox transformation used in steps 1 to 4 calculates an estimate for the Lambda value of 0.06, Minitab will work from a convenient rounded value, hence the value is 0.

By transforming the times and the specification, this allows a fit for the normal distribution and a calculation of Cpk.

While choosing to transform the data within the **Capability Analysis** dialog box, we can specify the value of Lambda to use or let Minitab pick the best value itself. Minitab will use the rounded value when it picks the best value.

There's more...

The Ppk value for the transformed results is 0.65. This is a slightly different result as compared to the previous recipe using the lognormal data. This is because we use the calculation of Cpk from a normal distribution here. The nonnormal capability uses an approximation based on the ISO method. Both the overall performance figures will be the same no matter what method is used to calculate capability.

The **Assistant** tool can also transform the data with a Box-Cox transformation. If the data is not normally distributed, the assistant will check the transformation and prompt us to ask if we would want to transform the results if it is possible. Note that we should not transform the data just because it is possible to; we should first investigate the cause of the data being nonnormal.

See also

▸   The *Capability analysis for normally distributed data* recipe

▸   The *Capability analysis for nonnormal distributions* recipe

▸   The *Using the Assistant tool for short-run capability analysis* recipe

Using a Johnson transformation for capability

Johnson transformations are used in a way similar to Box-Cox transformations. First, apply a transformation to the response, and then use the transformed data with a normal distribution to find capability.

As with using other distributions to fit to nonnormal data, we should investigate the reasons for our data being in the shape it is before attempting Johnson transformations. For more notes on what to look out for, see the *Capability analysis for nonnormal distributions* recipe.

The main benefit of Johnson transformations over Box-Cox transformations is the ability of the former to transform data with negative values or 0 values. They can also be useful in situations where a process or data set has an extreme boundary condition that makes other distributions difficult to fit to. One example of where this may be used is for breaking stresses.

As with the previous examples on nonnormal distributions and Box-Cox transformations, we will use the data on patient waiting times at an accident and emergency ward. To do this, let's compare the output with the lognormal distribution and the Box-Cox transformation.

We need to check that the transformation is appropriate with the Johnson transformation from the **Quality Tools** menu before running a normal capability analysis on the transformed results.

How to do it...

The following steps will help us use the Johnson transformation for our data:

1. Open the worksheet `Wait time.mtw` by using **Open Worksheet** from the **File** menu.
2. Navigate to **Stat | Quality Tools** and select **Johnson Transformation**.
3. Enter `Wait time (1 Mins)` in the **Single Column** field and click on **OK**.
4. Check the results in the chart to see if the transformation and the function used to transform the data will work.
5. Navigate to **Stat | Quality Tools | Capability** and select **Normal**.
6. Insert the wait time column in the **Single column** field.
7. Enter the **Subgroup sizes** as `1`.
8. In the **Upper spec** field, enter `240`.
9. Click on the **Transform** button.
10. Select the option **Johnson Transformation**.
11. Click on **OK** in each dialog box.

How it works...

Steps 1 to 3 are used to check if the Johnson transformation will work on the data and if we ran the distribution ID plots as in the *Capability analysis for nonnormal distributions* recipe. It would not be essential to check the transformation using the **Johnson Transformation** tool. This tool is used to show if the transformation will work and if this is the optimum transformation function. It also allows the transformed data to be stored directly in the worksheet. The graphical page displayed shows that Minitab searches for the highest P-value to find the transformation.

The Johnson transformation in Minitab considers three transformation functions. These are for bounded, lognormal, and unbounded functions. The parameters of the transformation function are found from the function that has the highest P-value that is greater than the decision level. The default value used here is 0.1.

By selecting the Johnson transformation from the transformation functions within the normal capability analysis, we will automatically find the best transformation. If no transformation is possible, it will return an untransformed result.

See also

▶ The *Capability analysis for normally distributed data* recipe

▶ The *Capability analysis for nonnormal distributions* recipe

Using the Assistant tool for short-run capability analysis

Short-run capability is run on the assumption that the data is taken from a single period of time. The idea is to view data from a single sample point without any information about time. There is no subgrouping of the data or time information as the results may come from a small batch of products. Because of this, no within standard deviation can be found, this means Cpk will not be calculated and only Ppk will be used.

The **Assistant** tool for capability analysis helps us find the type of study to run and provides guidance in term of output and preparation of the data. Like all the **Assistant** tools, the dialog box is presented without any options in order to make the choices simpler and easier to use.

Because the emphasis is on ease of use, with the **Assistant** tool, we will not use a sample data set for this recipe. Instead, try following the instructions with your own results.

How to do it...

The following instructions show the steps to choose the capability analysis in the assistant:

1. Go to the **Assistant** menu and select **Capability Analysis**.

2. From the decision tree, scroll to **Continuous** and select the **Capability Analysis** option at the bottom of the tree, as shown in the following screenshot:

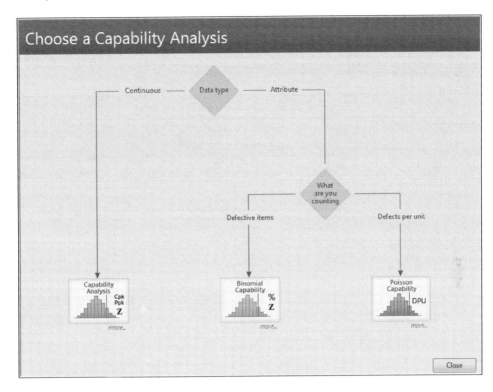

3. Change **Type of analysis** to **Snapshot**, and then enter your data column in the section labeled **Column**.

4. Enter the lower and upper specifications where indicated, and click on **OK**.

How it works...

As the snapshot considers data from a single time point, we do not produce Cpk. This is because Cpk is calculated from within the group variation that we cannot have with a snapshot of the data. Only Ppk for the overall variation of the samples is given.

The **Assistant** menu's capability tools offer a simplified dialog box to produce capability. If we had used a complete capability analysis, then **Assistant** would also produce control charts. This generates control charts for Xbar-R, Xbar-S, or I-MR, based on the subgroup's size.

While the Assistant tool does not offer a capability for nonnormal data, it will transform the results with the Box-Cox transformation. Minitab will ask before performing the transformation.

There's more...

We could generate the same capability measures from the **Stat** menu tools by turning off the options for calculating within capability and only displaying Ppk.

See also

▶ The *Capability analysis for normally distributed data* recipe

Comparing the capability of two processes using the Assistant tool

Multiple capability tools are available in both the **Stat** menu and the **Assistant** menu. The **Assistant** menu comparison tool will run a T-test and a two-variance test to compare the differences between means and standard deviations. The multiple variables capability within the **Stat** menu tools will allow more datasets to be used, but without the use of T-tests or tests of equal variances to check differences between the populations.

In the following recipe, we will look at comparing the fill volumes of syringes. The worksheet Volume4 uses two columns. The data is held in the columns before and after 75 syringes are measured from the process before a change. After an improvement has been made, the next 75 individual values are measured.

We will study the change in capability using the capability comparison tools from the **Assistant** menu. The subgroup size for both columns is 1.

How to do it...

The following steps will compare the capability of a process before and after a change; this will output how much of an improvement has been made:

1. Open the worksheet Volume4.mtw by using **Open Worksheet** from the **File** menu.

2. Go to the **Assistant** menu and select **Before/After Capability Analysis**.

3. Using the decision tree, follow the choice to the right for the **Capability Comparison** of **Continuous** data. Enter the Before and After columns as shown in the following screenshot. Enter the **Subgroup size** as 1 for both, the Before and After data.

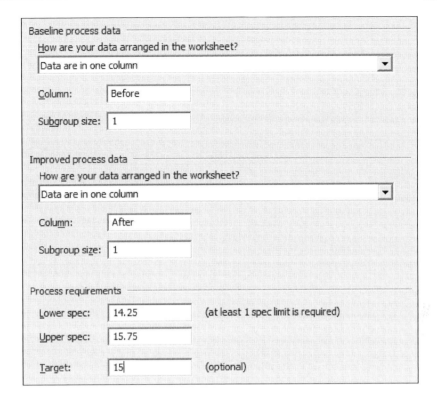

4. Enter the **Lower spec** as 14.25 and the **Upper spec** as 15.75. Enter the **Target** as 15.

5. Click on **OK** to run the reports.

How it works...

The **Assistant** menu's capability comparison tool will generate four report pages. The first page is a report card indicating the stability of the data, any issues with subgroups, normality, and amount of data.

The second page shows the process performance report. Both the capability histograms are displayed along with the metrics of Cpk, Ppk, Z.Bench, % out of spec, and the PPM figures.

The third report checks the process stability and normality of the data. Here, Minitab plots control charts and normality charts.

The final page is the summary report containing information on the capability stats once more. The change in capability is displayed along with two variance tests and a T-test on the mean to check for variation and mean changes.

There's more...

The **Assistant** menu does not have an option to use nonnormal data. Should our results not follow a normal distribution, they will try to find a transformation. This is restricted to using the Box-Cox transformation.

Minitab will warn us when the data is not normally distributed on running a capability via the **Assistant** tool. It will present the option to use the Box-Cox transformation if an appropriate value of Lambda will transform the data back to normal.

See also

▸ The *Capability analysis for normally distributed data* recipe

Creating an acceptance sampling plan for variable data

Acceptance sampling is used to check a lot or a batch of product to identify if it is acceptable to the customer. Typically, a customer or a regulatory body will require a guarantee of quality.

> AQL and RQL can change depending on the product and the industry. The **Food and Drug Agency** (**FDA**), has different guidelines for the use of the product. An example of these can be found in CFR 21 sec 800.10, where the AQL levels of surgical gloves and examination gloves are discussed.

The number of nonconforming product or nonconformities observed in a sample from the population can act as an indicator for the amount of problems in the whole lot. By observing fewer defects or defective items than the upper limit in the acceptance plan, we can state that the total of these in the population is likely to be less than the critical **Acceptable Quality Level** (**AQL**). If we observe more defects in the sample, then it is likely that the population does not meet the **Rejectable Quality Level** (**RQL**). In this recipe, we will find the number of samples and the critical distance to identify if a lot is acceptable.

Using the example of the syringe fill volumes, we have specifications of 14.25 ml and 15.75 ml. Each lot is of 5000 samples, and we will accept the lot if less than 0.1 percent is defective and reject if more than 1 percent is defective.

How to do it...

The following steps will generate a number of samples that should be collected from a population to verify the quality of that population:

1. Navigate to **Stat | Quality Tools | Acceptance Sampling by Variables** and select **Create/Compare**.
2. We will select **Create a Sampling plan** from the first drop-down list.
3. Select the **Units for quality levels** to be used as **Percent defective**.
4. Enter 0.1 in the **Acceptable quality level (AQL)** field.
5. Enter 1 in the **Rejectable quality level (RQL or LTPD)** field.
6. Enter the **Lower spec** as 14.25 and the **Upper spec** as 15.75.
7. Enter the **Lot Size** as 5000.
8. Click on **OK**.

How it works...

By creating an acceptance plan, we generate a series of charts to compare the performance of the plan and a table of results in the session window. We should obtain the result in the session window as shown in the following screenshot:

```
Sample Size                         67
Critical Distance (k Value)      2.66087
Maximum Standard Deviation (MSD)  0.259840

Z.LSL = (mean - lower spec)/standard deviation
Z.USL = (upper spec - mean)/standard deviation
Accept lot if standard deviation <= MSD, Z.LSL >= k and Z.USL >= k; otherwise reject.


  Percent   Probability  Probability
Defective    Accepting    Rejecting    AOQ     ATI
    0.1         0.952        0.048    0.094    304.6
    1.0         0.106        0.894    0.105   4475.6

Average outgoing quality limit (AOQL) = 0.200 at 0.394 percent defective.
```

The sample size and critical distance are found to satisfy the condition that if the percentage defective in the population is really 0.1 percent defective there is less than a 5 percent chance of rejecting the lot. And if the population is really 1 percent defective, then we would have a 90 percent chance of rejecting the lot.

The plan will generate four charts to indicate the performance of the acceptance sampling plan. The operating characteristic curve shows the chance of accepting lots with a population percent of a specification between 0.1 percent and 1 percent.

The AOQ specifies the average outgoing quality of a lot with the stated percent defective. This figure is arrived at by assuming the reinspection and rework of rejected lots.

Average Total Inspection (**ATI**) is a figure that represents how many items, including the defective ones, are inspected on average. Even with lots at 0.1 percent defective, there will be 304.6 items inspected per batch on an average due to the 5 percent chance of rejecting a batch at 1 percent defective.

The critical distance k is the number of standard deviations from the mean to the closest specification limit. Here, If the specification limits are further than 2.66 standard deviations away from the mean then we can pass the lot.

There's more...

The **Accept/Reject Lot...** tool for variable data can be used with the measured samples of an acceptance plan. This will return a reject or accept result based on the mean and standard deviation of the samples, and the critical distance of the plan.

We could compare a current acceptance sampling plan by using the **Compare user defined sampling plan** option. The output then evaluates the ability to accept or reject at the AQL and RQL values for the given number of samples and critical distance.

Acceptance sampling is often used with attribute data to identify if a binomial passes/fails or if the Poisson count of defects is acceptable.

See also

▶   The *Creating an acceptance sampling plan for attribute data* recipe

Creating an acceptance sampling plan for attribute data

Attribute acceptance sampling plans are used when the assessment of the samples is either a binomial judgment of pass/fail or a Poisson count of defects. We will want to generate a figure for the number of items that should be sampled in order to decide if a lot can be considered acceptable or not. The amount of items that need to be inspected will be based on the amount of defects or defective items that we can accept and the amount that we would reject in a lot.

Defective items can be specified as percent, proportion, or defectives per million. Defects can be specified as per unit, per hundred, or per million.

AQL and RQL are used here to define the acceptable quality level and the rejectable quality level. Here, we will use the same AQL, RQL, and lot number as in the *Creating an acceptance sampling plan for variable data* recipe. This will highlight the difference in the sample sizes between variable and attribute plans.

The response will be used as a binomial, samples being good or rejected, to create a sampling plan. We will identify the number of samples that need to be inspected from each lot in order to decide if the lot can be accepted.

A lot is judged on the percentage defective product; we will want to accept lots with less than 0.1 percent defective and reject lots with more than 1 percent defective. The total lot size being judged is 5000 items.

Getting ready

There is no datasheet to open for this recipe. We will use an AQL of 0.1 percent with an RQL of 1 percent.

How to do it...

The following steps will create an acceptance sampling plan for an AQL of 0.1 percent and an RQL of 1 percent with a total lot size of 5000 items. The producer's risk will be set at 0.05 percent and that of the consumers at 0.1 percent.

1. Navigate to **Stat | Quality tools** and select **Acceptance Sampling by Attributes**.
2. Use the drop-down menu to select **Create a Sampling Plan**.
3. **Measurement type** needs to be set to **Go/no go (defective)** for binomial data.
4. Set **Units for quality levels** as **Percent defective**.
5. Set the **AQL** to 0.1.
6. Set the **RQL** to 1.
7. Enter 5000 as the **Lot size**.
8. Click on **OK**.

How it works...

The results will indicate that we need to sample 531 items from a lot. A lot is acceptable if we observe two or fewer defective items from the sample.

This figure is much larger than the equivalent sampling plan by variables in the previous recipe. With attribute data, we lose information about the position that is collected with the variable data, and as such, this information is made up with more samples.

The acceptance plan that we have generated used binomial distribution to create the sampling plan. Our assumption is that the lot we are sampling comes from an ongoing process. The total number of items is very large. Occasionally, we may have a lot size that is finite, a one-off shipment, or product that is unique to each order. In these cases, we should select the hypergeometric distribution and not the binomial distribution. This is found from **Options** within the **Acceptance Sampling by Attributes** dialog box.

Another issue that arises here is the idea of an AQL and an RQL. The closer the two numbers, the more difficult it is to distinguish between them. To identify a result at 0.1 percent defective and a lot at 0.5 percent defective, we would need 1335 samples. To know definitively if a result is at 0.1 percent or is just above 0.1 percent, we would need to measure everything in the lot.

There's more...

Often, acceptance plans that talk about an acceptance number of zero are discussed. These are known as C= 0 plans and are commonly used as a check for outgoing lots of pharmaceutical products. These plans also use only one quality level, and this can cause confusion over the use of AQL and RQL. C = 0 plans are more commonly associated with one quality level. This is usually the RQL, although it can be referred to as the AQL, or rather, the **Lot Tolerance Percent Defective** (**LTPD**). For acceptance plans that only accept on zero defective items, see the next recipe.

See also

▸ The *Creating an acceptance sampling plan for variable data* recipe
▸ The *Comparing a previously defined sampling plan–C = 0 plans* recipe

Comparing a previously defined sampling plan – C = 0 plans

C = 0 refers to an acceptance sampling plan where the acceptance number is zero. When samples are collected from the lot, observing any rejected items will cause the whole lot to be rejected. The C = 0 acceptance plans tend to need fewer samples than other acceptance plans. The offset for this is that lots are only reliably accepted when the defective levels are very close to 0.

Here, we will compare a previously defined plan, using Minitab, to tell us how the acceptance plan will behave. We can use the same tool to create an acceptance sampling plan and compare plans that we currently use. This can be useful to check the chance of acceptance or rejecting lots at different levels of quality. Changing the plan to a comparison also allows us to see the impact of using an acceptance level of 0.

The current plan inspects 230 samples and rejects the lot if any defectives are found. This is for an RQL or LTPD of 1 percent. No AQL is defined for this plan.

Getting ready

There is no data to be opened for this recipe. The current acceptance plans takes 230 samples from a lot. The lot is rejected if any defective items are found. We want to compare the performance of this plan for an AQL of 0.1 percent and an RQL of 1 percent.

How to do it...

The following steps will identify the chance of accepting or rejecting lots with an AQL of 0.1 percent and an RQL of 1 percent for 230 samples, with an acceptance value of 0:

1. Navigate to **Stat | Quality Tools** and select **Acceptance Sampling by Attributes**.

2. Enter details in the dialog box as shown in the following screenshot:

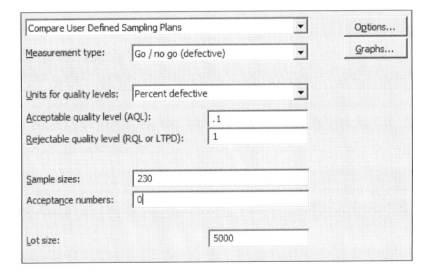

3. Click on **OK** to run the study.

How it works...

With C = 0 plans, the value of interest to define is the RQL or LTPD. LTPD is used to define the point at which we will reject lots. The outcome is that acceptable lots are the ones that tend to be 0 percent defective.

The graph of operating characteristics in the following screenshot will show a much steeper response with C = 0 plans than other acceptance plans. This shows that while we have a 90 percent chance of rejecting a lot with more than 1 percent defective, we roughly have only an 80 percent chance of accepting a lot with 0.1 percent defective. Notice that high levels of acceptance are only observed as the lot approaches 0 percent defective.

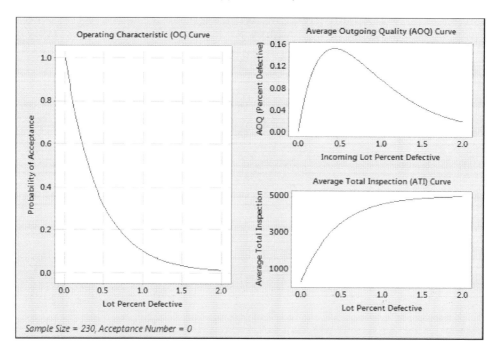

There's more...

There can be confusion over the use of the terms AQL or RQL. In C= 0 plans, we would set the RQL or LTPD value. In many pharmaceutical applications, a plan is used, where anything above the RQL is rejected, but this does not imply that lots below the RQL are accepted but not to a high degree.

We can also use the **Acceptance Sampling by Attributes** dialog box to create a C = 0 sampling plan. We need to enter the RQL or LTPD as normal, but for the AQL, we need to enter a low value. The dialog box must have a value for the AQL and it must be above 0. Entering `0.0001` for the AQL though, will generate a C = 0 plan.

See also

▸ The *Creating an acceptance sampling plan for variable data* recipe

▸ The *Creating an acceptance sampling plan for attribute data* recipe

Generating run charts

Run charts are similar in application to control charts. We are interested in finding nonrandom patterns in data over time. These patterns are identified as either runs about the median, or runs up or down. These rules identify clusterings, mixtures, trends, or oscillations in our data.

In this example, we will plot the time in the office of all the US Presidents. For ease of use, this data is supplied in a Minitab worksheet. The data was gathered from Wikipedia and the White House website. More up-to-date results can also be found from a more recent visit to these sites.

We will use a run chart to plot the time in office to check for evidence of clusterings, mixtures, trends, or oscillations.

How to do it...

The following steps will generate a run chart for the days in office of each President of the United States of America:

1. The data is saved in the worksheet `Presidents.mtw`. Go to **File** and then go to **Open Worksheet** to open the dataset.

2. Navigate to **Stat | Quality Tools** and select **Run Chart**.

3. Enter `Days` in the **Single column** field.

4. Enter the **Subgroup size** as `1`.

5. Click on **OK**.

How it works...

Run charts use the number of runs about the median and the number of runs up or down to identify patterns in the data. A run about the median refers to one or more consecutive points on one side of the median. A new run starts when the median line is crossed. The following diagram illustrates how runs are counted:

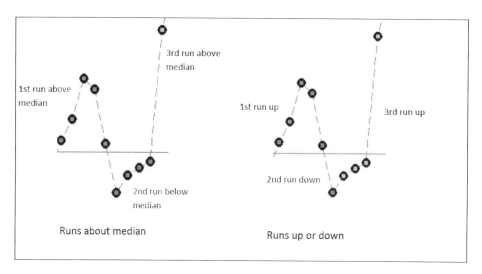

A run up or down refers to a number of points that continue in one direction. A new run begins when the data changes direction. More runs about the median than expected indicate clustering, less runs indicate mixtures.

Runs up or down that are more than expected suggest oscillations in the data; runs that are less than expected indicate trends.

There's more...

The president data does have an interesting pattern to it that the run chart does not reveal. Other means of displaying the data can be used and it is worth looking at histograms of the data or using a graphical summary, as used in *Chapter 3, Basic Statistical Tools*.

See also

 ▸ The *Xbar-R charts and applying stages to a control chart* recipe in *Chapter 6, Understanding Process Variation with Control Charts*

 ▸ The *Using I-MR charts* recipe in *Chapter 6, Understanding Process Variation with Control Charts*

 ▸ The *Producing a graphical summary of data* recipe in *Chapter 3, Basic Statistical Tools*

Generating tolerance intervals for summarized data

Tolerance intervals are used to find where a given percentage of the population can be expected to be found. For example, we could use a small sample taken from a population of results to inform us about where we can expect to find 95 percent of the population. Further, we can specify that we are 95 percent confident that 95 percent of the population would be found within the stated interval.

Here, we will use the tolerance interval tool to find the interval in which we expect a percentage of the population to be found. We have investigated capability with the fill weights of syringe volumes in the previous recipes of this chapter.

Summarized results for means, sample size, and standard deviation are supplied. From these, we want to know where we could expect to find 99 percent of the population of syringe fill volumes with a 95 percent confidence interval. From a recent trial, 30 samples were taken, and these had a mean of 15.15 and a standard deviation of 0.231.

How to do it...

The following steps will use the values of mean, standard deviation, and sample size to generate a tolerance interval that will show 99% of the population with a 95 percent confidence interval:

1. Navigate to **Stat | Quality Tools** and select **Tolerance Intervals**.
2. In the drop-down list for **Data**, select **Summarized data**.
3. Enter the **Sample size** as 30.
4. Enter the **Sample mean** as 15.15.
5. Enter the **Sample standard deviation** as 0.231.
6. Click on the **Options** button.
7. In the **Minimum percentage of population in the interval** field, enter 99.
8. Click on **OK**.

How it works...

The results generate a 95 percent tolerance for both a normal distribution and a nonparametric method. With summarized results from a mean, standard deviation, and sample size, we only obtain the normal method.

As we specified, 99 percent of the population between the interval of 14.374 to 15.926 show that we are 95 percent confident that 99 percent of the population may be found within this interval.

Here, we specified the summarized results. It is more advisable to use the raw data than the summarized results. Only referring to the mean and standard deviation does not reveal outliers in the data or other issues, such as time dependant errors.

Raw data is entered as a column, and this would then generate a graphical page showing a histogram of the data with confidence intervals and the normal probability plot.

See also

▸   The *Capability analysis for normally distributed data* recipe

▸   The *Capability analysis for nonnormal distributions* recipe

Datasets that do not transform or fit any distribution

Frequently, we obtain data that does not want to easily fit any distribution or any transformation. The key to using this data is often to understand the reasons for the data not fitting a distribution.

We can find many reasons for not fitting a distribution and the strategies for running a capability analysis can be varied, depending on the cause. For more on some of the issues that we should be careful of when declaring that our data is not normally distributed, see the *Capability analysis for nonnormal distributions* recipe.

The very first step in any analysis of data that is not normally distributed should be to understand why the data appears as it does.

This recipe explores several issues that may occur in data. This looks at a processing time example. Such data has the lower boundary at 0; this can give us a distribution skewed to the right. The other issue is that of discrete intervals in the data; the measurement system is not truly continuous for these.

Here, we will look at using the wait time data as they were used in the nonnormal examples earlier. This dataset contains wait times at the A&E department of a hospital across one day. Column one contains the data reported in one-minute intervals and column two contains the same data but rounded to the nearest five minutes.

For this recipe, we will use the column of wait time data that has been reported in five-minute intervals. We will try and find the right distribution to fit to the results using ID plots. This should reveal the discrete nature of the results before deciding on a solution to analyze the data in the *How it works...* section.

How to do it...

The following steps will generate the distribution ID plots for results given in the nearest five minutes:

1. Open the worksheet `Wait time.mtw` by using **Open Worksheet** from the **File** menu.

2. Navigate to **Stat | Quality Tools** and select **Individual Distribution Identification**.

3. Enter `Wait time (5 Mins)` in the **Single column** field.

4. Enter **Subgroup size** as 1.

5. Click on **OK** to generate probability plots for the 14 distributions and two transformations.

6. Check the probability plots to find a fit to the data.

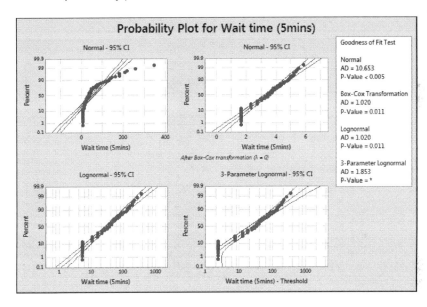

7. All available P-values will be below 0.05, indicating that we can prove that none of those distributions fit those results. Instead, find the closest fits visually.

How it works...

The ID plots will show P-values as below 0.05 for all distributions. The shape of the distributions also shows discrete intervals on most of the charts. In the preceding screenshot, you will notice the straight lines of the data points. The gaps and dots aligned are for the five-minute intervals. There is a large initial amount of data at five minutes, then a gap with no observations until the 10 minute result. The reason for not fitting any distribution is due to the data being discrete. Wait times really do not have exact five-minute gaps, but are an artifact of the measurement system.

In this recipe, we can still find the closest fit to the distribution graphically. As we know, the data has been split into discrete measurements and the actual times will really be from a continuous scale.

The lognormal distribution still provides a reasonable fit visually. Compare this to the result in the *Capability analysis for nonnormal distributions* recipe when using the one-minute interval data. In this case, we will analyze the data as a lognormal distribution. Run the five-minute interval column as a nonnormal capability analysis, follow the instructions for the earlier recipe, and substitute the five-minute interval data.

It is useful to compare the results either by using columns to see the effect that the discrete nature of the five-minute intervals has on the results. They will generate similar capability figures.

There's more...

Examples of other data that may not fit a distribution include unstable processes, where the data exhibits shifts in the mean or variance, or other special causes. The results could be declared as not normal because the tails of the data show too many results or because outliers make the data not normal. Ideally, we would want to find the reason behind the unstable process rather than trying to find a distribution or transformation to use.

Another common set of data are measurement systems that do not report values below a certain number. Typically, we might see these types of measurements on recording amount or size of particles as a measure of contamination. The measurement device reports all values below a threshold as 0. The actual results are too small to resolve, and we do not know the true value for any figure recorded as zero. It could be zero or any value in the intervals from zero to 0.02. Recording the figures at zero creates a dataset with a gap and some start point, say 0.02.

As the actual value is unknown, rather than reporting the value as zero, data from this sort of measurement system can be reported as missing below the threshold of resolution. Alternatively, the zero values can be adjusted by adding a random value. Find the variation of the measurement device from a Gage study. Then generate random values with a mean of zero and the standard deviation of the measurement device. Add these values to the zeroes to generate a pseudo data point. Any negative values should be left as zero.

See also

- The *Capability analysis of nonnormal distributions* recipe

8
Measurement Systems Analysis

In this chapter, we will be covering the following recipes:

- ▶ Analyzing a Type 1 Gage study
- ▶ Creating a Gage R&R worksheet
- ▶ Analyzing a crossed Gage R&R study
- ▶ Studying a nested Gage R&R
- ▶ Checking Gage linearity and bias
- ▶ Expanding a Gage study with extra factors
- ▶ Studying a go / no go measurement system
- ▶ Using the Assistant tool for Gage R&R
- ▶ Attribute Gage study from the Assistant menu

Introduction

A measurement system's analysis tools used here are to assess the precision and accuracy of the measurement system. Commonly, tools such as **Gage R&R** are used to assess the precision of both the measurement device and the operators to the variation in the process.

The R&R in Gage R&R stands for repeatability and reproducibility. These terms indicate the variation in measurements by the measuring device when performing repeated measures on items and the variation between operators.

Accuracy can be assessed by using Type 1 Gage studies and linearity and bias studies. Typically, they can include calibration studies to ensure that a measurement device is recording the correct values.

Finally, attribute studies can be used to assess the ability of appraisers to make visual inspections.

Gage R&R studies performed on paper or in applications such as Excel can often be held in a very different format to that of the columns in Minitab. To resolve this problem, the crossed Gage R&R example covers steps to convert the table layout used in Excel into a column format in Minitab.

Most of the tools presented here can be found within the **Quality Tools** menu and the **Gage Study** option. See the following screenshot to locate these in Minitab:

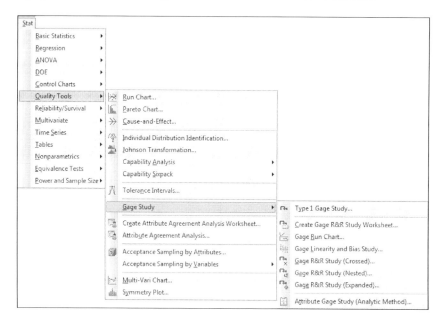

Analyzing a Type 1 Gage study

A Type 1 Gage study is used to evaluate the bias and repeatability of a measurement device by repeatedly measuring a known reference sample a number of times. By comparing the measurements recorded to the reference, we can evaluate the bias and repeatability of the measurement system. This can be compared to the tolerance to check if the variation in the measurement device is small enough to be acceptable.

In this study, we will look at measurements on fill volumes. A known volume of 15 ml is measured 20 times. The specifications for the process are 14.25 and 15.75. The worksheet Type 1 Gage.mtw contains 20 measurements on this syringe in the Measure column.

How to do it...

1. Open the worksheet `Type 1 Gage.mtw` by using **Open Worksheet...** from the **File** menu.

2. Navigate to **Stat | Quality Tools | Gage Study** and click on **Type 1 Gage Study**.

3. Enter `Measure` in the **Measurement data** field.

4. Enter `15` in the **Reference** field.

5. Under **Tolerance**, enter `1.5` in **Upper spec - lower Spec**.

6. Click on **OK**.

How it works...

Type 1 Gage studies will output a **Bias** measure and a **Capability** measure, namely **Cg** and **Cgk**. A one-sample T-test is run on the mean of the measurements against the reference value to check for bias. The results of this data should show a significant bias with a mean of `14.916`.

The run chart will display the measurements in the order they appear in the worksheet. The data should be presented in the collection order to allow a check for trends or patterns in the results.

The red lines plotted on the chart represent as 10 percent of the tolerance interval. Ideally, a good measurement device should have measurements well within the interval. Results exceeding the interval show a measurement device with too much variation. The measures displayed are as follows:

- ▶ **Cg**: This is calculated by dividing 20 percent of the tolerance width by the study variation: the width of the red lines divided by six times the standard deviation. The percent of the tolerance is given as 20 percent by default but can be changed within the Type 1 Gage study options.

- ▶ **Cgk**: This is calculated from the bias and the Gage variation. In this example, we should see that the results are close to, and cross the lower limit, causing **Cgk** to be much lower than **Cg**.

- ▶ **%Var(Repeatability)**: This compares the gage repeatability to 20 percent of the tolerance.

- ▶ **%Var(Repeatability and Bias)**: This compares both repeatability and bias with 20 percent of the tolerance.

Ideally, **Cgk** is above 1.33.

There's more...

The Type 1 study only checks the variation around one sample. As such, it only gives an indication of bias around the reference value. More in-depth checks of bias can be run with a Gage linearity and bias study, which checks the variation of the bias across a range of reference samples.

Usually, Type 1 studies are used as initial checks on a measurement device; uses, for example, might include assessing a new measurement device for suitability or assessing a current device for its suitability for use in a new application. One would then look at Gage R&R studies to examine operator variation, or bias and linearity studies to observe bias across a range.

See also

- ▸ The *Analyzing a crossed Gage R&R study* recipe
- ▸ The *Checking Gage linearity and bias* recipe

Creating a Gage R&R worksheet

Minitab contains a couple of methods to create a Gage R&R worksheet. They can be found either in the **Stat** menu under **Quality Tools**, or alternatively, with the **Assistant Measurement Systems Analysis (MSA)** section. Both are very easy to use and generate a worksheet for entering measurements. This can help produce worksheets ready for analysis of the data.

Here, we will create a Gage R&R study for two operators, 10 samples with two replicates on each sample by each operator, using the **Create Gage R&R Study Worksheet** option in the **Stat** menu.

How to do it...

The following instructions will create a new worksheet containing `Operators` and `Sample` columns ready to run **Gage R&R study (Crossed)**:

1. Navigate to **Stat | Quality Tools | Gage Study** and click on **Create Gage R&R Study Worksheet**.

2. On the top of the dialog box are selections for **Number of parts** and **Number of operators**; change **Number of Operators** to **2**.

3. In the table of operator, change the name for operator **1** to `Robert` and that for operator **2** to `Helen`.

4. Click on **Options**; check the box **Store standard run order in worksheet**.

5. Click on **OK** in each dialog box to create the worksheet.

How it works...

The worksheet creation tools are a quick way to generate a worksheet for a Gage R&R study (crossed). The default number of parts is 10, with three operators and two replicates—as suggested by the AIAG guidelines.

The **Automotive Industry Action Group** (**AIAG**) develops recommendations and practices of quality and process improvement in the automotive industry. The AIAG publish a series of manuals governing standards for the use of techniques and tools for quality.

Although primarily concerned with the automotive industry, they are frequently cited in other industries as well.

Even though the suggested number of samples in the study is 10, it can be useful to increase the number of parts in the study if we do not know the historical variation of the process. The higher the number of samples collected, the better the estimate of the population variation of the samples will be.

Here, we chose to store the standard run order in the worksheet. The StdOrder column shows the default, unrandomized order the design is generated in. The RunOrder column shows the randomized order we are requested to run the design in.

By default, the RunOrder column is randomized for the sequence of parts within operators. We could change this to randomize the entire worksheet or the operator sequence.

There's more...

As Minitab prefers working with columns, the worksheet is set out for all the results to be entered in a new column at the end of the design. We will name this column and enter the measurements as collected in the random order suggested.

This layout is different to the structure that may be used in Excel or texts on Gage R&R. It may happen that Gage R&R will have a table structure similar to the following screenshot:

	Trial	1	2	3	4	Part 5	6
Operator A	1						
	2						
	Means						
	Range						
Operator B	1						
	2						
	Means						
	Range						

These tables are easy to use for hand calculation and are often entered into Excel in this format. They can be a quick way to work with the mean and range calculations to estimate variation from parts and operators. We will look at an example of converting a Gage R&R table like the one displayed back into a Minitab-preferred format. This is dealt with in the upcoming recipes.

See also

▶ The *Analyzing a crossed Gage R&R study* recipe

Analyzing a crossed Gage R&R study

For this recipe we will analyze the results of a crossed Gage R&R study. The data is initially in a format that we may typically find in an Excel worksheet. In the first column, we have `Operator`, in the second one we have `Trial`, and columns `C3` to `C12` have the measurements on each part. This format is mentioned in the AIAG manual on measurement systems analysis. These instructions will show us how to convert this tabular form into a preferred format for Minitab.

The third row contains the mean result for `Helen`, the seventh row contains the mean for `Robert`. The fourth and eight rows contain the ranges of each operator. This data has already been imported from Excel; for more on opening data in Excel, see *Chapter 2, Tables and Graphs*.

We will initially remove the rows of `Means` and `Ranges` and then stack the data. After stacking the data, we will recreate the column for operator names. Then, we will run **Gage R&R Study (Crossed)**.

The specifications of 14.25 and 15.75 will also be entered into the study to generate percent tolerance and probabilities of misclassification.

 The worksheet `Gage R&R stacked.mtw` contains the data prepared in the Minitab format. We can skip steps 1 to 12 by using this dataset.

How to do it...

The following instructions take a table of results and format them into columns to analyze the columns with the **Gage R&R Study (Crossed)** option:

1. Open the worksheet `Gage R&R.mtw` by using **Open Worksheet** from the **File** menu.

2. Go to the **Data** menu and click on **Delete Rows**.

3. In **Rows to delete**, enter `3 4 7 8` to delete the rows of the means and ranges.

4. In the section **Columns from which to delete these rows**, select all the columns in the worksheet.

5. Click on **OK**.

6. Navigate to **Data | Stack** and click on **Columns**.

7. In the section **Stack the following columns:**, only enter the columns for the part numbers. The selection can be made easier by selecting columns C3 to C12. Then click on the **Select** button to move the columns across together as shown in the following screenshot:

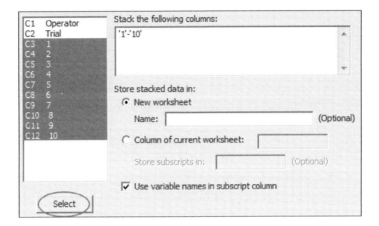

8. In the section **Name** under **New worksheet**, enter Stacked Data.

9. Click on **OK**.

10. In the new worksheet, name column C1 as Parts and column C2 as Measure.

11. Navigate to **Calc | Make Patterned Data** and click on **Text Values...**.

12. Enter data in the dialog box as shown in the following screenshot:

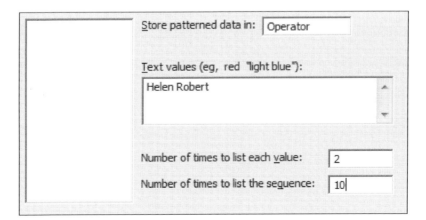

13. Click on **OK** to create the `Operator` column.
14. Navigate to **Stat | Quality Tools | Gage Study** and click on **Gage R&R Study (Crossed)**.
15. Enter `Parts` in the section **Part numbers**.
16. Enter `Operators` in the section **Operators**.
17. Enter `Measure` in the section **Measurement data**.
18. Click on the **Options** button.
19. Enter the **Lower spec** as `14.25`.
20. Enter the **Upper spec** as `15.75`.
21. Check the Box **Display probabilities of misclassification**.
22. Click on **OK** in each dialog box.

How it works...

Steps 1 to 12 are used to prepare the worksheet as the format is initially in a tabular form. They are useful for anyone importing their data from other sources.

The delete rows command is used to remove the rows of means and ranges to avoid including these in the calculations later. Rows can also be deleted by right-clicking the row number to highlight the entire row and clicking on **Delete** in the drop-down menu that appears.

We used the stack columns command, but this cannot stack the operator alongside the part numbers. The **Stack Blocks of Columns** command can stack the part numbers and the operators in one step, but will only allow eight sets of data to be stacked in the dialog box. Here we have 10 sets of data that need to be stacked.

To recreate the information on `Operator`, we use the **Make Patterned Data** tools. These are great for expanding information into a column. When the measurements are stacked, we know that there are two results for each `Operator`: the first and the second measurements on a sample. We list each value twice to state an operator twice in a row. Then, we repeat the pattern of `Helen Helen Robert Robert` for the 10 parts in the study.

These steps would not be needed if the data had been entered in the worksheet as described in the the *Creating a Gage R&R worksheet* recipe.

The output of the Gage R&R uses the ANOVA method as the default method of analysis. Studies previously calculated by hand use the Xbar and R method as this is a simpler technique than calculating sums of squares. Xbar and R calculations will not find interaction terms in the results whereas the ANOVA method will.

Entering specifications into `Options`, we calculate the percent tolerance. This could be entered as a lower and/or upper specification or just a tolerance interval. Using the limits rather than an interval allows the calculation of probabilities of misclassification. These are found by comparing the variation of the process and the measurement system to the specifications. Joint probabilities give the probability of identifying bad parts as good and good parts as bad. Conditional probability is the probability of misclassifying a part that is known to be out of spec as good or known to be in spec as bad.

Joint probability is based on not knowing if the tested sample is in spec or not, whereas conditional probability says that we know the tested part is good or bad.

When historical standard deviations are used, the Gage study will generate percent process to compare the measurement system variation to the historical process variation.

The value of the study variation used in Minitab's Gage R&R is given as 6 standard deviations. Those familiar with Gage studies from past AIAG manuals may be used to a value of 5.15 standard deviations. The third edition of the AIAG manual on measurement systems analysis uses the value of 6 standard deviations rather than 5.15. The default value used in Minitab has been updated to reflect this change. **Options...** allows us to change the value of study variation if we need to.

One final option that can be useful is the inclusion of confidence intervals. These are switched on from the **Conf int...** subdialog box. One-sided or two-sided intervals can be selected here.

There's more...

The **Stack Blocks of Columns** command, when used with the session commands, will allow more than just the eight sets of data that the dialog box allows. For more on session commands and macros, see *Chapter 11, Macro Writing*.

How many parts and operators should we use in a Gage study? The automotive guidelines recommend at least 10 parts and three operators with two replicates to give a total of 60 results. Ideally, the goal of the parts in the study is to represent the variation in the process. If a historical standard deviation is unknown, then it is suggested that more samples are collected. For more information on number of samples, refer to the discussion of this topic on the Minitab website. This information can be found in the answers database at `http://www.minitab.com/en-US/support/documentation/answers/NumberPartsOperatorsGageRR.pdf`.

The **Assistant** tool for Gage R&R also contains advice on the number of samples. Here, the recommended number of samples to estimate the process variation is between 15 to 35.

For more information on the **Assistant** tools, see the Minitab knowledgebase and answer ID 2613 at

`http://it.minitab.com/en-us/support/answers/answer.aspx?id=2613`

If the study has no operators and the measurement system is part of an automated system, then we can run a crossed Gage R&R without operators. We only need to enter the column for parts and measurements.

Studies can also be more complicated; comparison between measurement devices with operators can also be investigated. With additional factors, we can analyze the results by using an expanded Gage R&R study. This is covered later in this chapter.

See also

- The *Stacking several columns together* recipe in *Chapter 1, Worksheet, Data Management, and the Calculator*
- The *Stacking blocks of columns at the same time* recipe in *Chapter 1, Worksheet, Data Management, and the Calculator*
- The *Expanding a Gage study with extra factors* recipe
- The *Using the Assistant tool for Gage R&R* recipe

Studying a nested Gage R&R

A nested Gage R&R can be useful for studying destructive measurements. As obtaining a measurement destroys the sample being measured, repeating and reproducing measurements on the same item is not possible.

A nested Gage study depends on the ability to be able to use groups of samples that, if not identical, are at least similar.

The worksheet Gage nested contains a dataset loosely based around breaking the strength of a block of chocolate. A block of chocolate is assumed to be homogenous and is split into three identical bars. 12 blocks of chocolate are divided among the two operators with six blocks per operator. Each operator measures all the bars within its set of six blocks.

We will use the **Gage R&R Study (Nested)** option to investigate the measurement system error and sample variation.

How to do it...

The following instructions will run the nested Gage R&R study on the data for a destructive test:

1. Open the file Gage nested.mtw by using **Open Worksheet** option from the **File** menu.

2. Navigate to **Stat | Quality Tools | Gage Study** and click on **Gage R&R Study (Nested)**.

3. Enter `Block` in the **Part or batch numbers** field.

4. Enter `Operator` in the **Operators** field.

5. Enter `Strength(N)` in the **Measurement data** field.

6. Click on **OK** to run the study.

How it works...

The output from the nested Gage study will contain the same components as the crossed studies. We should have results that give us the percent study variable for the total Gage R&R, repeatability, reproducibility, part to part variation, and total variation.

We did not specify any tolerances or historical standard deviations, percent tolerance and percent process are not generated. As with the crossed studies, these could be entered from **Options**. See the **Gage R&R Study (Crossed)** option for more on these results.

The crossed Gage R&R estimates the reproducibility by comparing the results via the Operators field on the same samples. Differences by operator on a sample give reproducibility. In the nested design, operators measure different samples. In this case, we are estimating the operator effect on the difference between the means of all the measurements. This variation of the operator is found from a nested ANOVA, where the parts are nested within the operator.

There's more...

When using a nested study on destructive tests, variation within the batch or samples that should be identical will be confounded with the repeatability. As long as the variation within the batch is small, the study works fine. If the variation within the batch is high, then we cannot tell if the repeatability is due to variation within the sample or the measurement system.

See also

▸ The *Analyzing a crossed Gage R&R study* recipe

Checking Gage linearity and bias

Here, we will look at checking the accuracy of a measurement device over its range of measurements. The worksheet `Gage Linearity` has a study with five known reference samples, each measured 12 times. The actual result and the measured value are used to estimate the bias or linearity of the measurement device.

There is a historical process variation of two units that will be used to assess the size of the bias and linearity to the process variation.

How to do it...

The following instructions will check the accuracy for a range of standard samples:

1. Open the worksheet `Gage Linearity.mtw` by using the **Open Worksheet...** option from the **File** menu.
2. Navigate to **Stat | Quality Tools | Gage Study** and click on **Gage Linearity and Bias Study**.
3. Enter `Part` in the **Part numbers** field.
4. Enter `Reference` in the **Reference values** field.
5. Enter `Result` in the **Measurement data** field.
6. Enter the **Process variation** as `2`.
7. Click on **OK** to run the study.

How it works...

The AIAG suggests a linearity and bias study should comprise five reference parts with 12 measurements. This is to gather information on the mean bias for each reference value.

The results will plot the bias, difference between the measured value and the actual value on the chart on the left along with the mean bias at each reference value and a regression line. The plotted result is shown in the following screenshot:

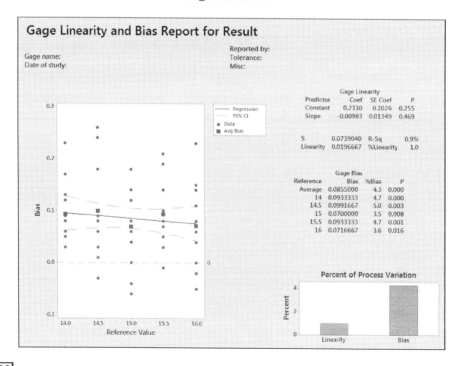

If the confidence interval of the regression line completely encloses the zero line, then our results can be judged as accurate. Should the confidence intervals not include the zero line completely, it could include a horizontal line so that we have a flat bias. Sloped lines would indicate that the measurement system has a changing bias across the results.

The output also includes P values on the bias and slope. The null hypothesis for these are 0 bias and 0 slope respectively.

There's more...

Quadratic problems with accuracy can also show up in this style of study; however, they can only be visually assessed.

See also

▶ The *Analyzing a Type 1 Gage study* recipe

Expanding a Gage study with extra factors

In expanded Gage studies, we are interested in including more than just an operator or part as factors in the Gage R&R. This is especially useful if the study is interested in investigating the differences across measurement devices, different labs, or even locations.

Here, we will look at a Gage R&R including one extra factor, a preparation method effect on the sample. In this recipe, the study looks at the force required to remove adhesive from a glass plate. The sample is a batch of adhesive, and the response is the force required to remove a test piece from a glass plate. Two operators prepare the samples and test the force of the adhesive.

Additionally, in this study, three different preparation methods are used to clean the glass plates before the adhesive is applied.

We will use the expanded Gage R&R to look at the effect of the preparation method, operator, and adhesive batch on the force measurements.

The worksheet contains the columns `Preparation Method`, `Sample`, `Operator`, and `Force (N)`.

The preparation method will be identified as an additional component to the part-to-part variation.

How to do it...

1. Open the worksheet `Gage R&R Expanded.mtw` by using **Open Worksheet** from the **File** menu.

2. Navigate to **Stat | Quality Tools | Gage Study** and select **Gage R&R Study (Expanded)**.

3. Enter the columns into the dialog box as shown in the following screenshot. Enter `Sample` in **Part numbers**, `Operator` in **Operators:**, `'Force (N)'` in **Measurement data**, `'Preparation Method'` should be entered into **Additional factors** and **Fixed factors**.

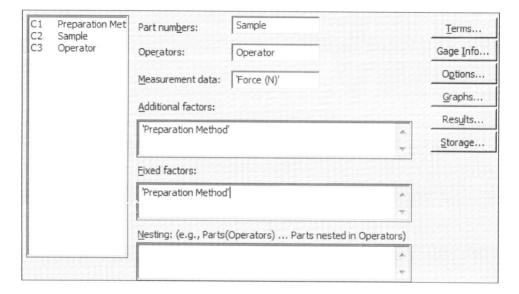

4. Click on the **Terms** button.

5. From the **Include terms in the model up through order** drop-down list, choose **2** to select all two-way interactions.

6. Click on the **Part-to-Part Variation** button.

7. Move **Preparation Method** and the **Sample*Preparation Method** interaction to the selected terms.

8. Click on **OK**.

9. Click on the **Graphs** button.

10. Enter `'Preparation Method'` into both the sections for **Plots of measurements by single factors** and **Plots of average measurements by two factors**.

11. Click on **OK** in each dialog box to run the Gage R&R.

How it works...

By entering the preparation method as an additional factor, we look at the effect of the three preparation methods on the measurements. With the expanded Gage R&R tools, factors are by default set to random factors, unless defined as fixed. As the preparation method is a choice of the three techniques, we are interested in finding the mean effect of each preparation method rather than the variation from the population of methods. Hence, we define the preparation method as a fixed factor.

With parts in a study, these are expected to be random as these are a random selection of samples from the larger population. Operators are also by default set to random factors, as the operators are assumed to be a small selection of operators in the population, and we wish to find the variation across the population of operators. The expanded Gage R&R study allows us to define operators or parts as fixed, unlike the crossed or nested studies, although it is unlikely that parts in a Gage R&R will be fixed.

The option **Terms** is used to identify which terms to include in the study. By entering all two-way interactions, we can look at the effect of `Sample*Operator`, `Preparation Method*Sample` and `Preparation Method*Operator`.

The study will automatically remove interactions that have a P-value greater than 0.25, this Alpha to remove interaction can be changed from within the **Options** button if required.

As the preparation method may affect the sample, it has been included as a part-to-part variation. If we had additional factors that contribute to the measurement rather than to the sample, these would be left as measurement system variations.

We are also able to choose the charts to be displayed. The **Graphs** option is used to include the charts for `Preparation Method` and the two-factor interactions, including `Preparation Method`. Xbar-R charts can also be included for additional factors.

There's more...

The expanded study can allow us to include nested factors as well. Consider comparing measurements across two different laboratories; we would nest operators within each lab.

See also

- ▸ The *Analyzing a crossed Gage R&R study* recipe
- ▸ The *Studying a nested Gage R&R* recipe

Studying a go / no go measurement system

Studies to check the accuracy of go / no go measurements systems are run from the **Attribute Gage Study (Analytic Method)** option. This is found within the **Gage Study** submenu of **Quality Tools**.

In this recipe, we will use data for a go / no go plug gage. The upper limit of the gage is 0.25 mm; 11 reference samples are checked 20 times against the gage and the accepted number is recorded.

We will type the data into the worksheet before running the **Attribute Gage Study (Analytic Method)** option.

Getting ready

Enter the data shown in the following screenshot into a new worksheet in Minitab:

	C1	C2	C3	C4
	Part	Reference	Accepted	Trials
	1	0.2500	20	20
	2	0.2505	19	20
	3	0.2510	16	20
	4	0.2515	11	20
	5	0.2520	5	20
	6	0.2525	4	20
	7	0.2530	1	20
	8	0.2535	0	20

How to do it...

1. Navigate to **Stat | Quality Tools | Gage Study** and click on **Attribute Gage Study (Analytic Method)**.
2. Enter Part into the **Part Numbers** field.
3. Enter Reference into the **Reference Values** field.
4. Enter Accepted into the **Summarized counts** field.
5. Enter Trials into the **Number of trials** field.
6. Enter the **Upper limit** as 0.25.
7. Click on **OK**.

How it works...

The output will plot the probability of acceptance against each reference value.

Bias is calculated from the upper limit and intercept/slope. The slope is found from the regression of the probabilities of acceptance on the reference values.

The **Options** dialog box allows us to choose between an AIAG method and a regression method for the test of bias. The AIAG method requires one part with 0 acceptances, one part with 20 acceptances, and six parts with acceptances between 0 and 20. The regression method isn't limited to eight reference values and the restrictions of one part with 0 acceptances and one part with 20 acceptances.

The bias will show the difference between the limit specified and the 50th percentile from the regression line.

Repeatability is the difference between the 0.995 and 0.005 proportions from the fitted line divided by an adjustment factor of 1.08.

This can be a useful tool in understanding the performance of go / no go gages. The ideal scenario would be reference values within the specifications that are accepted all the time. Reference values that are outside the specifications should be rejected every time they are tested.

The sharper the slope, the better the gage, and the closer the 50th percentile is to the specification, the more accurate the gage. The problems in accepting parts out of specification, or rejecting items within specification, can show distortion in the gage.

Using the Assistant tool for Gage R&R

The **Assistant** menu's tools also include a crossed Gage R&R. They offer a simpler dialog use and guidance with interpretation of the results in exchange for fewer options compared to the **Stat** menu tools.

Here, we will use the same data as in the crossed Gage R&R study earlier as a comparison with the crossed study within the **Stat** menu.

The data is on measuring fill volumes; we have two operators, 10 parts, and two replicates. We will use specifications of 14.25 and 15.75.

The crossed Gage study in the earlier recipe shows stacking a dataset that is set out in a format more typical to Excel. Rather than repeating these instructions, we will open the data in the worksheet `Gage R&R stacked.mtw`. This holds the worksheet ready for Minitab.

How to do it...

The following instructions will step through the **Assistant** menu to lead us to the Gage R&R:

1. Open the worksheet Gage R&R stacked.mtw by using **Open Worksheet** from the **File** menu.

2. Go to the **Assistant** menu and click on **Measurement Systems Analysis (MSA)**.

3. Follow the decision tree to the left, as shown in the following screenshot, for a data type of **Measurement** and an objective of **Analyze data**.

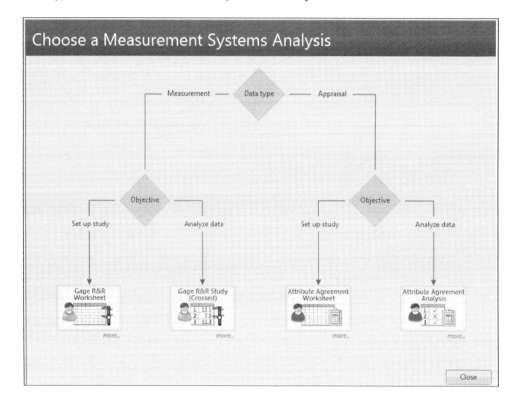

4. Select **Gage R&R Study (Crossed)**.

5. Enter Operator in **Operators**.

6. Enter Parts in **Parts**.

7. Enter Measure in **Measurements**.

8. In the section for **Process variation**, choose the option to **Estimate from parts in the study**.

9. Enter the **Lower spec:** as 14.25 and the **Upper spec:** as 15.75.

10. Click on **OK**.

How it works...

The assistant Gage R&R offers an easier to use dialog box without all the options that are offered in the **Gage R&R (Crossed)** option in the **Stat** menu. This makes it easier to use and offer guidance on the reports. There are four report cards generated for the Gage R&R.

The **Summary** report will indicate if the measurement system can assess process performance and tolerance. Process performance is judged by historical process variation if this report is used, and percent study is judged by percent process or study variation if the historical variation is not entered.

The adequacy of the gage is judged by the AIAG guidelines as follows: less than 10 percent is ideal, 10 percent to 30 percent is marginally acceptable, and greater than 30 percent is unacceptable.

The assistant Gage R&R will only use the ANOVA method for the analysis, not the Xbar-R method.

For more control over what output is displayed or what options to select (for example, the Xbar-R method and the number of standard deviations for the study variation) we should use the Gage R&R tools from the **Stat** menu.

There's more...

Like the crossed Gage R&R, the assistant will run an attribute agreement analysis. The attribute agreement analysis is shown in the next recipe.

See also

- ▸ The *Attribute Gage study from the Assistant menu* recipe
- ▸ The *Analyzing a crossed Gage R&R study* recipe

Attribute Gage study from the Assistant menu

The attribute studies are used where, instead of a measurement device, operators or appraisers make a judgment on the acceptability of items. The study here is used to assess the appraisers' ability to agree with themselves and the standards in a study.

For this recipe, we will use data for an inspection on car bumpers. The appraisers inspect the bumpers to check for a color match with the vehicle they are to be fitted to.

A total of 30 samples are tested by three appraisers with two replicates. A standard was identified for the results in the study, and this is given in the sixth column. We will use the attribute study to compare the ability of appraisers to agree with their own results and to the standards.

Here, we will use the **Assistant** menu to run the attribute studies; a similar study can be run from the **Stat** menu and **Quality Tools**.

How to do it...

Here, the instructions will show us how to navigate the assistant decisions and lead us to the attribute gage study. Then, using the following steps, we will produce results examining the consistency and accuracy of the appraisers' answers:

1. Open the worksheet `Attribute gage study.mtw` by using **Open Worksheet** from the **File** menu.

2. Go to the **Assistant** menu and select **Measurement Systems Analysis (MSA)**.

3. Follow the decision tree to the right for a data type of **Appraisal**; the decision tree is shown in the previous recipe.

4. For the objective, follow **Analyze data**.

5. Select **Attribute Agreement Analysis**.

6. Enter `Appraisers` into the section **Appraisers**.

7. Enter `Test Items` into the section **Test Items**.

8. Enter `Results` into the section **Appraisal Results**.

9. Enter `Standards` into the section **Known Standards**.

10. Select **Pass** as the **Value of good or acceptable items:**.

11. Click on **OK**.

How it works...

The assistant attribute study will create four output cards. The first is a report card about the mix of items in the study and how the accuracy and error rates are calculated. The second shows a misclassification report. This indicates the appraisers' errors and samples that are misclassified.

The third page is a report on the accuracy of the appraisers and the accuracy of responding pass or fail.

The final page gives a summary report, indicating the overall percentage accuracy and error rates.

The assistant uses percentage accuracy and error to convey the ability of the appraisers to agree. If we are interested in producing Kappa statistics, then the **Attribute agreement analysis**, found in the **Stat** menu, and **Quality Tools** should be used.

The assistant study will only be able to use binomial responses, and needs a standard to compare the responses to.

Attribute agreement analysis from the **Stat** menu allows us to use ordinal or nominal data and does not need a standard to use. For ordinal data, the **Stat** menu tool can also output Kendall's coefficients.

There are also tools to create worksheet to generate attribute gage study worksheets in the **Assistant** and the **Stat** menu.

There's more...

We used the **Assistant** tool here for the attribute agreement studies, as the output is easily interpreted and very graphical. Should we have a study without a known standard, or a response that is not binomial, then the **Attribute agreement analysis** from within the **Stat** menu, and **Quality Tools** provide an alternative study. This will generate Kappa or Kendall's coefficients.

Attribute gage studies are not recommended with fewer than 20 samples due to confidence intervals on results being large. Another consideration is that as the number of samples is reduced, the ability of the appraisers to be able to remember the given samples and results is higher. This can increase measurement bias if operators are able to remember details about the samples.

9
Multivariate Statistics

In this chapter, we will cover the following recipes:

- Finding the principal components of a set of data
- Using factor analysis to identify the underlying factors
- Analyzing the consistency of a test paper using item analysis
- Finding similarity in results by rows using cluster observations
- Finding similarity across columns using cluster variables
- Identifying groups in data using cluster K-means
- The discriminant analysis
- Analyzing two-way contingency tables with a simple correspondence analysis
- Studying complex contingency tables with a multiple correspondence analysis

Introduction

Multivariate tools can be useful in exploring large datasets. They help us find patterns and correlations in the data; or, try to identify groups from within a larger dataset.

Tools such as principal components analysis and factor analysis are used as a way to identify underlying correlations or factors that are hidden in the data. The clustering tools try to find a similarity between observations or columns; for example, finding the similarity between how close the rows and variables are to each other.

Correspondence analysis helps us investigate relationships between two-way tables and even more complex tabular data.

We may find the use of multivariate tools as a precursor to modeling data in regression or ANOVA as these techniques can often lead to an understanding of the relationships between variables and the dimensionality of our results.

The data files used in the recipes are available for download on the Packt website.

The Multivariate tools are found under the **Stat** menu as shown in the following screenshot:

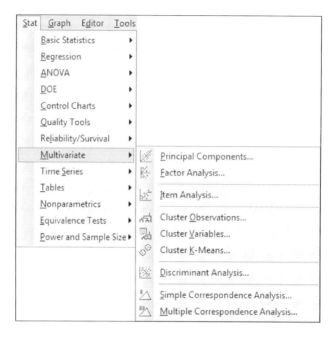

Finding the principal components of a set of data

With **Principal Components Analysis** (**PCA**), we can try to explain the variance-covariance structure of a set of variables. We will use PCA to investigate linear associations between a large number of variables; or rather, we will change the dimensionality of a large dataset to a reduced number of variables. This can help identify the relationships in a dataset that are not immediately apparent.

As such, PCA can be a useful exploratory tool in data analysis and can often lead to more in-depth analysis.

This example looks at the tax revenue in the UK from April 2008 to June 2013.

How to do it...

The following steps will generate the principal components of the input factors and also plots to evaluate the impact of the first two principal components:

1. Open the `Tax Revenue.MTW` worksheet.
2. Go to the **Stat** menu, click on **Multivariate**, and select **Principal Components...**
3. For the **Variables:** section, select the numeric columns from `PAYE Income` to `Customs duty`.
4. In the **Number of components to compute:** section, enter `5`.
5. Click on the **Graphs...** button and select all the charts.
6. Click on **OK** in each dialog box.

How it works...

In our study, we have a set of variables that correlate with each other to varying degrees. Using PCA, we convert these variables into a new set of linearly uncorrelated variables. We identify the first principal component by seeking to explain the largest possible variance in our data. The second component then seeks to explain the highest amount of variability in the remaining data, under the constraint that the second component is orthogonal to the first. Each successive component then must be orthogonal to the preceding components.

Ideally, this can help reduce many variables to fewer components, thereby reducing the dimensionality of the data down to a few principle components. The next step is the interpretation of the components that are then generated.

The results of the principal components, as shown in the following screenshot, give us an indication of the correlations between the variables. Next, we should study the principal components and their construction from the variables. Ideally, we would be able to identify a theme for the components.

The output in the session window will list an eigenanalysis of the correlation matrix plus the variables and their coefficients in the principal components.

In the following screenshot, we should observe that PC1 accounts for a proportion of 0.233 of the overall variation and PC2, 0.426:

Variable	PC1	PC2
PAYE income	0.226	0.036
SA income	0.134	0.333
CGT	0.041	0.322
Tax credits	0.179	-0.106
NICs	0.266	0.212
VAT	0.366	0.163
Corp tax	0.305	0.178
Petroleum tax	-0.093	-0.076
Fuel duty	0.149	-0.288
IHT	0.155	-0.145
Stamp taxes	0.228	-0.184
Tobacco Duty	0.291	-0.017
Spirit Duty	0.159	-0.270
Beer Duty	0.171	-0.263
Wine Duty	0.206	-0.310
Cider duty	0.183	-0.282
Betting & Gambling	0.173	0.085
Air passenger duty	0.200	-0.191
Insurance premium	-0.011	0.134
Landfill tax	0.335	0.193
Climate change Levy	-0.024	0.182
Aggregates levy	0.291	0.240
Customs duty	0.102	-0.134

The coefficients for PC1 reveal a negative value for **Petroleum tax** with positive coefficients for tobacco, alcohol duties, income tax, corporation taxes, and others. A low score in PC1 indicates a high petroleum tax revenue with low income-tax-based revenues; high scores for PC1 would indicate higher employment-based taxes and social taxes such as alcohol duties and tobacco duties. PC1 may be representing an overall income-based tax.

PC2 shows us the positive values of the revenues of **climate change levy** (**CCL**), insurance premium taxes, **Self Assessment** (**SA**) income, and **Capital Gains Tax** (**CGT**). SA income and CGT are not collected automatically via wages paid to employees, but are taxes that have to be declared by an individual at specific times of the year.

The option for PCA allows us to choose between using a correlation matrix or a covariance matrix to analyze the data. A correlation matrix will standardize the variables while the covariance matrix will not. A covariance matrix is often best applied when we know that the data has similar scales. When the covariance matrix is used with variables of differing scales or variation, PC1 tends to get associated with the variable that has the highest variation. Using descriptive statistics from the **Basic Statistics** menu in **Stat**, we will observe that corporation tax has the highest standard deviation. If we were to run the PCA again with a covariance matrix, then we would observe the first principal component that is aligned strongly with corporation tax.

The following screenshot shows us the **Scree Plot** of eigenvalues of each component, where the highest eigenvalues are associated with components **1** and **2**:

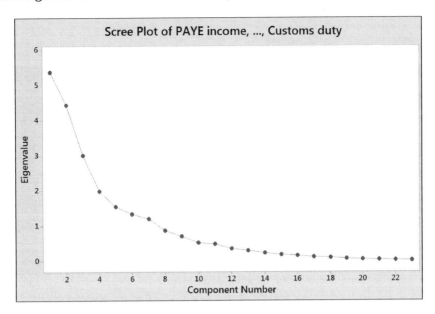

The following screenshot displays the **Score Plot** of the first two principal components; the graph is divided into quadrants for the positive and negative values of PC1 and PC2.

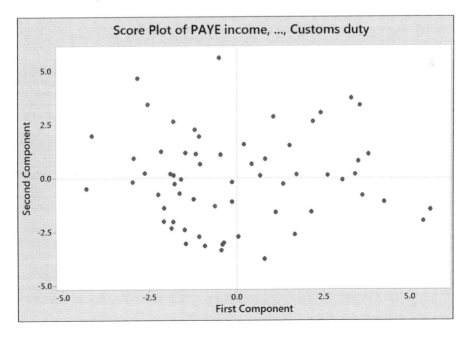

To help with the interpretation of the score plot, it would be useful to either apply a grouping variable by editing the points or brush the chart. The following steps can be used to turn the brush tool on and identify the country behind each point on the chart:

1. Right-click on the score plot and select **Brush** from the menu.

2. Right-click on the chart once again and select **Set ID variables...**.

3. Double-click on the columns for `Years` and `Month` into the **Variables:** section.

4. Click on **OK**.

5. Use the cursor to highlight points on the chart.

Another option is to add data labels to the score plot. The following steps show us how to label each point with the country's name:

1. Right-click on the chart and go to the **Add** menu and select **Data Labels...**.

2. Select the **Use labels from column:** option.

3. Enter `Month` into the section for labels.

4. Click on **OK**.

> If the brushing tool is still active, the right-click menu will show us options that are relevant to brushing the chart. We must return the chart to the select mode before running the preceding steps.

Comparing the score plot to the loading plot helps us understand the effect of the variables on the first two components. In the following screenshot, we can see the negative association between agricultural employment and PC1. Countries with negative PC1 will tend to have a high percentage of their population employed in agriculture.

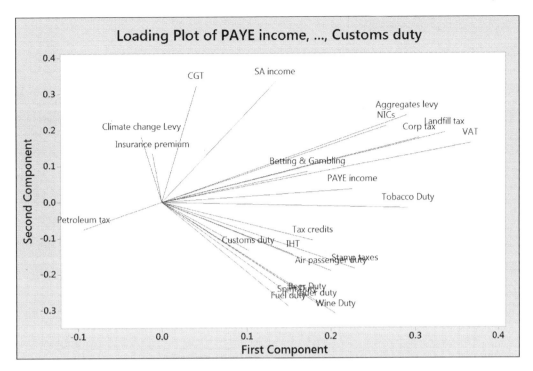

The upper-right corner of the loading and score plots are associated with higher taxes from self-declared income. The lower-right corner is associated with taxes from alcohol, stamp duty, and air passenger duties.

The biplot is useful in that it combines the loading and the score plots. The downside to the biplot is that the brushing tool does not work with it and we can't add data labels as well.

There's more...

The graphs generated for loading as well as the biplots from the dialog box use only PC1 and PC2. We can use the **Storage** option to store the scores for other components. If we wanted to store the scores for the first four principal components, we would enter four columns into the section for scores.

This can allow us to create scatterplots for the other components.

See also

▸ The *Using factor analysis to identify the underlying factors* recipe

Using factor analysis to identify the underlying factors

Factor analysis can be thought of as an extension to principal components. Here, we are interested in identifying the underlying factors that might explain a large number of variables. By finding the correlations between a group of variables, we look to find the underlying factors that describe them. The difference between the two techniques is that we are only interested in the correlations of the variables in PCA. Here, in factor analysis, we want to find the underlying factors that are not being described in the data currently. As such, rotations on the factors can be used to closely align the factors with structure in the variables.

The data has been collected from different automobile manufacturers. The variables look at weights of vehicles, fuel efficiency, engine power, capacity, and CO2 emissions.

We will use factor analysis to try and understand the underlying factors in the study. First, we try and identify the number of factors involved, and then we evaluate the study. Finally, we step through different methods and rotations to check for a suitable alignment between the factors and the component variables.

How to do it...

The following steps will help us identify the underlying factors in the jobs dataset:

1. Open the `mpg.MTW` worksheet.

2. Go to **Stat**, click on **Multivariate**, and select **Factor Analysis**.

3. Enter `CO2`, `Cylinders`, `Weight`, `Combined mpg`, `Max hp`, and `Capacity` into the **Variables:** section.

4. Select the **Graphs...** button and select **Scree plot**.

5. Click on **OK** in each dialog box.

6. Check the results in the scree plot and the session window to assess the number of factors, as shown in the following screenshots:

```
Principal Component Factor Analysis of the Correlation Matrix


Unrotated Factor Loadings and Communalities

Variable        Factor1   Factor2   Factor3   Factor4   Factor5   Factor6   Communality
CO2             0.953    -0.223    -0.155    -0.032     0.103     0.072      1.000
Cylinders       0.866    -0.022     0.383    -0.306    -0.090    -0.008      1.000
Weight          0.555     0.735    -0.381    -0.078    -0.014    -0.002      1.000
Combined mpg   -0.781     0.442     0.435     0.036    -0.010     0.052      1.000
Max hp          0.941     0.005     0.078     0.255    -0.211     0.008      1.000
Capacity        0.892     0.185     0.330     0.143     0.200    -0.030      1.000

Variance        4.2583    0.8212    0.6209    0.1873    0.1033    0.0090     6.0000
% Var           0.710     0.137     0.103     0.031     0.017     0.002      1.000


Factor Score Coefficients

Variable        Factor1   Factor2   Factor3   Factor4   Factor5   Factor6
CO2             0.224    -0.272    -0.250    -0.170     1.000     8.015
Cylinders       0.203    -0.026     0.617    -1.634    -0.875    -0.914
Weight          0.130     0.896    -0.614    -0.416    -0.137    -0.257
Combined mpg   -0.183     0.539     0.701     0.192    -0.094     5.822
Max hp          0.221     0.006     0.125     1.359    -2.038     0.890
Capacity        0.209     0.225     0.532     0.762     1.932    -3.358
```

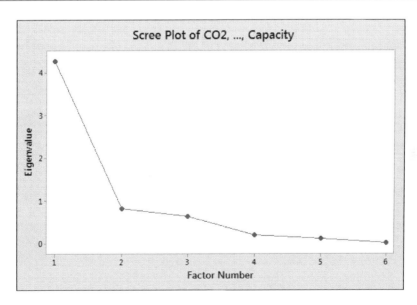

7. Here, the results indicate that factors **1** and **2** account for a majority of the variation, factors **3** and **4** account for a similar amount, and the components beyond factor **4** are small.

8. Next, we should assess how useful the factors are likely to be. The loadings for factor 1 have high values across most factors and pay particular attention to high CO_2 and `Max hp` values, with a strong negative combined mpg.

9. Assess the model with only the first two factors by returning to the last dialog box by pressing *Ctrl + E*.

10. Enter 2 in the **Number of factors to extract:** section. Click on the **Graphs...** button and select **Loading plot**.

11. Click on **OK** to generate the loading plot for the first two factors.

12. Next, we will assess the model with a rotation. Do we see the same structure using an orthogonal rotation? Press *Ctrl + E* to return to the last dialog box.

13. Change the type of rotation to **Varimax**.

14. Click on **OK**.

15. Compare the loading plot from the varimax rotation to the original loading plot. The same structure should be observed with a rotation between the two factors.

16. Next, compare the results from the Maximum likelihood and Varimax rotation. Press *Ctrl + E* to return to the last dialog box and select the option for **Maximum likelihood**. Click on **OK**.

17. Compare the loading plots. All loading plots show a similar structure, but with our variables aligned differently to the factors across each rotation and method. The loading plot from the principal components study, using the varimax rotation, may be desirable as PC1 is closely tied to `Combined Mpg`, with PC2 showing a strong association with `Weight`; the factors associated with `Capacity`, `cylinders`, `hp`, and `CO2` tend to the upper-right corner of the chart.

18. Press *Ctrl + E* to return to the last dialog box, select **Principal components** for **Method of Extraction**, and **Varimax** for **Type of Rotation**.

19. Click on the **Graphs...** button and select **Score plot** and **Biplot** to study the results.

20. Click on **OK** in each dialog box.

How it works...

The steps run through several steps to iteratively compare the factor analysis. The strategy of checking different fitting methods and rotations to settle on the most suitable technique is discussed in "*Applied Multivariate Statistical Analysis 5th Edition*",*Richard A. Johnson* and *Dean W. Wichern*, Prentice Hall, *page 517*.

The method and type of rotation is probably a less crucial decision, but one that can be useful in separating the loading of variables into the different factors rather than having two factors that are a mix of many component variables.

The strategy, as discussed by Johnson and Wichern in brief, is as follows:

1. Perform an analysis of a principal component.
2. Try a varimax rotation.
3. Perform maximum likelihood factor analysis and try a varimax rotation.
4. Compare the solutions to check whether the loadings are grouped together in a similar manner.
5. Repeat the previous steps for a different set of factors.

In this example, we will get similar groups of loadings with both fitting methods and rotations. The loadings will be different with each rotation, but they group in a similar way; we can observe this from the loading plot.

The suggestion that the principal components method with Varimax rotation is suitable for this data comes from the line along factor **1** and **2** in the loading plot, as shown in the following figure:

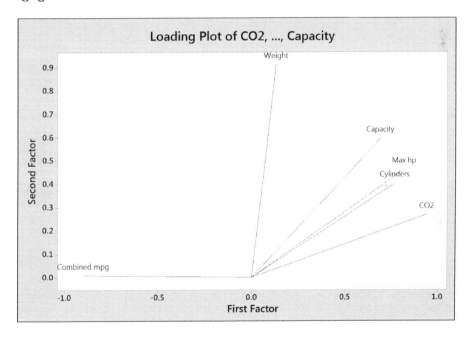

Factor **1** appears to be associated with fuel efficiency versus power and factor **2** with vehicle weight.

Minitab offers Equimax, Varimax, Quartimax rotations, and Orthomax, where the rotation gamma can be chosen by the user.

The storage option allow us to store loadings, coefficients, scores, and matrices. Stored loadings can be used to predict factor scores of new data by entering the stored loadings into the loadings section of the initial solution within options.

See also

▸ The *Finding the principal components of a set of data* recipe

Analyzing consistency of a test paper using item analysis

Typically, item analysis is used to check the test structure or questionnaires for internal consistency and reliability of the results. Cronbach's alpha is generated for item analysis and is usually referred to as a measure of internal consistency or reliability of the survey.

In this example, we use item analysis to compare the results of students' answers on a test paper. We are interested in investigating the correlation of the question results with each other and the consistency of the results.

The data is in the form of a short exam. 20 students are asked five questions. The results are 1 for a correct answer and 0 for an incorrect one.

How to do it...

The following steps will check the consistency of questions in a short test paper given to students:

1. Open the `Item analysis.MTW` worksheet.
2. Go to the **Stat** menu, click on **Multivariate**, and select **Item Analysis...**.
3. Enter the columns from Q1 to Q5 in the **Variables:** section.
4. Click on **OK** to run the study.

How it works...

Item analysis will display the correlation matrix and the matrix plot to look at the association between variables. A covariance matrix can also be displayed from the **Results...** option.

Cronbach's alpha is displayed along with an alpha table for one variable removed at a time. With the results observed here, removing Q2 from the study would increase alpha to 0.5797.

There's more...

Cronbach's alpha is often referred to as a measure of internal consistency or reliability of the tests or questions. Values of 0.6 to 0.7 are thought to indicate a good level of consistency.

 Care must be taken with the use of Cronbach's alpha in isolation. A discussion, *On the use, the misuse, and the Very Limited Usefulness of Cronbach's Alpha*, by *Klaas Sijtsma* can be found at the following URL:

http://www.ncbi.nlm.nih.gov/pmc/articles/PMC2792363/

See also

▶ The *Analyzing two-way contingency tables with simple correspondence analysis* recipe

▶ The *Studying complex contingency tables with multiple correspondence analysis* recipe

Finding similarity in results by rows using cluster observations

The clustering tools look for similarities or distances in the data to form groups of results. Cluster observations find groups among the rows of the data, while variables look to find groups among the columns.

For both Cluster Observations and Variables, we will investigate a dataset on car fuel efficiency. Cars are listed as observations and we will look to find groups among the different vehicles.

How to do it...

The following steps will cluster vehicle types together to identify similar vehicles that are identified by rows and then label the dendrogram with a column of vehicle and fuel type:

1. Open the mpg.mtw worksheet .

2. Go to the **Calc** menu and select **Calculator...**.

3. In **Store result in variable:**, enter the name of the new column as Group.

4. In **Expression:**, enter the values as shown in the following screenshot. Then click on **OK** to create the `Group` column.

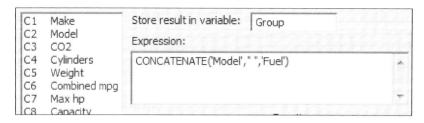

5. Go to the **Stat** menu, click on **Multivariate**, and select **Cluster Observations...**.

6. Enter `CO2`, `Cylinders`, `Weight`, `Combined mpg`, `Max hp`, and `Capacity` into **Variables or distance matrix:**.

7. Check the to **Show dendrogram** box.

8. Click on the **Customize...** button.

9. In **Case labels:**, enter `Group`.

10. Click on **OK** in each dialog box.

11. Check the following dendrogram figure to identify the number of groups that may exist in the data:

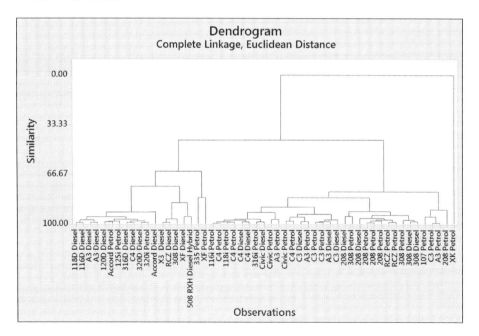

12. From the chart, we may decide to investigate how observations are clustered together using a similarity of 90.

13. Press *Ctrl + E* to return to the last dialog box.

14. Choose the **Specify Final Partition by Similarity level:** option and enter 90.

15. Store the group membership by going to the **Storage...** option. Enter a column name as `Clusters` within the **Cluster membership column:** section.

16. Click on **Ok**.

How it works...

With the single linkage method used in this example, Minitab will try to find the first cluster by looking at the differences between pairs of observations. The pair with the minimum distance is joined. With the second step, we look to find the next minimum distance. At each step, we join clusters by looking at the minimum distance between an item in one cluster and a single item or another cluster.

While the single linkage method looks for the minimum distance between observations, there are other linkage methods that we can use in Minitab. These are averages, centroids, maximum distances between the pairs of observations between clusters, medians, and more.

We can also choose a distance measure to link clusters from the following measures:

▶ **Euclidean**: This is the square root of the sum of squared distances

▶ **Pearson**: This is the square root of the sum of the squared distances divided by the variances

▶ **Manhattan**: This is the sum of the absolute differences

▶ **Square Euclidean**: This is the sum of the squared distances

▶ **Squared Pearson**: This is the sum of the squared distances divided by the variances

By observing the dendrogram, we can visually identify clusters of observations, use a similarity level, or ask to find a fixed number of groups in the data. Here, we used a similarity of 90 to define clusters. This gives us six clusters in the cars dataset.

It is advised that we be careful in the interpretation of the clusters to ensure that they make sense. By investigating the other linkage methods, we can compare the groupings that are found and try and identify the grouping that makes the most sense.

The **Case labels** option from the **Customize...** option allows us to use a column to name the rows displayed on the dendrogram. If this was not used, we would just display the row names.

There's more...

Different linkage methods can have different patterns and effects to watch out for. A single linkage, for example, can end up grouping the observations into long chains (as individual items can be close to each other) whereas the average-based methods can be influenced more by outliers in the data.

See also

▸ The *Finding similarity across columns using cluster variables* recipe

▸ The *Identifying groups in data using cluster K-means* recipe

Finding similarity across columns using cluster variables

Cluster variables work in a manner that is similar to cluster observations. Here, we are interested in the columns and variables in the worksheet rather than grouping the observations and rows.

We will look at the dataset for car fuel efficiency to identify groups of variables, or rather identify the columns that are similar to each other.

This dataset was collected from manufacturer-stated specifications.

How to do it...

1. Open the `mpg.MTW` worksheet.

2. Go to the **Stat** menu, click on **Multivariate**, and select **Cluster Variables...**.

3. Enter the columns for `CO2`, `Cylinders`, `Weight`, `Combined mpg`, `Max hp`, and `Capacity` into the **Variables or distance matrix:** section.

4. Check the **Show dendrogram** option.

5. Click on **OK** to create the results.

6. Inspect the dendrogram to identify groups in the result. The higher the value of similarity along the the y axis, the greater the similarity between columns, as shown in the following figure:

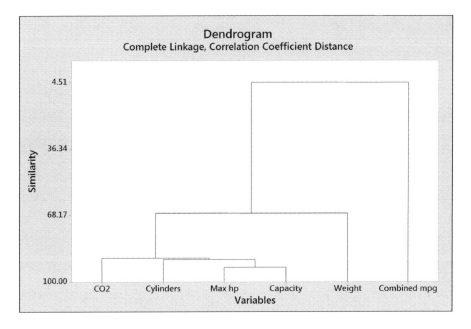

7. It looks like there are three main groups of variables. Press *Ctrl + E* to return to the last dialog box.

8. Under **Number of clusters:**, select **3**.

9. Click on **OK**.

How it works...

As with cluster observations, we have used the single linkage method by default. We have the same options for the linkage method and distance measure as the ones used in cluster observations.

The results for the variables here show us that the combined mpg is very different when compared to the other variables.

For larger numbers of variables, dendrograms can be split into separate graphs by clusters. The **Customize...** option for the dendrogram can be set to the maximum number of observations per graph.

See also

▸ The *Finding similarity in results by rows using cluster observations* recipe

▸ The *Identifying groups in data using cluster K-means* recipe

Identifying groups in data using cluster K-means

Cluster K-means is a nonhierarchical technique to cluster items into groups based on their distances from the group centroid. Minitab uses the MacQueens algorithm to identify groups.

Here, we will look at finding groups of tax revenues for the UK from April 2008 until June 2013 in the data. The value of * for row 49 onwards, next to the dates in the second column, indicates provisional data.

The values are in millions of pounds sterling. We might expect tax revenue patterns to exhibit a measure of seasonality. We will use cluster K-means as a way of grouping the months of the year. As this is expected to be based on the month within a quarter, we will initially set the clusters to three.

In the *How it works...* section, we will compare the identified clusters with the results of a PCA for this data.

How to do it...

The following steps will identify the observations into three groups within the data, based on their distances from the centroids group:

1. Open the `Tax Revenue.MTW` worksheet by using **Open Worksheet...** from the **File** menu.

2. Go to the **Stat** menu, click on **Multivariate**, and select **Cluster K-Means...**.

3. Enter all the columns from `C4 PAYE` income to `C32 Child Benefit` into the **Variables:** section.

4. In **Number of clusters:**, enter 3.

5. Check the **Standardize variables** option.

6. Click on the **Storage...** button.

7. In **Cluster Membership column:**, enter `Group`.

8. Click on **OK** in each dialog box.

How it works...

The output will generate tables to indicate the clusters and observations within each cluster. Minitab will create groups based on their average distance from centroids and maximum distances of centroids of each cluster.

It is useful to standardize the results in this example as the tax revenue has very different scales for each variable. Income-tax-based revenue has a much greater value and range than climate change levies.

By storing the cluster membership into a new column called `Group`, the worksheet will label each row 1, 2, or 3 in this column. To understand the implication of groupings in the data, compare the new column to the months in the second column. We should see that the group 123 is a repeating pattern. April is 1, May is 2, June is 3, then July is 1, and so on. April is the start of the second quarter of the year, May is the middle, and Jun is the end of the quarter.

In this example, we let the algorithm identify its own grouping in the data, and this is related to the exact month in a quarter. A more useful method is to provide a seed or starter group to identify the grouping in the data. To do this, we would need to use an indicator column to identify a group for an item in the worksheet.

To do this, create a column of zeroes and then enter a group number on known lines to seed the cluster K-means algorithm. The seed points form the basis of each group. The seed column needs to be the same length as the other columns in the study, hence the requirement to complete the column with.

The following steps will create a seed column that can be used with the tax revenue data:

1. A column of zeroes can be quickly created using the **Make Patterned Data** tools and **Simple Set of Numbers...** from within the **Calc** menu.

2. Name a column `Seed` within the **Store patterned data in:** section.

3. Enter 0 in the **From first value:** and **To last value:** boxes. In the **Number of times to list the sequence:** section, enter 63.

4. Then in the worksheet, change the values of 0 in the seed column to 1, 2, and 3 in rows 1, 2, and 3.

The final partitions found by cluster K-means will depend a lot on the specified initial conditions. Hence, the use of this tool is best when we have an idea of the number of groups we are looking for and some initial seed conditions to start each group.

There's more...

As additional checks on the data, we can check the results by coding the months in the second column and using this column on the score plot from the principal components analysis. Use **Text to Text...** by navigating to the **Data | Code** menus. By completing the dialog box shown in the following screenshot, we will code the months to the start, middle, and end of a financial quarter:

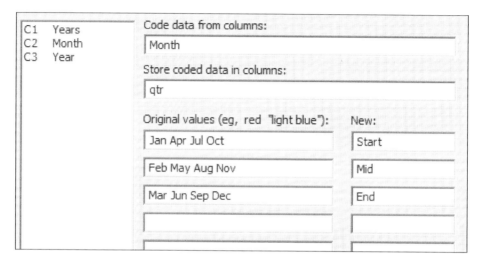

When comparing the coded values, we should see that they match the Group column identified in cluster K-means.

Next, use the **Principal Components...** analysis with loading and score plots from the **Multivariate** menu and enter columns C4 to C32 in the **Variables:** section.

Under the **Graph...** option, select the score plot and the loading plot and run the study.

To see the effect of the groups identified in cluster K-means, double-click on one of the data points on the score plot. Select the **Groups** tab and in the **Categorical variables for grouping:** section, enter either the Group column or the qtr column.

The resultant score plot should clearly separate the three stages in each quarter.

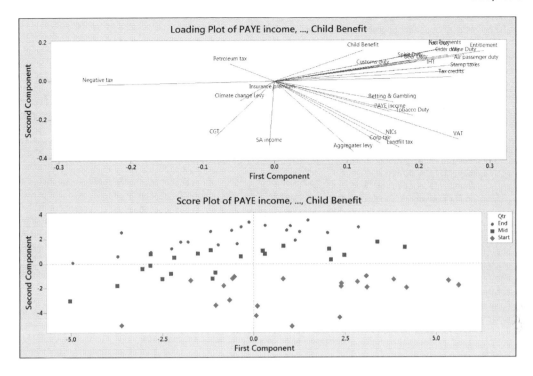

See also

▶ The *Finding the principal components of a set of data* recipe

The discriminant analysis

Discriminant analysis is a technique to classify observations into different groups. Here, we will use a linear discriminant function to predict the outcome of the battles in World War II. The example for this data is based on the study *Discriminant Analysis: A Case Study of a War Dataset* by *Dr Nikolaos V. Karadimmas*, *M. Chalikias*, *G Kaimakais*, and *M Adam*. This can be found at the following link for more details:

```
http://www.academia.edu/193503/Discriminant_Analysis_-_a_case_study_
of_a_war_data_set
```

Wikipedia was used as a source to obtain the data in the worksheet. We should verify the correctness of this before drawing conclusions from the dataset.

Here, we will obtain the troop and tank ratios for each battle from the calculator before constructing the linear discriminant function as a method to predict the outcome of the battle.

Enter the results into the worksheet, as shown in the following screenshot:

C1-T	C2-T	C3	C4	C5	C6	C7-T	C8	C9	C10
Battle	Combatant	Troops	Tanks	Aircraft	Losses	Outcome	Opposing Troops	Opposing Tanks	Opposing Aircraft
Stalingrad	Axis	1040000	500	732	850000	Loss	1143000	2400	1115
Stalingrad	Allies	1143000	2400	1115	1120000	Win	1040000	500	732
Kursk	Axis	912460	2928	2110	54182	Loss	1910361	5128	3000
Kursk	Allies	1910361	5128	3000	177847	Win	912460	2928	2110
Monte Cassino	Axis	140000	*	*	20000	Loss	240000	1900	4000
Monte Cassino	Allies	240000	1900	4000	55000	Win	140000	*	*
Battle of the Bulge	Axis	300000	440	2400	100000	Loss	665000	1616	6000
Battle of the Bulge	Allies	665000	1616	6000	90900	Win	300000	440	2400
El Alamein, Egypt I	Axis	96000	70	500	10000	Loss	150000	179	1500
El Alamein, Egypt I	Allies	150000	179	1500	13250	Win	96000	70	500
El Alamein, Egypt II	Axis	116000	547	480	30542	Loss	195000	1029	530
El Alamein, Egypt II	Allies	195000	1029	530	13560	Win	116000	547	480
Normandy	Axis	380000	0	*	209875	Loss	1452000	0	*
Normandy	Allies	1452000	0	*	226386	Win	380000	0	*
Battle of France	Axis	3350000	2445	5638	163650	Win	3300000	3383	2935
Battle of France	Allies	3300000	3383	2935	2260000	Loss	3350000	2445	5638
Battle of the Netherlands	Axis	750000	759	830	11000	Win	280000	1	145
Battle of the Netherlands	Allies	280000	1	145	11600	Loss	750000	759	830

These figures are also included in the `World War II.MTW` worksheet.

The following steps will generate columns of `Troop` and `Tank` ratios for the results before finding a linear discriminant function to identify the outcome of a battle:

1. Go to the **Calc** menu and select **Calculator...**.
2. In **Store result in variable:**, enter `Troop Ratio`.
3. In **Expression:**, enter `'Troops'/'Opposing troops'`.
4. Click on **OK** to create the column.
5. Press *Ctrl + E* to return to the previous dialog box.
6. Press *F3* to reset the dialog box to blank settings.
7. In **Store result in variable:**, enter `Tank Ratio`.
8. In **Expression:**, enter `'Tanks'/'Opposing Tanks'`.
9. Click on **OK** to create the column.

Note that the calculator will generate an error message as two battles had zero tanks. This is just a warning message that is missing in the resulting value in the worksheet. Click on **Cancel** to continue.

10. Go to the **Stat** menu, click on **Multivariate**, and select **Discriminant Analysis....**

11. Enter Outcome in **Groups:**.

12. In **Predictors:**, enter Troop Ratio and Tank Ratio.

13. Click on **OK** to run the study.

How it works...

The results in the session window will give us a summary of classification, as shown in the following screenshot:.

```
Summary of classification

                 True Group
Put into Group   Loss     Win
Loss                7       2
Win                 0       5
Total N             7       7
N correct           7       5
Proportion      1.000   0.714

N = 14           N Correct = 12          Proportion Correct = 0.857
```

Only 14 of the 18 results are used, as four lines have missing values for the tank ratio. The summary table indicates the correctly identified number. Out of this study, two results were misclassified. The session window will indicate that these are row 2 and row 15.

The linear discriminant function is generated to classify the group. This is shown as follows:

```
Linear Discriminant Function for Groups

                   Loss       Win
Constant         -1.549   -10.158
Troop Ratio       4.899    12.451
Tank Ratio       -0.007    -0.015
```

We have two linear expressions. One for loss and one for win. We can construct a column in the worksheet called `Loss` and use the following expression:

$$Loss = -1.549 + 4.899 * Troop\ Ratio - 0.007 * Tank\ Ratio$$

Then we can create a `Win` column and use the following expression:

$$Win = -10.158 + 12.451 * Troop\ Ratio - 0.015 * Tank\ Ratio$$

We would classify a result as a loss if the `Loss` column has a greater value than the `Win` column. If `Win` is greater, the result is classified as a win.

The linear discriminant function uses the assumption that the covariance matrices are equal for all groups. If the covariance matrices are not equal for all groups, then the quadratic discriminant function is more appropriate.

The discriminant analysis can often show overly optimistic values when predicting the dataset used. To check how good the analysis really is, we could split the dataset into two parts. One part is used as a training dataset and the other part is used to predict the group membership by using the discriminant function from the training dataset. An alternative is to use cross validation. Cross validation will leave one result out of the study at each round and try and predict the group when the result is left out.

There's more...

We may want to use discriminant analysis to predict group membership for new observations. If we had a set troop number and tank number for battles where the outcome was unknown, then we would enter this in **Options...**.

The discriminant analysis tool allows the use of prior probabilities and entries for columns to predict group membership from within the **Options...** section.

Analyzing two-way contingency tables with a simple correspondence analysis

We will use simple correspondence analysis to investigate the associations in a two-way contingency table. This is a technique to investigate frequencies of observations within the table.

The example dataset that is used is from the data and stat library and looks at the characteristics that students find important in a good teacher for academic success.

Here, we will use simple correspondence analysis to investigate the relationship between the behaviors in the rows and the count of how often they are identified as **important (IM)**, **neither important nor unimportant (NU)**, and **not important (NI)**.

Getting ready

The data is available at the following link:

`http://lib.stat.cmu.edu/DASL/Datafiles/InstructorBehavior.html`

First, copy the data into Minitab. This will copy and paste the data directly, but use the information window to check the number of rows of data. Pasting the results may result in an extra blank cell at the end of the behavior column. Delete this cell before continuing.

The `instructor behaviour.MTW` worksheet also contains this data.

How to do it...

1. In the worksheet, create a new column in C5 and name this column `names`.

2. In the new column, enter the values IM, NU, and NI in rows 1 to 3.

3. Go to the **Stat** menu, click on **Multivariate**, and select **Simple Correspondence Analysis....**

4. In the dialog box, select the **Columns of a contingency table:** option.

5. Enter the columns of IM, NU, and NI into the **Columns of a contingency table:** section, as shown in the following screenshot:

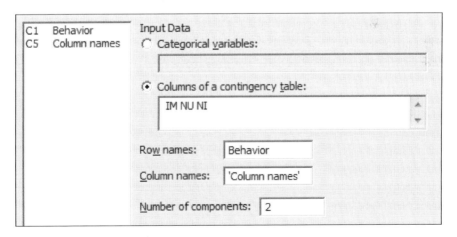

6. Enter `Behavior` into the **Row names:** section.

7. Enter `'Column names'` into the **Column names:** section.

8. Click on the **Results...** button.

9. Check the boxes for **Row profiles**.

10. Click on **OK**.

11. Click on the **Graphs...** button.

12. Check the option for **Symmetric plot showing rows only**, **Symmetric plot showing columns only** and **Symmetric plot showing rows and columns**.

13. Click on **OK** in each dialog box.

How it works...

Using two components, we are attempting to plot a two-dimensional representation of our results. The output in the session window will give us **Analysis of Contingency Table**, which will show us the inertia and proportion of the inertia explained by the two components, as shown in the following screenshot:

```
Analysis of Contingency Table

Axis  Inertia  Proportion  Cumulative  Histogram
   1   0.2495      0.9065      0.9065  *****************************
   2   0.0257      0.0935      1.0000  ***
Total  0.2752
```

Inertia is the chi-squared statistic divided by n; it represents the amount of information retained in each dimension. Here, axis 1 accounts for over 90 percent of the inertia.

By checking the option for **Row profiles** in **Results...**, we will produce a table that indicates the proportion of each of the row categories by columns. We should see that the first questions have the highest proportions associated with IM and the last questions have increasing proportions associated with NU or NI.

The `profiles`, `Expected`, `Observed-Expected` and `Chi Square` column's values can also be generated from the **Results...** option.

Row contribution and column contribution tables are used to indicate how the rows and columns of the data are related to the components in the study.

Quality is a measure of the proportion of the inertia explained by the two components of that row. In this example, the total proportion of inertia explained by the two components was `1`, hence all quality values are `1`.

The `Coordinate` column is used to indicate the coordinates of component 1 and 2 for this row.

The `Corr` column is used to show the contribution to the inertia of that row or column. The example used here for quality is 1 for all rows; the total inertia explained by the two components is 1 for each row. The values of `Corr` for component 1 and 2 will, therefore, add to 1.

The `Contribution` column gives us the contribution to the inertia.

The **Graph...** option allows the use of symmetric or asymmetric plots. Here, we generated just the symmetric plots.

The column plot, which is shown in the following screenshot, shows NI as low in component 1 and IM as high in component 1. NU is shown as high in component 2.

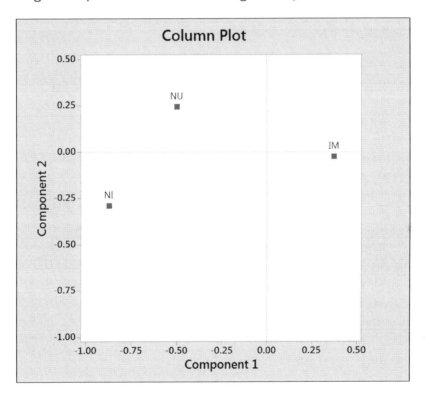

Comparing this to the row plot reveals the questions related to behaviors that are ranked as important and unimportant. We should also notice that with the behaviors labeled in longhand, the text on the charts, including the row, is difficult to read.

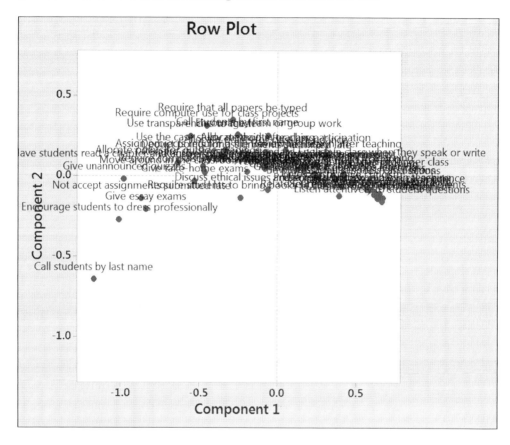

There are a few methods available to help tidy the results on charts such as the one shown in the previous screenshot. By leaving the `Behavior` column out of row names, the study will use the row numbers for the plot labels. Likewise, if we did not enter the column names as indicated in the fifth column, then Minitab would just report a number for each variable. Using row numbers instead of names can make the interpretation of this chart easier when we have a large number of variables.

We can also double-click on the labels on any of the charts to adjust the font size. Double-click on a label to go to the **Font** option and then type a value of 4 in the **Size:** section to reduce the fonts to a more manageable size.

There's more...

Supplementary data allows us to add extra information from other studies. The supplementary data is scored using the results from the main dataset and can be added to the charts as a comparison.

Supplementary rows must be entered as columns. For example, if we had an additional behavior to evaluate, it would be entered in a new column with the number of rows in this column equal to the number of columns in the contingency table.

Let's say we have a new behavior of `Dress Casually`; this would be entered as a column with three rows for the responses, as shown in the following screenshot:

Column name	Dress Casually
IM	56
NU	450
NI	229

Here, a supplementary column would be required to have the same number of rows as the main data.

Axes on the charts can be changed by choosing the component that is plotted as y and x. In the **Graph...** option, this is initially set as 2 1. Here, 2 is our y axis and 1 is the x axis. If we have 3 2, then that would indicate that the component 3 is y and 2 is x. We can enter more components and they would be entered as y x pairs; all values are separated by a space.

We could also use more than two categories in a simple correspondence analysis. The **Combine...** option allows us to combine different categories into a single one to convert the results back into a two-way contingency table.

See also

▶ The *Studying complex contingency tables with multiple correspondence analysis* recipe

Studying complex contingency tables with a multiple correspondence analysis

We use multiple correspondence analyses on tables of three or more categorical variables. This expands the study of a simple correspondence analysis from the two-way table to more variables. One downside of this technique is the loss of how rows and columns relate.

The data that we will look at is based on a study of students and their gender—whether they live in urban, suburban, or rural locations—and their goals to be popular, that is, being good at sports or getting good grades.

This is a simplified dataset that is taken from the original located at DASL. The full dataset can be found at the following location:

`http://lib.stat.cmu.edu/DASL/Datafiles/PopularKids.html`

We will tally the results of the columns to observe the value order of the columns and then we need to create a categorical list of the labels for each item in the factor columns. We will list these figures in the fourth column in the correct value order before running the multiple correspondence analysis.

How to do it...

The following steps use Tally to identify the categories in the tables and then use them to identify student priorities:

1. Open the `MCorrespondance.MTW` worksheet.
2. Go to **Stat**, click on **Tables**, and select **Tally Individual Variables...**.
3. Enter the columns `Gender`, `Urban/Rural`, and `Goals` in **Variables:**.
4. Click on **OK**.

Gender	Count	Urban/Rural	Count	Goals	Count
boy	227	Rural	149	Grades	247
girl	251	Suburban	151	Popular	141
N=	478	Urban	178	Sports	90
		N=	478	N=	478

 The output will show that Minitab lists the text in columns alphabetically. We can change this by right-clicking on a column and selecting **Value Order** from the **Column** option.

5. Return to the worksheet and name the fourth column as `Categories`.

6. In the fourth column, enter the categories of the factors as shown in the following screenshot, where categories must be listed in the order shown in the tally:

Gender	Urban/Rural	Goals	Categories
boy	Rural	Sports	Boy
boy	Rural	Popular	Girl
girl	Rural	Popular	Rural
girl	Rural	Popular	Suburban
girl	Rural	Popular	Urban
girl	Rural	Popular	Grades
girl	Rural	Popular	Popular
girl	Rural	Grades	Sport
girl	Rural	Sports	
girl	Rural	Sports	
girl	Rural	Sports	

7. Go to the **Stat** menu, click on **Multivariate**, and select **Multiple Correspondence analysis...**.

8. In the **Categorical names:** section, enter the columns of Gender, Urban/Rural, and Goals.

9. In the **Category names:** section, enter Categories.

10. Select the **Results...** button and check the option for **Burt table**.

11. Click on **OK**.

12. Click on the **Graphs...** button and check the **Display column plot** option.

13. Click on **OK** in each dialog box.

How it works...

As Minitab does not take the names of the categories inside the columns, we need to specify them in a separate column. Hence, we create the fourth column as Categories, in the study to specify the names in the dialog box.

Tally can be a useful step to check the order of the text as seen by Minitab. This is alphabetical by default. We can adjust this order by right-clicking on a text column and selecting **Value Order...** from the **Column** section.

The output of the multiple correspondence analysis will generate tables of the indicator matrix's analysis. Inertia and proportion can help identify the usefulness of the study. Column contributions are also generated to identify the effect of each of the categories.

Each of the levels of a factor are converted into an `Indicator` column internally by the multiple correspondence analysis commands. Hence, the levels of boy, girl, rural, urban and so on, are referred to as columns.

We could have used a worksheet generated as a set of indicator variables directly. Each column would be a `0 1` column that indicates the presence of that value. To create indicator columns very quickly, use the **Make Indicator Variables...** tool in the **Calc** menu.

Entering the `Gender` column into **Make Indicator Variables** will create a column for `boy` and a column for `girl`.

There's more...

As with simple correspondence analysis, we could include supplementary data.

We could also return to a two-way table structure in a worksheet of three or more categories using the **Combine...** option from **Simple Correspondence Analysis**. This would allow us to define how the variables are combined and whether they relate to rows or columns.

We cross the variables of gender `(boy/girl)` and urban/rural `(Rural/SubUrban/Urban)`; this will create a combined variable in the order that is shown in the following screenshot:

| boy/Rural |
| boy/suburban |
| boy/urban |
| girl/rural |
| girl/suburban |
| girl/urban |

See also

▸ The *Analyzing two-way contingency tables with simple correspondence analysis* recipe

10
Time Series Analysis

In this chapter, we will be covering the following recipes:

- ▶ Fitting a trend to data
- ▶ Fitting to seasonal variation
- ▶ Time series predictions without trends or seasonal variations

Introduction

With time series, we will observe the variation in our data over time. We will also look at forecasting data from these techniques.

The **Time Series** tools are found in the **Stat** menu, as shown in the following screenshot. It is worth pointing out that the **Time Series Plot** option in the **Stat** menu is the same as the **Time Series Plot** in the **Graph** menu. We will not use this option here as it has already been covered in *Chapter 2, Tables and Graphs*.

In this chapter, we will focus on the tools that help us smooth the data over time or fit trends and seasonality.

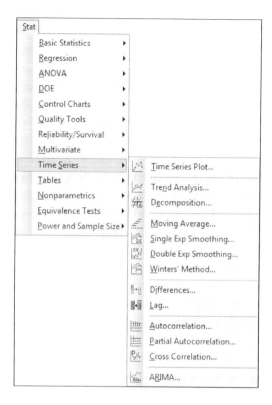

To fit trends, we will use trend analysis and double exponential smoothing; seasonality will use the Winters method and Decomposition. Finally, when no trend or seasonality is apparent, we will use single exponential smoothing and moving average tools to smooth the series.

The datasets used in this chapter are provided as support files on the Packt website.

Fitting a trend to data

There are two tools for fitting trends in Minitab: Trend analysis and double exponential smoothing. Both of these are used to look at the trends in healthcare expenditure in the U.S. The dataset we will look at runs from 1995 to 2011. The values each year are given as a percentage of the GDP and per capita values in dollars.

We will compare the results of a trend analysis plotting a linear trend with double exponential smoothing and produce forecasts for the next three years.

This data was obtained from `www.quandl.com`.

How to do it...

The following steps will plot the trend and double exponential smoothing results with three years of future forecasts.

1. Open the `Healthcare.mtw` worksheet.

2. For the trend analysis, go to the **Stat** menu, then **Time Series** option and select **Trend Analysis**.

3. Enter `'Value (%)'` in the **Variable** section.

4. Check the box for **Generate forecasts**, and in **Number of forecasts,** enter 3.

5. Click on the **Time** button. Select the radio button for the **Stamp** section and enter `Year` into the **Stamp** section.

6. Click on **OK**.

7. Click on the **Graphs** button and select the **Four in one** residuals option. Click on **OK** in each dialog box.

8. For double exponential smoothing, go back to the **Time Series** menu and select **Double Exp Smoothing**.

9. Enter `'Value (%)'` in the **Variable:** section.

10. Follow steps 3 to 6 to stamp the axis with the year and generate residual plots.

How it works...

Trend analysis can fit trends for Linear, Quadratic, Exponential, and S-Curve models, and works work best when there is a constant trend of the previous types to model in the data. The trend analysis tools use a regression model to fit our data over time.

Double exponential smoothing is best used when the trend varies over time. With the `'Value (%)'` data, we should see a change in the trend slope for the period from 2000 to 2003. Because of this, the trend analysis models will not provide an adequate fit to the varying trends in our data.

Double exponential smoothing will use a trend component and a level component to fit to the data. The level is used to fit to the variation around the trend, and the trend is used to fit to the trend line. The fitted line is generated from two exponential formulas. The fitted value at time t is given by the addition of the level and trend components as shown in the following equation:

$$Y_t = L_{t-1} + T_{t-1}$$

Here, the level at time t is given as follows:

$$L_t = \propto Y_t + (1 - \propto)(L_{t-1} + T_{t-1})$$

Also, the trend at time t is given as follows:

$$T_t = \gamma(L_t - L_{t-1}) + (1 - \gamma)T_{t-1}$$

Higher values of weight for the level will, therefore, place more emphasis on the most recent results. This makes the double exponential smoothing react more quickly to variations in the data.

Higher trend values will make the trend line react more quickly to changes in the trend; lower values will give a smoother trend line. Lower values for trend will approach the linear trend.

Minitab will calculate the optimal ARIMA weights from an ARIMA (0,2,2) model looking to minimize the sum of squared errors.

For both trend analysis and double exponential smoothing, it is appropriate to check residual plots to verify the assumptions of the analysis.

The accuracy measures in the output form a useful way of comparing the models to each other The measures shown in the output form are as follows:

▶ **Mean Absolute Percentage Error (MAPE)**: This represents the error as a percentage

▶ **Mean Absolute Deviation (MAD)**: This allows us to observe the error in the units of the data

▶ **Mean Squared Deviation (MSD)**: This gives the variance of the study

When comparing different models, the lower these figures, the better the fit to the data.

There's more...

Here, we should see that double exponential smoothing provides a better fit as we have changes in the trend of the data. We can compare the percentage results to the per capita data and check whether the double exponential or the trend analysis provides a better approach for this new column.

With trend analysis, we can enter historical parameter estimates in options. This will generate a comparison of the new trend and the prior values. The prior and new values can also be blended with each other by specifying a weight for the blending. Parameters and weights must be entered in the order displayed in the trend analysis. If in a previous study, we had obtained a trend of $Y_t = 2500 + 200 * t$, then this would be entered into the **Prior parameter values** section as shown in the following screenshot. The weights for blending each term can be entered as well; these values should be between 0 and 1.

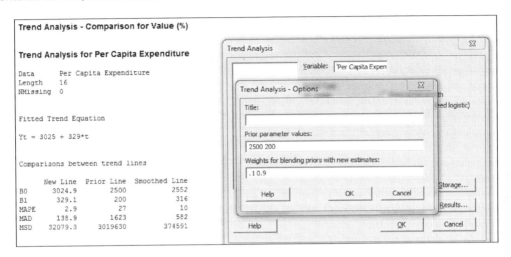

See also

▶ The *Fitting to seasonal variation* recipe

▶ The *Time series predictions without trends or seasonal variations* recipe

Fitting to seasonal variation

We can use the Decomposition or the Winters' method in Minitab to fit to the trends and seasonality in our data. It is generally recommended that we have at least four to five seasons in our data to be able to estimate seasonality.

Here, we will look at the results for temperature from the Oxford weather station. The data can be obtained from the Met Office website:

`http://www.metoffice.gov.uk/climate/uk/stationdata/.`

The data is also provided in the `Oxford weather (cleaned).mtw` worksheet. We should expect a strong seasonal pattern for temperature. As the complete dataset starts in 1853, we will use a small subset for the period 2000 to 2013 for our purposes.

While we know that the seasonal variation has a 12 month pattern, we are going to verify this with autocorrelation. We will then compare the results using the Decomposition and Winters' method tools.

In earlier examples, we obtained the data directly from the Met Office website. For our convenience, we will open a prepared dataset in a Minitab worksheet.

How to do it...

1. Open the `Oxford weather (cleaned).mtw` worksheet by using **Open Worksheet** from the **File** menu. To subset the worksheet, go to the **Data** menu and select **Subset Worksheet**.

2. Enter `2000 onwards` in the **Name** section of the worksheet.

3. Select **Condition** and set the condition to include rows as shown in the following screenshot:

4. Click on **OK** in each dialog box.

5. To run autocorrelation, go to the **Stat** menu, then to **Time Series**, and select **Autocorrelation**.

6. Enter `'T Max'` in the **Series** section and click on **OK**.

   The chart for the autocorrelation should show strong positive correlations at every 12 month interval and negative correlations at each 6-month interval. Next, we will run Decomposition.

7. To run Decomposition, return to the **Time Series** menu and select **Decomposition**.

8. Enter `'T Max'` in the **Variable** section and `12` in the **Seasonal length:** section.

9. Check the **Generate forecasts** option and enter `12` to run forecasts for the next 12 months.

10. Click the **Time** button and select the **Stamp** option; enter `Year` and `Month` into the space available.

11. Click on **OK** to run Decomposition. Next, run the Winters' method.

12. To run the Winters' method, return to the **Time Series** menu and select **Winters' Method**.

13. Enter `'T Max'` in the **Variable** section and enter `12` in the **Seasonal length:** section.

14. Click on the **Time** button.

15. Select the **Calendar** option and choose **Month Year**.

16. In **Start value**, enter 1 2000.

17. Click on **OK** in each dialog box.

How it works...

Autocorrelation can be a useful step in identifying seasonality in data. Peaks in the autocorrelation identify where the dataset correlates with itself after a number of lags. In the weather data, we can see peaks regularly at 12-month intervals and negative peaks at 6 month intervals.

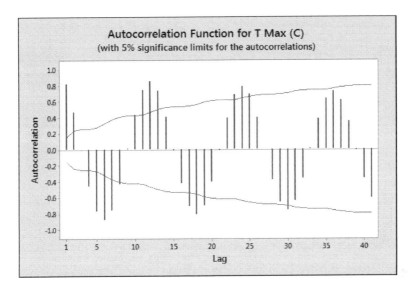

This identifies a 12 month long seasonal pattern. Entering the seasonal length into either Decomposition or Winter's method allows us to fit both trends and seasonality.

High positive peaks at one lag would tend to indicate a dataset that trends in one direction or follows a previous value. For example, if we see a result that decreases, we may expect its resultant values to be decreased.

Decomposition will fit a trend line to the data and use either an additive or multiplicative model to find the seasonal value. The additive model gives each month a value to add or remove from the trend line as a fit to the data.

The multiplicative model gives each period, or month in this case, a multiplier to be used on the trend line. Multiplicative models are best used when seasonal variation is expected to scale with the trend. If the seasonal variation remains constant, then the additive model would be mode applicable.

Decomposition will also generate a panel of charts to investigate the seasonal effects and one to reveal the data after trends or seasonality have been removed. Both the Component Analysis page and the Seasonal Analysis page can help identify problems with fitting to the model and give us similar outputs to the residuals plots.

As with fitting to trends, MAPE, MAD, and MSD are used to evaluate the closest fitting model. Again, we would want to find a model with the lowest values for these measures.

The Winters' method, which is sometimes referred to as the Holt-Winters method, uses a triple exponential smoothing formula. We include a seasonality component along with level and trend for exponential smoothing. Fitted values are generated in a similar manner to the double exponential smoothing function, but with the additional seasonal component. Additive or multiplicative models can be selected, as was done in Decomposition, and they function in the same manner.

Smoothing constants can be selected to have values between 0 and 1, although they tend to be between 0.02 and 0.2. Ideally, we want to obtain a model where the weights for level, trend, and seasonality give the smallest square errors across the time series. Minitab does not offer a fitting method to estimate the values of the smoothing constants, and it can be difficult to settle on a unique solution for the weightings. We can expect several possible combinations of weights to give reasonable results.

As with double exponential smoothing, weights that tend to zero give less value to recent observations; weights approaching one increase the emphasis of recent results, reducing the influence of past values.

There's more...

While looking at the data for Oxford from 2000 onwards, we appear to reveal a negative trend. I am sure that, given the nature of the data, this may elicit some response from the reader. Before declaring a statement about climate change, we should examine data from other weather stations globally, and look for other influencing factors.

For instance, try running the same study on the complete dataset. Then, look at the result for the trends. We may want to run the study with the trend component removed and only fit to seasonality. We can then look at the residual plots to see if there is evidence that we need to include in the trend component.

See also

> ▸ The *Fitting a trend to data* recipe

Time series predictions without trends or seasonal variations

When we observe no clear trend or seasonality in the data, we can use either moving average or single exponential smoothing tools for forecasting.

The data we will use in this example are the GDP figures for the UK from 2009 to 2013. The data is provided for us in the `GDP figures all.mtw` worksheet and is available in the code bundle; it contains data from 1955 to 2013. We will initially subset the data for results from 2009 onwards. Then, we will use quarterly growth percentage, comparing the results from both moving average and single exponential smoothing.

The data was originally obtained from the Guardian website and is available at

`http://www.theguardian.com/news/datablog/2009/nov/25/gdp-uk-1948-growth-economy`.

How to do it...

The following steps will generate a moving average chart and a single exponential smoothing chart:

1. Open the `GDP figures all.mtw` worksheet.
2. Go to the **Data** menu and select **Subset Worksheet**.
3. Enter `2009 onwards` in the **Name** section.
4. Click on the **Condition** button.
5. Enter `Year >= 2009` in the **Condition** section.
6. Click on **OK** in each dialog box.
7. Create the moving average chart first by going to the **Stat** menu, then to **Time Series**, and selecting **Moving Average**.
8. Enter `GDP, Quarterly growth` in the **Variable** section and 2 in the **MA length** section.
9. Check the button for **Generate forecasts** and enter 4 for the **Number of forecasts:**.
10. Click on the **Time** button.
11. For **Time Scale**, choose the **Calendar** option and select **Quarter Year** from the drop-down list.

12. For the start value, type `1  2009`, the dialog box for which should appear as follows:

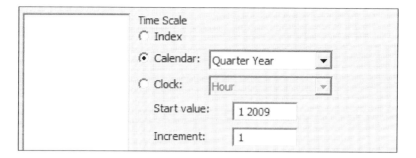

13. Click on **OK**.

14. Click on the **Graphs** button and select the option for the **Four in one** residual plots.

15. Click on **OK** in each dialog box.

16. For the single exponential smoothing, go back to the **Time Series** menu and select **Single Exp Smoothing**.

17. For the **Variable** section, enter `GDP, Quarterly growth`.

18. Follow steps 8 to 14 to select residual plots and enter the quarter and year on the x axis of the chart.

How it works...

On the moving average chart, the fits are the average of the previous *n* data points, where *n* is the moving average length. The length of the moving average can be used to specify how smoothed or how responsive the fitted values are. The higher the moving average, the greater the smoothing on the fitted values. Here, we used a moving average length of 2, and the fitted values are then the mean of the previous two values.

Single exponential smoothing uses the level component to generate fitted values. As with the moving average, by using the weight, we control how responsive or smoothed the results are. The weight can be between 0 and 2. Low weights result in smoothed data; higher weights can react more quickly to changes in the series.

Forecasting for both the techniques takes the value of the fitted result at the origin of the time point and continues this value forward for the number of forecasts. The default origin for fitted values is the last time point of the data. It is possible to reset the origin for the forecasted results, and by resetting the origin to a specific time point within the series, we can compare how useful the forecasts would have been for our data.

We should note that forecasts are an extrapolation, and the further ahead the forecasts, the less reliable they are. Also, forecasting only sees the data in the period we have been studying; it does not know about any unusual events that may occur in the future.

The time options within both tools allow us to change the display on the time scale. Here, we used the calendar to set the scale to quarter and year. By indicating the start value at `1 2009`, we tell the charts to start at quarter 1 in 2009. A space is all that is needed to separate the values. We could have also used the `Year/Quarter` column in **C1** by using the **Stamp** option instead. The trend analysis example illustrates using a column to stamp the **Time** axis.

See also

> ▸ The *Fitting a trend to data* recipe

11
Macro Writing

In this chapter, we will cover the following recipes:

- ▶ Exec macros to repeat simple commands
- ▶ Building a Global macro to create a custom graph layout
- ▶ Obtaining input from the session window with a Global macro
- ▶ Creating a Local macro
- ▶ Local macros with subcommands, submacros, and control statements

Introduction

Minitab does have a macro language that can be used to automate simple tasks or run more sophisticated functions. Here, we will explore the three different types of macro in Minitab. The recipes follow a set of commands that are used to create a panel of charts. In each recipe, we will build on the previous example until we get to the final, complicated, but sophisticated, Local macro. This will show you the differences between the macro types and why you may want to use one type over another.

The macro language in Minitab shares a lot of similarities with Fortran, and here Minitab shows its pedigree. The first version was written in Fortran at Penn State University in 1972!

Minitab also has an **Application Programming Interface** (**API**) that can be programmed to use Visual Basic and other languages. Anyone looking to use the API will find Minitab type libraries and references that they can use as part of the installation of Minitab. Programming the API, though, goes beyond the scope of this book.

What is the difference between the macro types?

Exec macros are just the command language in a text file. When Minitab reads this command language, it will run the steps in order. You cannot use any control statements, such as the `IF` statements or `DO` loops within an Exec. Execs, though, can be quite useful as a very quick way of repeating the same steps on new data. They work directly in the worksheet in Minitab. They use the `*.MTB` file extension.

Global macros are one step more advanced than Execs. They allow for the use of control statements. Like Exec files, they work directly from the worksheet in Minitab. Both Execs and Global macros will refer to columns in the worksheet either by column number, such as `C10`, or by a column name. Those columns must exist in the worksheet in the same format for the macros to run properly. They use the `*.MAC` file extension.

Local macros, when called, are told which columns, constants, or matrices to use, and they take this information into the macro. We have to specify the data types for columns and constants within these macros as we use them. Local macros are more typical of a programming language. They are more flexible to use, as by calling the macro, we identify which data to use from the worksheet. They can work on any worksheet and are not limited to using the same column, either by name or number. The `*.MAC` file extension is used for Local macros as well.

Furthermore, we can call macros from within other macros. These can be held in the same macro file or can call external macro files. In calling other macros, we have to be aware of which macro types can call other macro types. The following table can be used to see how macros can call other macros:

	EXEC	**GLOBAL**	**LOCAL**
EXEC	X	X	X
GLOBAL		X	X
LOCAL			X

The rows show you the macro that is running, and the columns show you the macro being called.

Useful information for writing macros

The history folder in Minitab is an invaluable help in writing macros. Most of the commands that we use in the menus have text commands associated with them; as we run the commands in the **Stat** or **Graph** menus, this text is stored in the history folder.

We could, however, type the text commands directly into Minitab to create charts or studies without the use of the menus. For instance, the `PLOT C1*C2` command will create a scatterplot of column 1 and column 2.

These commands can be entered either into the session window or the command-line editor. To enter commands in the session window, we need to enable the use of the command language. To achieve this, select the session window, go to the **Editor** menu, and select **Enable Commands**. This should switch on a MTB > command prompt in the session window. Commands can be entered after this prompt and you can then click on enter to run them. The command language for the session window is disabled by default, but we can change this within options and the section for the session window.

The command-line editor can be accessed from the **Edit** menu or by pressing *Ctrl + L*. The benefit of the command-line editor is that it remembers the previous commands that were used. We can also type several lines into the command-line editor and run them in one step by clicking on **Submit Commands**. This can be useful to test small sections of code.

Macros can be written in any text editor. Notepad is used here as it is freely available and offers a simple interface. The macros must be saved correctly though, and when using **Save As...** in Notepad, it will add a *.TXT file extension to every file unless we specify that the file type should be save as **All files**.

Notepad does not allow users to highlight syntax. To see the structure of the macro, spaces are used, which helps follow code, subcommands, and sections for If and Do loops. Other text editors will allow us to color the code.

When writing a macro, it is possible to use Minitab to generate as much of the syntax as possible. By running the command from the menus, we can go to the history folder and take the code from there.

The help files within Minitab also contain a great resource for most of the commands that we can use in macros. From the main help screen, we should select macros from the references section. Then, from the top of the **Using Macros** help page, select the **See also** link. The **Alphabetical command list** option is a great location to read up on most of Minitab's commands.

Preparing to run macros

To run Exec files, navigate to **File | Other Files | Run an Exec...**; or, we could enter the Execute command with the path and the file name to run the Exec. This is shown as follows:

```
Execute "C:\Users\...\Macros\Report.mtb" 1.
```

Macros are run by entering a % symbol in front of the path and filename, as shown in the following command:

```
%"C:\Users\...\Macros\montecarlo.mac"
```

This can be simplified by specifying the folder where macros are saved in **Options...**. Under the **Tools** menu, select **Options...**. The **Macro location:** section can be used to point to macros.

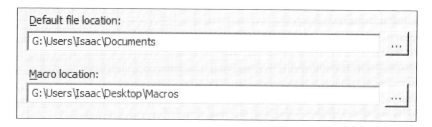

Macros saved in the macro location folder only need to be referred to with % and the filename. The recipes here will assume that we have set the macro location and that our macros are saved within this location.

Debugging

Many times, a macro will fail to run because of a small syntax error. Typically, a missing ; symbol or the incorrect use of " instead of ' can cause all sorts of problems. To help with debugging, the following commands prove invaluable:

▶ PLUG: This command is used to tell a macro to run and ignore errors in the code that would cause it to not run. It will run through the macro until it hits a problem.

▶ NOPLUG: This command turns PLUG off.

▶ ECHO: This command is used to print each line into the session window while it is run.

▶ NOECHO: This command turns Echo off.

▶ NOTE: This command is written after a note is printed in the session window. Using NOTE and a number, for instance, can tell where you have reached in the macro.

▶ #: This is used to enter notes into the macro. Anything written after # will not be read.

Exec macros to repeat simple commands

Exec macros are the simplest form of macros that can be written in Minitab. They are only session commands that are saved in a text file. Exec files must use the *.MTB file extension.

Here, we will use data in the Macro data.mtw worksheet to create an Exec file to automate the running of several charts. If we regularly work from a set of data in the same format each week or each month, then we can use a simple Exec such as this one to run all the commands that we would use in the menus.

The Exec file will generate **probability**, **histogram**, and **time series plots** and will then run **1 sample t-test** and a **1 Variance** test on the data.

We will run the tools from the menus in Minitab in sequence, before using the commands from the history folder to save them as an Exec file.

Getting ready

Open the `Macro Data.MTW` worksheet by going to the **File** menu and selecting **Open worksheet...**.

How to do it...

The following instructions will use the history folder to build a simple Exec file to generate a series of graphs:

1. Go to the **Graph** menu and select **Probability Plot...**.
2. Select the **Single** plot.
3. Enter `Data` in the **Graph variables:** section.
4. Click on **OK**.
5. Go to the **Graph** menu and select **Time Series Plot...**.
6. Select the **Simple** chart.
7. Enter `Data` in the **Series:** section.
8. Click on **OK**.
9. Go to the **Graph** menu and select **Histogram...**.
10. Select the **With Fit and Groups** option.
11. Enter `Data` in the **Graph Variables:** section.
12. Click on **OK**.
13. Navigate to **Stat | Basic statistics** and select **1-sample t-test**.
14. Enter `Data` in the **One or more samples, each in a column:** section.
15. Check the option for **Perform hypothesis test** and enter `10` for **Hypothesized mean:**.
16. Click on **OK**.
17. Navigate to **Stat | Basic statistics** and select **1 Variance...**.
18. Enter `Data` in the **One or more samples, each in a column:** section.
19. Check the option for **Perform hypothesis test**.
20. Enter `2` in **Value:**.
21. Click on **OK**.

22. Go to the history folder, which is the yellow icon on the project manager toolbar, as shown in the following screenshot:

23. Highlight the commands from **PPlot** to the end of the **OneVariance** test, as shown in the following screenshot:

```
PPlot 'Data';
  Normal;
  Symbol;
  FitD;
  Grid 2;
  Grid 1;
  MGrid 1.
TSPlot 'Data';
  Symbol;
  Connect.
Histogram 'Data';
  Bar;
  Distribution;
    Normal.
OneT 'Data';
  Test 10;
  Confidence 95.0;
  Alternative 0.
OneVariance 'Data';
  STest 2;
  Confidence 95.0;
  Alternative 0.
```

24. Right-click on the selected commands and go to **Save As...**.

25. Name the file as `Report` and choose the **Save as type:** option as `Exec Files – ANSI (*.MTB)`.

26. Navigate to the macro directory and click on **Save**.

27. To run the macro, go to the **File** menu and select **Other Files** and **Run an Exec...**.

28. Click on **Select File**.

29. Navigate to the macro folder and select the `Report.mtb` file.

30. Click on **Open** to run the Exec file.

How it works...

The Exec file is only a text file and can be edited by opening it in Notepad or any other text editor. Exec files can be created by writing or pasting the commands directly into Notepad as well as saving them directly from the history folder. The ANSI denomination on the file is short for American National Standards Institute. Typically, saving the Exec file as an ANSI formatted text should avoid any issues with compatibility.

Minitab will run commands in the order that they are saved in the Exec file. In this manner, they can be created very quickly and simply by using the menus to generate the desired output and then selecting the commands from the history folder.

After following the previous steps, the Exec will always look for a column labeled `Data` to generate the output. If a worksheet does not contain a column of this name, the Exec file will not work. As an alternative, we can use the column references, `C`, and the column number to point to a specific column.

The **Number of times to execute:** field allows an iterative Exec to be run. This can be useful as a simple way to run a simulation. If we want to estimate a parameter with a Monte Carlo simulation, we can use the number of times the file is executed as a way of taking multiple sample points.

There's more...

There are several commands that can be added to help an output in Minitab. The `XWORD` command will output the charts and session window to Word, and `XPPOINT` will output to PowerPoint. Adding either of these to the end of the Exec file will send everything in the session window and all charts directly into either application.

Graphs can be sent into the Report pad within Minitab by use of the `GMANAGER` command with an `APPEND` subcommand. This works only for graphs in the project and not for results in the session window.

We can use the Exec file to split the worksheet, subset the worksheet, and more. These data tools generate new worksheets. The macro will continue running within the active worksheet after splitting or subsetting it. Should we need to swap to a different worksheet, then the `Worksheet` command used with the worksheet name can be used to swap between worksheets in a project. Constants, columns, and matrices remain unique to a worksheet; storing a constant in one worksheet will not be available in a second worksheet.

See also

- The *Using probability plots to check the distribution of two sets of data* recipe in *Chapter 2, Tables and Graphs*

- The *Creating a time series plot* recipe in *Chapter 2, Tables and Graphs*

- The *Comparing the population mean to a target with a 1-Sample t-test* recipe in *Chapter 3, Basic Statistical Tools*

Building a Global macro to create a custom graph layout

In this recipe, we will generate a custom layout of graphs. We will convert the previous recipe's Exec file into a Global macro and place all the charts on one page.

Global macros are similar to Exec files in that they look at the worksheet for the datasets. Like Exec files, they will use column names or references to identify the data to be used.

A benefit of Global macros over Execs is the ability to specify control statements such as DO and IF.

We will edit the `report.MTB` file generated in the previous example to place the histogram, probability, and time series plot into a single graphical layout. We will also edit the time series chart, add specification limits, and adjust the color and type of the reference line.

Getting ready

Open the `Macro Data.MTW` worksheet in Minitab and open the Exec file created in the previous recipe or the catch-up `report.MTB` file in Notepad.

How to do it...

The following steps will convert the Exec file created in the previous recipe into a Global macro. We will also place the graphs into a single graph page:

1. In the `Report.MTB` Exec file, add `GMACRO` to the top line in Notepad and as a second line, add `GLAYOUT`.

2. On the last line, add `ENDMACRO` so the macro looks like the following screenshot:

```
GMACRO
GLAYOUT

PPlot 'Data';
  Normal;
  Symbol;
  FitD;
  Grid 2;
  Grid 1;
  MGrid 1.

TSPlot 'Data';
  Symbol;
  Connect.

Histogram 'Data';
  Bar;
  Distribution;
    Normal.

Onet 'Data';
  Test 10.

OneVariance 'Data';
  STest 2;
  Confidence 95.0;
  Alternative 0.

ENDMACRO
```

3. Save the file in the macro directory with the name `Glayout.mac`.

4. Press *Ctrl + L* to bring up the command-line editor. Enter the `%glayout` command and click on the **Submit** command.

It is good practice to test macros as they are being worked on to see if they still run. If the macro fails to run, check if the macro directory is specified correctly. Also check if there is a column named `Data` in the worksheet.

5. Select the time series plot that the macro generated and right-click on the chart. From the right-click menu, go to **Add** and then select **Add Reference Lines...**.

6. In the **Show reference lines at Y values:** section, enter `12.5` and click on **OK**.

7. Double-click on the reference line that is generated and change the line to a **Custom** type. Select a dashed line, a red color, and make the size of the line **2**.

8. Click on **OK**.

9. Double-click on the label of **12.5** on the reference line.

10. Change the **Text:** value to `USL` and click on **OK**.

11. Go to the **Editor** menu and select the **Copy Command Language** option.

    The **Editor** menu is context specific and will only show options that are relevant to the selected window. If the **Copy Command Language** option is not available, left-click on the chart and go back to the **Editor** menu.

    Return to the macro in Notepad.

    Delete the text for the time series plot. This should start with `TSPlot Data;` and continue to the line `Connect;`.

    Paste the copied commands into the section where the old `TSPlot` command was. The command for the time series plot should now look like the following screenshot:

```
Tsplot Data;
  Index;
  Connect;
  Symbol;
  Reference 2 12.5;
    Type 2;
    Color 28;
    Size 2;
    MODEL 1;
    Label "USL";
  Title;
  Footnote;
    FPanel;
  NoDTitle.
```

12. To start a graph layout, enter `Layout` before the `PPlot` probability plot command.

13. To finish the graph layout, enter `Endlayout` after the `Histogram` command.

14. The graphs will need to be positioned on the layout page. For the `PPlot` command, add the `Figure 0 0.5 0 0.5;` line as a subcommand.

15. For a histogram, add the `Figure 0.5 1 0 0.5;` command-line.

16. For the time series plot, add `Figure 0 1 0.5 1;` to ensure that the macro looks similar to the following screenshot:

```
GMACRO
GLAYOUT

LAYOUT

PPlot 'Data';
  FIGURE 0 0.5 0 0.5;
  Normal;
  Symbol;
  FitD;
  Grid 2;
  Grid 1;
  MGrid 1.

Tsplot Data;
  Index;
  Connect;
  FIGURE 0 1 0.5 1;
  Symbol;
  Reference 2 12.5;
    Type 2;
    Color 2;
    Size 2;
    MODEL 1;
    Label "USL";
  Title;
  Footnote;
    FPanel;
  NoDTitle.

Histogram 'Data';
  Bar;
  FIGURE 0.5 1 0 0.5;|
  Distribution;
    Normal.

ENDLAYOUT

OneT 'Data';
  Test 10;
  Confidence 95.0;
  Alternative 0.

OneVariance 'Data';
  STest 2;
  Confidence 95.0;
  Alternative 0.

ENDMACRO
```

17. Save the macro and test it to see if it works by going back to Minitab.

18. Press *Ctrl + L* to open the command-line editor and enter `%glayout` and click on **Submit Commands** to run the macro.

How it works...

Global macros use the `GMacro` header to identify whether they are Global macros. They also require the second line to be a name for the macro. Finally, macros must finish with the `EndMacro` command.

The macro's name is relevant only if several macros are used in the same file; for an example, see the *Local macros with subcommands, submacros, and control statements* recipe. The name of the macro is used to call that macro. To invoke a macro saved in the same file, we would use the `Call Macroname` command. If we are invoking a macro saved as a separate file, we would use the `%Macroname` command.

The copy command language functionality is an excellent method to edit charts visually and then obtain the text of those commands to use them in a macro.

Copy command language is a function that works only for the updating graphs in Minitab. This includes only the charts that we create from the **Graph** menu and the control charts. Most graphs created from the **Stat** menu do not update and have fewer subcommands. The `Figure` subcommand that we have used here, for instance, is only available for updating charts.

For a list of the subcommands that can be used by charts in either the **Stat** or the **Graph** menu, see the **Help** section and the **Alphabetical command** list, as discussed in the *Introduction* section.

The command and subcommand structure is defined by the use of full stops and semicolons. A full stop is used to end a command and a semicolon continues the command on the next line with a new subcommand. Any command that is only run on one line does not need the full stop to end the command. The following is an example of such a command line:

```
Plot C1*C2
```

If we were to include a regression fit to the scatterplot, the command would then need to be as follows:

```
Plot C1*C2;
Regress.
```

The `Figure` commands in this example used a semicolon to continue the subcommands. If the `Figure` commands are the last line of the command, they should be followed by a full stop.

Subcommands do not have any requirement to be placed in a specific order. `Figure` could be entered as the first or the last subcommand, or anywhere in between. Although, it must be noted that subcommands of subcommands must be included in the relevant section, as shown in the following screenshot:

```
Tsplot Data;
  Index;
  Connect;
  FIGURE 0 1 0.5 1;
  Symbol;
  Reference 2 12.5;
    Type 2;
    Color 28;
    Size 2;
    MODEL 1;
    Label "USL";
  Title;
  Footnote;
    FPanel;
  NoDTitle.
```

The reference subcommand for the time series plot places the reference line on the y axis, and the subcommands, such as `Type`, `Color`, and `Size`, all detail properties of that line. If `Type` does not follow the reference section, the `Tsplot` command will generate an error.

In the preceding code, `Index`, `Connect`, `Symbol`, and `Reference` could be entered in any order. `Type`, `Color`, `Size`, `Model`, and `Label` refer to the `Reference` subcommand and must appear with a reference.

The `Layout` command has two parts. `Layout` starts a graphical layout; any new chart that is created will be held waiting until the `Endlayout` command is given. All graphs created between those two commands are placed on the same page. If we do not position the graphs with the `Figure` subcommand, they would all be placed on top of each other. The `Figure` command defines the page position in the following way:

Figure X1 X2 Y1 Y2

Here, 0 0 0 0 defines the bottom-left corner of the chart and 1 1 1 1 is the top-right corner.

There's more...

In general, spaces, tabs, and capitalization do not make any difference to how the macro runs. The commands are not case sensitive and while spaces are used to separate values as in `Figure X1 X2 Y1 Y2` or `Reference Axis Value`, if we included two or more spaces, it would not affect the macro. The preceding time series plot code could remove all the leading spaces on each line and would work exactly the same as if it had been entered with spacing.

The commands that we copy across from the history folder or from **Copy Command Language** automatically space out subcommands. This is not essential for Minitab to understand the macro. It is convenient for us to identify subcommands while creating the macro. Similarly, it is recommended that we space out the commands in a `Do` loop or an `If` statement to ensure ease of reading the macro, when using control statements later.

Spaces are used to separate items and are only essential to pay attention to when used with functions such as greater than or equal to. This is entered as `>=`, with a space between the two, which will recognize it as separate functions.

A fiddly method of overlaying different charts is to use the layout to drop all the charts on one page. But as graph and figure regions on the charts are shaded, all but the first chart must be set to use no fill; otherwise, the last graph hides all the previous graphs. The graphs are placed in sequence of first to last and back to front. This is a tricky overlay method as care must be taken to position the axes of the data regions correctly.

The command language that is outputted to the history folder includes the full command text. Minitab only really needs to use the first four letters of any command. We could use a command of `Histogram` or `Hist` and both will run the same function.

See also

▸ The *Exec macros to repeat simple commands* recipe

▸ The *Obtaining input from the session window with a Global macro* recipe

Obtaining input from the session window with a Global macro

In the previous recipe, the macro used a fixed specification limit of `12.5`. Here, we will add commands to ask for the specification and then group the points on the time series plot. This grouping is used to color points based on whether they are inside or outside the specification.

Allowing input from the session window can be helpful when running a macro. This can be a great way to add some flexibility to the macro. This uses the `Set` command to ask for input from the session window.

 We can only use the `Set` command to read from the session window if commands are enabled. If the **MTB>** is not showing in the session window, re-enable this by going to the **Editor** menu and selecting **Enable Commands**.

Getting ready

We will need to open the macro from the previous recipe or the catch-up macro, `Glayout. mac`. Open this file in Notepad. Next, open the `Macro Data.MTW` worksheet.

How to do it...

The following steps will add a command to ask for input from the session window in Minitab. This is then used to identify if the data is above or below this number.

1. Rename the GLayout macro and save the file as GSession.mac.

2. Add the following lines after the macro name and before the Layout command:

```
GMACRO
GSESSION

Note --------------------------
Note Enter a Specification Limit
Note --------------------------

#Read a single value into column 100
SET C100;
   FILE "TERMINAL";
   NOBS 1.

#Copy the value in C100 into constant K1
Let K1 = c100

#Delete column 100
ERASE C100

#Create a new column called group to identify results outside of specification
NAME C2 "Group"
LET C2 = IF(DATA > K1, "Above Spec", "within Spec")

LAYOUT
```

3. Find the Tsplot command in the macro. Change the Reference 2 12.5; line to Reference 2 K1;.

4. Add a Legend subcommand and a grouping symbol to the time series plot as shown in the following screenshot:

```
Tsplot Data;
  Index;
  Connect;
  FIGURE 0 1 0.5 1;
  Legend;
   Section 1;
  Symbol Group;
  Reference 2 k1;
   Type 2;
   Color 28;
   Size 2;
   MODEL 1;
   Label "USL";
  Title;
  Footnote;
   FPanel;
  NoDTitle.
```

5. Save the macro and return to Minitab.

6. Press *Ctrl + L* to bring up the command-line editor and type `%GSession` and click on **Submit Commands** to run the macro.

How it works...

The `Set` command can be used to open data within ASCII files. Using the filename as a terminal, it specifies the session window as the data source. We could use a `FORMAT` subcommand with `Set`. The `Format` subcommand is used to set the format of the data; `F` specifies numeric values, `A` specifies the alphanumeric values, and `DT` specifies the date/time; more information on the format items can be found in Minitab's help section.

`F5` tells Minitab to look for a five-digit number. Characters are included in that amount; for example, `12.5` is four characters. We could use the `F3.1` format and it would read in three values, the last value being the first decimal place. For example, entering `123` with the `F3.1` format would give us `12.3`.

When the `Format` subcommand is not used, the `Set` command will only read in numeric values.

The last `NObs` subcommand is the number of observations. By fixing this to `1`, we only look for one data entry. When the `Set` command is run, the session window will be given more focus and the prompt session will change to `Data >`; entering a value and pressing *Enter* will continue the macro.

The `Set` command can only read into columns, not constants. Because of this, we had to read into a column in the worksheet. It can be a safe practice to save the new data into columns that are away from the rest of the data to avoid any overwrites in new worksheets while storing data. The `Let` command then takes the value from `C100` and enters this into the `K1` constant. If there was more than one value in `C100`, we would specify the row with this syntax: `C100[1]`.

We have used the # symbol to enter comments into the macro. Any text following a # is ignored by the macro. This can be in the line of the code as well.

We manually entered new subcommands to the time series plot command to group the symbols by the new group column. Alternatively, we could have made the changes on the graph and copied the command language. This is detailed in the previous recipe.

The `Let` command uses an `IF` statement as a calculator function. See the *Calculator – using an if statement* recipe in *Chapter 1, Worksheet, Data Management, and the Calculator*, to on how to calculate `if` statements. This is not the same as the `IF` session command that will be used in the *Local macros with subcommands, submacros, and control statements* recipe.

The `Note` command is a quick way to output notes into the session window. Any text that follows a note is printed to the session window. The `Print` command has a similar functionality but can also print columns or constants. The `Print "Hello world"` command will output text to the session window within the double quotes. The `Print K1` command will print the value in the `K1` constant.

There's more...

The reference line has been updated in this activity to take user input from the session window. Alternatively, we could place a reference line from the mean of the data. To do this, we would need to store the mean in a constant and use this constant for the reference line. The **Column Statistics...** tools under the **Calc** menu can be used to store values directly into constants.

Most of the **Stat** menu tools also offer us the ability to store values in the worksheet. These will be stored in the columns of the worksheet. This way, we can use many of the generated values and report them out on a new graphical page.

We may want the value that is generated by a function from a capability analysis such as Cpk, but may not want to generate the typical set of charts. In those cases, we can use the `BRIEF` command.

The `BRIEF` command can be used to limit or expand the output from results in Minitab. `BRIEF 0` is no output; `BRIEF 2` is the default level of output. The level of `BRIEF` relates to the options available in the results of many tools.

Some tools also have the `NOCHART` subcommand to suppress the graphical output.

See also

- The *Calculator – using an if statement* recipe in *Chapter 1, Worksheet, Data Management, and the Calculator*
- The *Local macros with subcommands, submacros, and control statements* recipe

Creating a Local macro

Local macros help create more general functions than Global macros or Execs. Rather than running from column references in the worksheet, we send data to a Local macro. This is run internally. On running a Local macro, we identify the data to be sent into the macro. We also need to declare the data type of variables used within the macro.

Here, we will convert the GSession macro from the previous recipe into a Local macro. This will allow us to tell the macro to use a column instead of looking for a specific column name or reference.

At this step, we will also simplify the function by removing the commands for the one sample t-test and one variance test.

Getting ready

Open the `Macro data.MTW` worksheet by using an open worksheet in the file menu. Then open the `Gsession.mac` file, which was created in Notepad in the previous recipe. Or, open the provided catch-up file.

How to do it...

The following commands will convert the Global macro from the previous recipe into a Local macro.

1. Go to the `GSession.mac` file. To prepare the file for our changes, save it as `LLayout.mac` in the macro directory.

2. In Notepad, remove the `G` from the start of `GMACRO`.

3. On the second line, change the name of the macro to `LLAYOUT Col Spec`.

4. Delete the commands associated with reading the data from the session window and replace these with the `MColumn Col Group` and `MConstant Spec` declarations. The initial lines of the macro till `Layout` should look as follows:

    ```
    MACRO
    LLayout COL Spec

    MCOLUMN GROUP
    MCONSTANT SPEC

    LET C2 = IF(DATA > K1, "Above Spec", "Within Spec")

    LAYOUT
    ```

5. Replace all references of `Data` or `'Data'` with `Col`.

6. Replace all references of `K1` with `Spec`.

7. Replace any references of `C2` with `Group`.

8. Delete the commands for the `Onet` One Sample t-test, and the `OneVariance` One Variance test.

9. Check if the macro looks similar to the following screenshot:

```
MACRO
LLayout Col Spec

MColumn Col Group
MConstant Spec

#Identify results outside of specification for column Group

Let Group = if(Col > Spec, "Above Spec", "Within Spec")

LAYOUT

PPlot Col;
  FIGURE 0 0.5 0 0.5;
  Normal;
  Symbol;
  FitD;
  Grid 2;
  Grid 1;
  MGrid 1.

Tsplot Col;
  Index;
  Connect;
  FIGURE 0 1 0.5 1;
  Legend;
    Section 1;
  Symbol Group;|
  Reference 2 Spec;
    Type 2;
    Color 28;
    Size 2;
    MODEL 1;
    Label "USL";
  Title;
  Footnote;
    FPanel;
  NoDTitle.

Histogram Col;
  Bar;
  FIGURE 0.5 1 0 0.5;
  Distribution;
    Normal.

ENDLAYOUT

ENDMACRO
```

10. Save the macro and then go back to Minitab.

11. Press *Ctrl + L* to call up the command-line editor.

12. Enter `%LLayout c1 12.5` into the command-line editor and click on **Submit Commands** to run the macro.

How it works...

The variables on the name line of the macro define how many items we need to specify when we run the macro; or rather, what information is passed to the macro. The `Col` command is the first value to be passed to the macro and `Spec`, the second.

Any variable used in the macro has to be declared. The `MColumn` command declares columns; `MConstant` is used for `Spec` to declare a constant. There are also `MFree` and `MMatrix`. The `MFree` command will allow the variable to be defined when the macro is invoked and is dependent on the variable type passed to the macro.

Variables can have any name as long as they do not clash with any of the commands in Minitab.

There's more...

Here, we have a macro that creates a panel of charts for any column that we send to the macro:

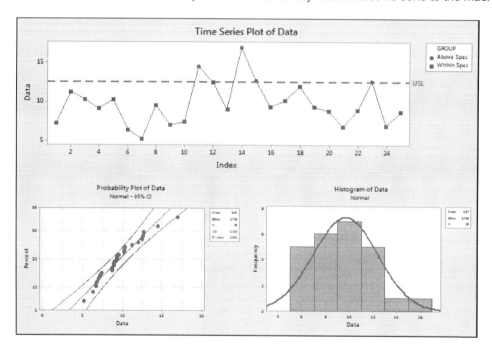

We can improve on this macro by allowing any number of columns to be used and making specifications optional.

The one sample t-test and one variance test were removed from the macro to simplify the example. If we wanted to keep the two tests, we could pass variables for the hypothesized mean and variance into the macro. When calling the macro, we would specify the data column, the specification, the mean, and the variance.

Another option to handle a lot of extra variables is to use subcommands on the macro name. Means and variances could be supplied as an optional command. If they are not used, the tests are not run; if they are supplied, then we would run the two tests. See the next recipe for an example of subcommands on the macro name.

See also

▶ The *Local macros with subcommands, submacros, and control statements* recipe

Local macros with subcommands, submacros, and control statements

This recipe will create a complicated macro using control statements and subcommands on the main macro command.

The following macro will be able to accept any number of columns on the main command line and generate a layout for each column. Specifications can be optional; they can be entered as a column or a single value. We will use a column for the specifications to allow different specifications for each column of data, or a constant to use the same specification for each column. The macro will be able to choose between the layout with or without specifications and perform an error check to see if the right number of specifications have been entered. This will cover several nested IF statements and DO loops.

Finally, we will copy the Llayout macro from the previous recipe into Notepad twice and edit this macro to create two submacros. One will be used to generate a layout for specifications and we will edit the other to create a layout when no specifications are used.

Getting ready

We will need the Llayout.mac file from the *Creating a Local macro* recipe or the catch-up file, Llayout.mac.

How to do it...

The following steps will convert the Llayout macro to use any number of columns as an input. We will also add a subcommand to use specifications as either a constant or a column:

1. Open a new Notepad and save the file as LSub.mac in the macro folder.

2. Enter the values shown in the following screenshot into Notepad for the macro name, subcommand, and variables to be defined.

```
MACRO
LSUB Col.1-Col.N;
  Specs SPC.

#Define Variables
MColumn Col.1-Col.N Group
MConstant N LP VTYPE SND CNT
MFree SPC
```

3. Enter the first part of the IF statements as a way to check if the specification subcommand has been used and to identify if it is a constant.

```
# If statement checks to see if specifications have been used.

IF Specs = 1  #specifications are used
  MTYPE SPC VTyPE  #Check variable type of the spec

  IF VTYPE = 1  #Spec Variable is type 1, a constant. Create charts with single spec

    DO LP = 1:N
      Call Llayout Col.N SPC
    ENDDO
```

4. Enter the next section for the specifications that have been used as a column and to check if the number of specifications and the number of columns are the same.

```
  ELSEIF VTYPE = 2  #Spec Variable is type 2, column. Create charts with seperate spec
#Count number of specifications
    Let CNT = Count(SPC)

    IF CNT NE N  #If the number of specifications does not equal Columns, exit macro.
      NOTE ------------------------------------------------
      NOTE Number of specifications does not equal columns
      NOTE Macro Exiting
      NOTE ------------------------------------------------
      EXIT
    ENDIF

#Call the Layout without limit if a missing value is entered as the spec
#Or call the layout with specifications

    DO LP = 1:N
      IF SPC[LP] = miss()
        Call NOSPEC COL.N
      Else
        LET SND = SPC[LP]
        Call Llayout COL.LP SND
      ENDIF
    ENDDO

  ENDIF
```

5. Finish the macro by entering the next section for no specifications used and ending the macro.

```
#when the specification subcommand isnt used, create charts without the spec line
ELSE
  DO LP = 1:N
    Call NOSPEC COL.N
  ENDDO
ENDIF

ENDMACRO
```

6. Copy the entire Llayout macro and paste this after ENDMACRO.

7. Paste the Llayout macro a second time.

8. For the second Llayout commands, change the macro name to NOSPEC.

9. Delete all references to SPEC and GROUP from the NOSPEC macro.

10. Change the header section and declarations to the commands shown in the following screenshot:

```
MACRO
NOSPEC Col

MCOLUMN COL
```

11. Change the TSPLOT commands by removing the GROUP and Reference subcommands. Ensure that the TSPLOT command appears as follows:

```
Tsplot Col;
  Index;
  Connect;
  Symbol;
  FIGURE 0 1 0.5 1;
  Title;
  Footnote;
    FPanel;
  NODTitle.
```

12. Save the macro.

13. Return to Minitab and test the macro by first generating random data. Go to the **Calc** menu, then **Random Data**, and then select **Normal....**

14. In **Number of rows of data to generate:**, enter 30.

15. In the **Store in column(s):** section, enter c1-c5.

16. For the **Mean:** section, enter 10.

17. Click on **OK**.

18. In the worksheet, create a new column called `Specifications`.

19. Enter `11 11.5 * 12.5 13` in the `Specifications` column.

20. Press *Ctrl* + *L* to open the command-line editor.

21. Enter the `%LSub c1-c5;` command and press *Enter* to go to the next line.

22. Enter `Specs c6.` and click on **Submit Commands**.

How it works...

Subcommands that are entered on the macro name line allow optional commands to be entered. When running the macro, we can decide whether we want to use specifications or not.

The use of the `Mfree` command here allows a single specification to be entered as a constant; if separate specifications are desired, we can enter a column from the worksheet because `Mfree` will set its variable type based on the variable that is being passed to the macro. The `Mtype` command is then used to ask what variable type we have in `SPC`.

The first `IF` statement checks if the `SPECS` subcommand was used. If it was, then we check if the specifications were entered as a constant or column. If they are entered as a column, then we check if the number of specifications match the number of columns with the count of `SPC` compared to `N`.

To avoid rewriting the graph code several times, we store this in two separate macros: Llayout and Nospecs. If we want to remove excess code, we could further tidy this by placing the `Pplot` and the `Histogram` command in a third macro. As these commands haven't used specifications, using a third submacro could reduce the number of lines used.

The `Miss()` function is used to identify the missing values in the worksheet. It has been used here to identify when missing values have been entered for specifications. This allows us to not include a specification for some columns.

There's more...

The `Default` command can be used to fix the values of constants in subcommands. This allows us to set a value for these constants if they have not been specified when calling the macro. The `Default` command, though, must come directly after the declaration statements.

Navigating Minitab and Useful Shortcuts

The following are a list of navigation tools on the Project Manager toolbar. These are used within the recipes to return to the relevant section.

The Project Manager toolbar

The following screenshot shows the Project Manager toolbar:

Each of the toolbar buttons shown return to a different section within Minitab.

Show Session Folder

Selecting the session folder returns us to the session window for statistical and graphical output.

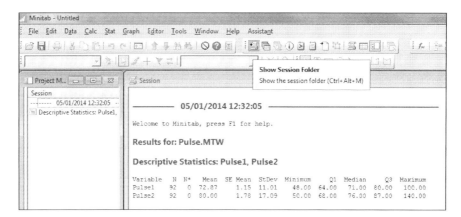

The session window is displayed on the right; the left-hand pane displays the graphs and also the items in the session window. Double-click to select an item to be displayed.

Show Worksheets Folder

Selecting the worksheet folder returns the worksheets in the project on the left and the active worksheet on the right. The following screenshot displays the two worksheets within the project:

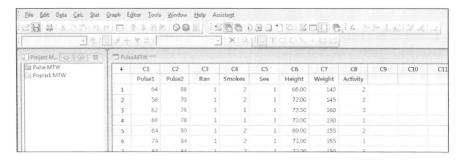

Show Graphs Folder

Selecting the graphs folder gives a list of graphs in the project on the left, and the selected graph on the right.

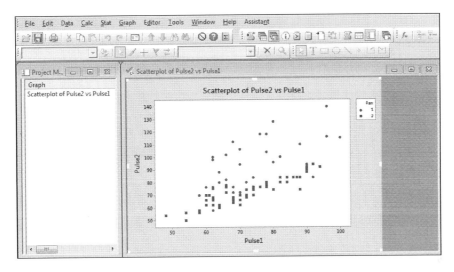

Show Info

The info window returns information on the columns within the active worksheet. This can be an especially useful place to start when opening a worksheet. While using Minitab, we will often find tools that require columns to be of the same length. The info window can be an important aid in identifying the columns that are missing data.

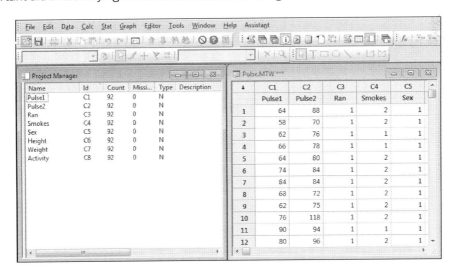

Show History

The history folder displays a list of commands generated from the menus or entered directly into the session or the command-line editor.

Show ReportPad

The Report pad can be used to store output and make notes on a study.

Changing default settings in Minitab

Minitab has a large set of default settings that can be adjusted using **Options**. These are located in the **Tools** menu and under **Options**.

It is possible to adjust the default start values in the directories where Minitab will look for datasets, macro directories, and lots more; for example, default graph colors and styles, statistics used within functions such as control charts, and even the type of boxplot that is plotted. Navigate to the locations shown in the following screenshot to adjust some useful settings:

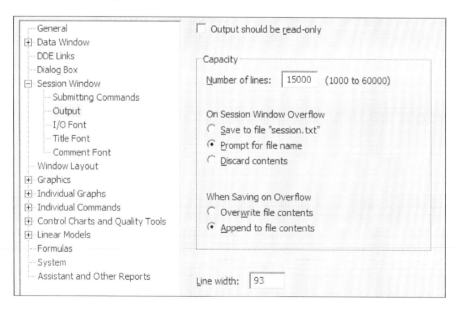

▶ **Session Window | Output**: The session window's default line width is 93 characters wide in release 17 (79 in release 16). The maximum width is 132 characters. Changing this setting to 132 characters can help large tables fit better into the session window.

▶ **Graphics | Annotation | My Footnote**: **My Footnote** controls the information automatically generated as a footnote in the charts. The project and worksheet names, as well as the date and time of the last modification to the charts, can be switched on from here.

▶ **Individual Graphs| Boxplots**: This allows us to choose between percentiles, hinges, or quartiles to use for boxplots.

▶ **Control Charts and Quality Tools| Tests**: Here, we can choose the default tests to use for control charts and the values for these tests. Other options within the **Control Charts and Quality Tools** section allow us to change the methods for estimating standard deviation on control charts.

Useful keyboard shortcuts

There are a lot of key presses that can be used within Minitab. This is not an extensive list, just the shortcuts used with this book. More keyboard shortcuts can be found and customized within Minitab from the **Tools** menu and by selecting **Customize**.

▶ *Ctrl + E*: This is used to return to the last dialog box

▶ *Ctrl + L*: This is used to open the command-line editor

▶ *Ctrl + D*: This is used to bring the data window to the front

▶ *Ctrl + M*: This is used to bring the session window to the front

▶ *Ctrl + I*: This is used to bring the Project Manager to the front

Links to data, and sites used in the book

We have tried to use data from many different locations to give a good variety of topics. The following is a list of the locations for these data sets:

▶ The MET office website is used for the Oxford weather station data
`http://www.metoffice.gov.uk/climate/uk/stationdata/`.

▶ The atmospheric pressure difference data is taken from the Climatic Research Unit's website: `http://www.cru.uea.ac.uk/data`.

▶ The Statistical Science portal provides a useful link to many data sets: `http://www.statsci.org/index.html`.

▶ UK economy figures can be obtained from the Guardian website: `http://www.guardian.co.uk/news/datablog/2009/nov/25/gdp-uk-1948-growth-economy`.

▶ The Data and Story Library forms a rich resource for anyone looking for examples: `http://lib.stat.cmu.edu/DASL/`.

Index

bar chart
 creating, of categorical data 39-41
 creating, with numeric response 42, 43
binary logistic regression
 overview 142-144
blocks of columns
 stacking 15, 16
Box-Cox transformation
 about 198
 using, for capability 198-200

C

C = 0 plans 186, 210
calculator
 text column, cleaning up with 30-32
capability
 Box-Cox transformation,
  using for 198-200
 Johnson transformation, using for 201
capability analysis
 for nonnormal distributions 193-197
 for normally distributed data 189-192
capability analysis sixpack 187
capability histograms
 generating 187
Capital Gains Tax (CGT) 244
categorical column
 Tally, finding of 34, 35
 worksheet, splitting of 18, 19
categorical data
 bar chart, creating of 39-41
Chi-Square test
 using 85, 86
climate change levy (CCL) 244
cluster K-means
 about 258
 used, for identifying
  groups in data 258-260
cluster observations
 used, for finding similarity in
  results by rows 253-255
cluster variables
 used, for finding similarity across columns
  256, 257
columns
 transposing, of worksheet 17, 18

commands, macros
 # 288
 ECHO 288
 NOECHO 288
 NOPLUG 288
 NOTE 288
 PLUG 288
complex contingency tables
 studying, with multiple
  correspondence analysis 269-272
complicated macro
 creating, control statements used 305-308
 creating, subcommands used 305-308
control charts
 about 154
 and Laney U' chart 175
 creating, Assistant tool used 165
 CUSUM charts 176
 EWMA chart 177
 G charts 182
 I-MR charts 161
 Laney P' chart 171
 proportion chart 168
 stages, applying 154-156
 T charts 180
 u-chart 173
 Xbar-R charts 154
 Xbar-S charts 157
control statements
 used, for creating complicated
  macro 305-308
correlation
 finding, between multiple variables 76
covariance
 analyzing 113-115
Cpk
 generating 187
critical F-statistic
 about 121
 finding 121, 122
critical t-statistics
 about 74
 finding, probability distribution plot used 75
Cronbach's alpha 252
crossed Gage R&R study
 analyzing 224-226

Cross tabulation tool
using 86
custom graph layout creation
Global macro, building for 292-297
CUSUM charts
about 176
generating 176
working 177

D

data
normality test, performing for 63, 64
opening, from Access 11, 12
trend, fitting to 274-276
Data and Story Library forms
URL 314
data set
principal components, finding of 242-247
data sets
locations 313
data subset
creating, in worksheet 19-22
date/time column
values, extracting from 22, 23
default settings, Minitab
modifying 312, 313
descriptive statistics
table, building of 36, 37
discriminant analysis
overview 261-264
distribution ID plots
generating 217, 218

E

e-calculator tool
about 24
using 25, 26
ECHO command 288
equal variances
testing for 99-101
Equimax 251
equivalence tests
about 87
used, for proving zero difference between
mean and target 87, 88

Estimate tool 188
Euclidean measure 255
EWMA charts
about 177
example 177
generating 178
working 179
Excel file
opening, in Minitab 8-11
Exec file
working 291
Exec macros
about 286, 288
simple commands, repeating 289-291

F

factor analysis
used, for identifying
underlying factors 248-252
fitted line plots
simple regressions, visualizing with 127, 128
Food and Drug Agency (FDA) 206

G

Gage bias
checking 229, 230
Gage linearity
checking 229, 230
Gage R&R
about 219, 220
Assistant tool, using for 235, 237
Gage R&R worksheet
creating 222-224
Gage study
expanding, with factors 231, 233
G charts
about 182
generating 182
working 182
General Linear Model tools 92
GLM (General Linear Model)
about 108, 152
using, for unbalanced designs 108-113
Global macro
about 286

multiple variables
   correlation, finding between 76
multivariate tools 241, 242

N

NAO 93
nested design
   analyzing 116, 117
nested Gage R&R
   about 228
   studying 228, 229
NOECHO command 288
nonlinear regression
   fitting 146-151
nonlinear regression tools 146
nonnormal distributions,
      capability analysis 193-197
NOPLUG command 288
normality test
   performing, for data 63, 64
normality tests
   generating 187
normally distributed data, capability analysis
      189-192
Normit transformation 144
North Atlantic Oscillation. *See* **NAO**
NOTE command 288
numeric column
   coding, to text values 28, 29
numeric columns
   stacking, simultaneously 12-14
numeric response
   bar chart, creating with 42, 43

O

ODBC
   used, for opening data from Access 11, 12
one-way ANOVA
   power, calculating 95, 96
   running, Assistant tools used 97, 98
   using, with unstacked columns 93-95
Open Database Connectivity. *See* **ODBC**
Options tool 188
orthogonal regression 126
Orthomax 251

P

paneled Boxplot
   generating 46-48
Pareto chart
   about 37
   creating 38
partial least square regression 126
P-chart (proportion chart)
   about 168, 171
   creating 169
   working 169-171
Pearson measure 255
PLUG command 288
Poisson Regression 126
population mean to target
   comparing, with 1-Sample t-test 64-66
population proportions
   testing, with 2 Proportions test 81, 82
power
   calculating, of one-way ANOVA 95, 96
Power and Sample Size tool
   using, for 1 Proportion test 79, 80
   using, for 1-Sample t-test 67, 68
   using, for 2 Proportions test 82
   using, for 2-Sample t-test 72, 73
Ppk
   generating 187
predictors
   selecting, for regression model 139-141
previously defined sampling plan
   defining 210, 211
principal components
   finding, of data set 242-247
Principal Components Analysis (PCA) 242
probability 288
probability distribution plot
   used, for finding critical t-statistics 75
probability plots
   used, for checking
   distribution of data sets 51, 52
process capability
   comparing, Assistant tool
   used 204-206
Project Manager toolbar
   about 309
   History folder 312

test paper consistency
analyzing, item analysis used 252
Tests tool 188
text column
cleaning up, with calculator 30-32
text values
numeric columns, coding to 28, 29
time series plot
about 54
creating 54-56
secondary axis, adding to 56-58
time series plots 288
time series predictions
without seasonal variations 281, 282
without trends variations 281, 282
Time Series tools 273
tolerance intervals
about 215
generating, for summarized data 215, 216
tools, capability studies
Estimate 188
Options 188
Tests 188
Transform 188
Transform tool 188
trend
fitting, to data 274-276
two-way contingency tables
analyzing, with simple correspondence analysis 264-269
Type 1 Gage study
about 220
analyzing 221

U

u-chart
about 173
creating 173, 174
working 174, 175
unbalanced designs
GLM, using for 108-113
underlying factors
identifying, factor analysis used 248-251
unstacked columns
one-way ANOVA, using with 93-95

V

values
extracting, from date/time column 22, 23
variable data
acceptance sampling, creating for 206, 207
variables
scatter plot, creating of 44, 45
Variance inflation factors (VIF) 134
Varimax 251

W

worksheet
columns, transposing of 17, 18
data subset, creating in 19-22
splitting, by categorical column 18, 19

X

Xbar-R charts
about 154
creating 155, 156
features 157
generating 187
working 156, 157
Xbar-S chart
about 157
creating 158, 159
features 160
options 159
using 157
working 159

Z

Z LSL 192
Z USL 192

Thank you for buying
Minitab Cookbook

About Packt Publishing

Packt, pronounced 'packed', published its first book "*Mastering phpMyAdmin for Effective MySQL Management*" in April 2004 and subsequently continued to specialize in publishing highly focused books on specific technologies and solutions.

Our books and publications share the experiences of your fellow IT professionals in adapting and customizing today's systems, applications, and frameworks. Our solution-based books give you the knowledge and power to customize the software and technologies you're using to get the job done. Packt books are more specific and less general than the IT books you have seen in the past. Our unique business model allows us to bring you more focused information, giving you more of what you need to know, and less of what you don't.

Packt is a modern, yet unique publishing company, which focuses on producing quality, cutting-edge books for communities of developers, administrators, and newbies alike. For more information, please visit our website: www.PacktPub.com.

About Packt Enterprise

In 2010, Packt launched two new brands, Packt Enterprise and Packt Open Source, in order to continue its focus on specialization. This book is part of the Packt Enterprise brand, home to books published on enterprise software – software created by major vendors, including (but not limited to) IBM, Microsoft and Oracle, often for use in other corporations. Its titles will offer information relevant to a range of users of this software, including administrators, developers, architects, and end users.

Writing for Packt

We welcome all inquiries from people who are interested in authoring. Book proposals should be sent to author@packtpub.com. If your book idea is still at an early stage and you would like to discuss it first before writing a formal book proposal, contact us; one of our commissioning editors will get in touch with you.

We're not just looking for published authors; if you have strong technical skills but no writing experience, our experienced editors can help you develop a writing career, or simply get some additional reward for your expertise.

Learning RStudio for R Statistical Computing

ISBN: 978-1-78216-060-1   Paperback: 126 pages

Learn to effectively perform R development, statistical analysis, and reporting with the most popular R IDE

1. A complete practical tutorial for RStudio, designed keeping in mind the needs of analysts and R developers alike.

2. Step-by-step examples that apply the principles of reproducible research and good programming practices to R projects.

3. Learn to effectively generate reports, create graphics, and perform analysis, and even build R-packages with RStudio.

Statistical Analysis with R

ISBN: 978-1-84951-208-4   Paperback: 300 pages

Take control of your data and produce superior statistical analyses with R

1. An easy introduction for people who are new to R, with plenty of strong examples for you to work through.

2. This book will take you on a journey to learn R as the strategist for an ancient Chinese kingdom!

3. A step-by-step guide to understand R, its benefits, and how to use it to maximize the impact of your data analysis.

4. A practical guide to conduct and communicate your data analysis with R in the most effective manner.

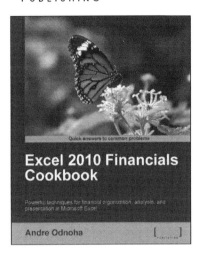

Excel 2010 Financials Cookbook

ISBN: 978-1-84969-118-5   Paperback: 260 pages

Poweful techniques for financial organization, analysis, and presentation in Microsoft Excel

1. Harness the power of Excel to help manage your business finances.

2. Build useful financial analysis systems on top of Excel.

3. Covers normalizing, analyzing, and presenting financial data.

4. Clear and practical with straight forward, step-by-step instructions.

Microsoft Dynamics GP 2013 Cookbook

ISBN: 978-1-84968-938-0   Paperback: 348 pages

Over 110 immediately usable and effective recipes to solve real-world Dynamics GP problems

1. Understand the various tips and tricks to master Dynamics GP, and improve your system's stability in order to enable you to get work done faster.

2. Discover how to solve real-world problems in Microsoft Dynamics GP 2013 with easy-to-understand and practical recipes.

3. Access proven and effective Dynamics GP techniques from authors with vast and rich experience in Dynamics GP.

Please check **www.PacktPub.com** for information on our titles

Made in the USA
Lexington, KY
27 September 2014